Issues in the
Spanish-Speaking World

Issues in the Spanish-Speaking World

JANICE W. RANDLE

GREENWOOD PRESS

Westport, Connecticut • London

Library of Congress Cataloging-in-Publication Data

Randle, Janice W.
    Issues in the Spanish-speaking world / Janice W. Randle.
        p.   cm.
    Includes bibliographical references and index.
    ISBN 0–313–31974–X (alk. paper)
    1. Latin America—Politics and government—21st century.   2. Spain—
Politics and government—21st century.   3. Latin America—Social
conditions—21st century.   4. Spain—Social conditions—21st century.
I. Title.
    F1414.2.R27   2003
    909'.0975661—dc21   2002192777

British Library Cataloguing in Publication Data is available.

Library of Congress Catalog Card Number: 2002192777
ISBN: 0–313–31974–X

First published in 2003

Greenwood Press, 88 Post Road West, Westport, CT 06881
An imprint of Greenwood Publishing Group, Inc.
www.greenwood.com

Printed in the United States of America

The paper used in this book complies with the
Permanent Paper Standard issued by the National
Information Standards Organization (Z39.48–1984).

10 9 8 7 6 5 4 3 2 1

In memory of my parents, Jack and Clara,
and to Richard, for encouragement and patience

Contents

Acknowledgments

This book is the product of many years of interest in the Spanish language and the cultures of Spanish speakers. Teachers and advisors at the University of Texas at Austin, especially John Brodie and Mildred Boyer, and later Carlos Solé and Vicente Cantarino, encouraged and supported my belated discovery of Spanish and interest in teaching. I owe much to the Fulbright Commission for my first introduction to Spain as a junior lecturer in Valladolid and for my first acquaintance with Peru some 25 years later as a participant in a summer seminar, and in between as a participant in a National Endowment for the Humanities summer seminar on indigenous literatures and cultures of Mesoamerica and the Andes headed by Fran Kartunnen, a remarkable scholar and writer. Friends and acquaintances in Spain, Mexico, Ecuador and Peru have helped me to see their societies—at least to the degree I have been able—through other eyes.

To the members of my family, past and present, I owe a debt of gratitude for encouraging me to pursue my interests. St. Edward's University has helped to make possible a half dozen visits to Spain and the Andean region of South America. Good colleagues and my former dean, Marcia Kinsey, have given me much support over the years, and my students have given me a reason to keep learning. Wendi Schnaufer proposed the book project to me and patiently shepherded me through its writing. I thank them all.

Introduction

Spain and the Hispanic nations of Latin America are linked together by more than 300 years of colonial history, which gave them a common language, a common religion and many other shared cultural traits and customs that have survived nearly 200 years of political separation and development since the Wars of Independence in the early nineteenth century.

Nevertheless, the two regions exhibit some striking differences. Spanish culture did not expand in a vacuum in the Western Hemisphere. The soldiers, explorers, colonists, artisans, churchmen and administrators who arrived in the New World to establish Spain's empire encountered an astonishing array of indigenous cultures, ranging in social and technological complexity from nomadic hunter-gatherers to elaborate and wealthy empires, ruled by semi-divine kings and priestly castes that perpetuated complicated mythologies and rituals. The territory eventually claimed by the Spanish crown was immense, stretching from the Grand Canyon to the tip of South America, and encompassed every kind of physical environment the planet has to offer, from the second highest mountain range to coastal mangroves and Amazonian lowlands, deserts and jungles, glaciers, grasslands and rainforests. The centers of colonial power were separated from each other and from Spain itself by impossibly long distances and uncertain means of communication. As the Spaniards advanced from each new beachhead, they encountered different degrees of resistance to the imposition of their rule and their religion. No wonder there are important differences between Spain and its former colonies and between Latin American nations themselves today.

Although Spain used to be famous for its regional differences and loyalty to the *patria chica* (little homeland, the locality), recent changes, such as immigration to the large cities, increased foreign and domestic travel and closer identification with Europe through the European Union, have muted this divergence. Still, Spain is far from homogenous in several important ways. In three regions—Cataluña, Galicia and Euskadi, formerly known as the Basque country—you will hear languages other than Spanish spoken by large numbers of people. Regional languages, which lost speakers to Castilian during the eighteenth and nineteenth centuries and which were suppressed under the dictatorship of Francisco Franco, have become a symbol of local, "national" pride for many Catalans, Gallegos and Basques. The autonomous communities (political subdivisions much like our states) around the periphery have flexed their muscles after generations of domination and central control in Madrid. Regional pride, in some respects, is at an all-time high. In addition to language differences, some regional nationalities, the Catalans in particular, see themselves as more progressive, more hard working, and more European and are likely to diverge from the Castilian center on a number of issues. Spain also has smaller minorities, such as the Gypsies, or Rom, who have lived in Spain since at least the fifteenth century and, more recently, immigrants from many countries, but especially North Africa and Latin America.

In Latin America, the coexistence and commingling of people from radically different cultures is much more pronounced. From the initial, brutal shock of conquest and then the collapse of the native population, largely due to European diseases, the Indian majority became servants in their own lands. Although there were many indigenous rebellions throughout Hispanic America, the Spanish or their daughter republics were, in every case, eventually successful in crushing them. Indians retreated, when they could, to the mountains, jungles or other marginal areas, withdrawing as much as possible from contact with the colonial administration while still trying to protect their rights through the courts. In many areas, particularly the Caribbean islands and lowlands of Central and South America, African slaves were brought in to replace the rapidly declining indigenous labor force.

Miscegenation (racial mixing) began with the first contacts between Europeans and Indians or Africans. By the time of independence, *mestizos* and *mulattos* (people of mixed indigenous-European or African-European ancestry) had grown to outnumber their "parent" groups, and today in many of the Latin American republics they form the majority of the population. Race, however, has never been neutral in Latin America. White skin has always been an advantage; the political and economic elites of Latin America are nearly always European in origin (or claim to be), and color and social class are often closely linked. Orthodoxy, in the form of religious practice, family structure and gender roles, as well as language and education, are important in determining a person's place in society.

Just as people mingled their genes, so too cultures mixed in Latin America. The introduction of new plants and animals from Europe and Africa gave rise to a distinct cuisine in the New World. African and indigenous peoples often continued their own religious beliefs and practices behind a facade that sufficed to assure the Spanish that they had at least done their duty. Artistic tastes and techniques combined, and music and dance flourished in the cultural mixture of New Spain and the Viceroyalty of Peru, and later in the independent nations of Hispanic America. Today this fusion of cultures continues, as it has since independence—in some respects, at a faster pace. Modern life has injected new elements and new values into Latin American culture, from hip-hop music to consumerism and global commerce. Immigration to large cities has made daily life much more of a competitive struggle. Globalization, the computer revolution and air travel seem to have produced a greater gap, in many ways, between the rich and the poor now than 100 years—or even 20 years—ago.

Are these changes for the good or not? Time will tell in some instances, but people inside and outside of the Hispanic world have differing opinions about many of the issues that affect the two regions today. Spain and Latin America share numerous challenges with other nations: deterioration of the environment, immigration, sustaining economic development, the treatment of ethnic minorities or indigenous peoples, a growing concern about the effects of crime, alcohol, tobacco and drugs on societies and the individual, and establishing peace and justice within a workable governmental structure. On the other hand, some of the issues that surface in Spain and Latin America have special qualities because of the legacy of Spain's past: its strong identification with Roman Catholicism, the Iberian (or Mediterranean) concept of gender roles, the bullfight, the monarchy, and the role of Spain in the discovery and destruction of indigenous cultures in the New World.

Because we live in a world of instant communication, it is more important than ever that we try to develop an understanding of the world we live in and our own ability to communicate outside our borders. Some of you who use this book will become businessmen and women, others Peace Corps volunteers, government workers, teachers and politicians. You will have access to Spanish language television, newspapers and a wealth of information on the Internet— direct access to news that may express a point of view different from our news media and official sources. Hopefully, this book will help you to prepare to understand and use that information. In considering both sides of issues and in defending our point of view, we sharpen our ability to express ideas through language and to develop critical reasoning skills.

A book that focuses on issues, which by definition involve some question or controversy, will contain some material that is unpleasant or unflattering. To be aware of and to consider problems or controversies concerning Spain and Latin America does not imply that we cannot admire and enjoy the beautiful, inspiring, admirable and entertaining aspects of their societies, past and present. However, much of the art and literature of Hispanic nations—the Latin American nations in particular—has a strong component of social and political awareness. The Colombian novelist and short story writer Gabriel García Márquez was awarded the Nobel Prize for Literature in 1982 "for his novels and short stories, in which the fantastic and the realistic are combined in a richly composed world of imagination, reflecting a continent's life and conflicts."[1] In his acceptance speech, García Márquez spoke of the larger-than-life, fantastic quality of many of Latin America's heroes and villians, beauties and problems:

I dare to think that it is this outsized reality, and not just its literary expression, that has deserved the attention of the Swedish Academy of Letters. A reality not of paper, but one that lives within us and determines each instant of our countless daily deaths, and that nourishes a source of insatiable creativity, full of sorrow and beauty, of which this roving and nostalgic Colombian is but one cipher more, singled out by fortune. Poets and beggars, musicians and prophets, warriors and scoundrels, all creatures of that unbridled reality, we have had to ask but little of imagination, for our crucial problem has been a lack of conventional means to render our lives believable.[2]

In developing this book, no attempt was made to include each and every one of the independent Hispanic republics of Latin America and Puerto Rico, although issues are raised that mention specific instances in more than two-thirds of them. Instead, most of the topics the reader will find here were chosen for their relevance to both Spain and a number of the New World nations, without intending to suggest that every country faces the same challenges to the same degree or in exactly the same way. In a few instances, the chapter's discussion is limited to a focus on one country: the war on drugs in Colombia, the issue of Basque independence and terrorism, and the monarchy in Spain, for example.

Each chapter begins with a section that provides some background and three or four questions about the contemporary issue. A discussion of both sides of each question follows, along with questions and activities for students, a vocabulary list that could be useful in discussing the issue and a short list of sources, including print, Internet and video.

In addition to the specific Internet sites mentioned at the end of each chapter, students and teachers will find the following searchable Web sites useful for study and research: Latin American Network Information Center (LANIC), http://www.lanic.utexas.edu, the most complete collection of Web sites on Latin America, organized by topic and country; *Sí* Spain, http://www.sispain.org, a collection of pages on Spanish history, political organization and culture with links to many other sources, a project of the Embassy of Spain in Canada; and *Tecla*, http://www.sgci.mec.es/uk/Pub/tecla.html, articles in Spanish written for students on Spanish and Latin American topics, published weekly by the Office of Education of the Spanish Ministry of Culture, Education and Sports in the United Kingdom and Ireland (Consejería de Educación en Reino Unido e Irlanda del Ministerio de Cultura, Eduación y Deporte).

Issues in the
Spanish-Speaking World

Chapter 1

The "Best" Spanish

Most of us are rather sensitive when it comes to ranking the best in language—especially our own. We think that our own way of speaking is perfectly good, logical or the most natural, at the very least. If someone criticizes or makes fun of the way we speak, our first reaction is to feel hurt, defensive or angry. Language is such a part of our being that we react to criticism about the way we speak as though we ourselves were the targets of the criticism. That's one reason why tempers flare when discussion turns to which variety of Spanish is the best one, or the one that should be taught in the schools or taught as a foreign language. For many years in the United States, teachers and their students were told that Castilian Spanish was *the* variety of Spanish that should be taught and learned. Today, there's a broader choice, but controversy still exists.

BACKGROUND

Castilian is one variety or dialect of Spanish. Nowadays, the Castilian variety of Spanish is also the official language of Spain, although the regional language is co-official in three of Spain's autonomous communities: Catalonia, Euskadi (or the Basque Community) and Galicia. Catalan and Galician (*gallego*) are about as different from Spanish as Portuguese or French and cannot necessarily be understood by Spanish speakers who are unfamiliar with them. Basque is even more different, since it is unrelated to any existing languages elsewhere in Europe. Inside of Spain today there are people who oppose the co-equal status of regional languages.[1] They say that Spanish—that is, Castilian—ought to be Spain's one and only official language. Others, especially those in the minority language regions, vigorously support not only the maintenance of these languages in the home but their co-equal status with Castilian in their home regions.

Linguists define the term "dialect" as one of several varieties of a single language. It's important in this discussion to remember the linguists' definition, because the common, man-on-the-street meaning of "dialect" is "an inferior or *substandard* variety" of a language. As we will see, *everyone* speaks a dialect, all the way up to the Queen of England (or for that matter, the Queen of Spain).

Usually, speakers of one dialect can understand speakers of another. However, if you've seen movies made in other English-language countries such as England or Ireland, you know that it is sometimes very difficult to understand speakers of another dialect with whom you do not have frequent contact. Even in the United States there are dialects that most of us may not *easily* understand. Dialects can differ from each other in vocabulary (*pop* versus *soda* versus *soft drink*), in pronunciation (*greasy* with an "s" sound versus a "z" sound), in grammar (acceptance or rejection of grammatical constructions such as *I might could go* or *you-all*) or in meaning (the *trunk* of a car is its *bonnet* in England).

There are two kinds of dialects: geographical and social. Geographical dialects arise because communities of speakers become isolated from one another by geographic or political boundaries. Two major divisions within Spain include the Castilian of the *meseta* (the central plateau) and the Castilian of the south, or Andalucía. In the dialect of the *meseta*, c before e or i and the letter z are pronounced like English "th." (In Spanish this sound is called the *theta*.). This is the most distinctive aspect of Castilian pronunciation (and it's not the result of a lisp of one of Spain's monarchs!). In the South, in Andalucía, most of Extremadura and Murcia, the local population usually pronounces words with these same letters as if they were spelled with "s." In addition, in much of the *meseta*, the letter *ll* is pronounced "el-ye" but elsewhere (including most of the people under 30 in Madrid) this letter is pronounced as though it were the letter *y*. This, too, is a geographical distinction.

However, the two geographical dialects also became distinguished socially to some degree because of the influence of the central government and the school system, two entities that often play an important role in determining which varieties of language move up the social scale and are accorded more prestige. All over the peninsula, the dialect of the Castilian *meseta* became the prestige variety and educated people began to use the prestige pronunciation even if they came from areas where /s/ and /y/ were more commonly used.

Latin America, conquered and colonized largely by people from Extremadura and Andalucía (especially during the formative first century of colonial rule), became a region where the southern variety of Castilian, not the Castilian of the central *meseta,* was spoken. For this reason, all of the Latin American dialects resemble the southern variety of *castellano*, especially in pronunciation, and when Latin Americans say that they speak *castellano*, they are referring to the transplanted Southern variety. As time went on, further differentiation took place. Latin American dialects all settled on *ustedes* as the plural form of *tú* rather than *vosotros*, which is the norm everywhere in Spain today. This is a second important difference between peninsular and Latin American Spanish. Colonial settlements were relatively isolated from each other. Gradually each area developed its own norms of pronunciation, some words took on new meanings and, occasionally, differences in grammatical structures developed. The capital cities of Lima, Mexico, Santiago, Buenos Aires, Bogotá, Santo Domingo and so forth, each with its schools, government offices and commercial establishments, became the regional centers of prestige language in the New World. Today there are many regional standard dialects, often called regional or national norms.

However, language variation doesn't stop with noticeable differences from one place to another, but it also includes differences in the speech of speakers who live in the same locality. For a variety of reasons, clusters of pronunciation, grammatical and lexical features become typical of the speech of one group or another, creating social dialects. Social dialects are variants that correlate with some sociological characteristics, such as level of education, economic status, urban versus rural locality, ethnic or religious group, and so on. The prestige dialect is usually the one spoken by the group with higher levels of education, high social status, or the economically advantaged. These speakers are more likely to live (or work) in urban areas and to belong to the dominant ethnic group, if there is one. When the prestige dialect is widely adopted, it is often called the "standard dialect" and then it becomes the one by which all others are judged. The upper classes in England learned the "King's English" with tutors or in the British public schools. Often the middle class strives hardest to master the standard dialect as a conscious or unconscious means of moving up the social ladder. In many cultures women are more likely than men to learn and use "markers" of the social dialect(s) that are higher on the prestige scale.

We are all familiar with dialects of American English that are associated with low prestige: limited education, low income, "less desirable" neighborhoods or "the sticks," and so on. Unfortunately, it is all too easy to use attitudes concerning language to stereotype a person as unreliable, dumb, dangerous, lazy, thieving, or indifferent (or, conversely, stuck-up, arrogant or vacuous). This occurs just as much in Spanish-speaking countries as it does in English-language areas.

One more complicating factor in this Tower of Babel is the interaction of languages. When speakers of two or more different languages live alongside each other or interact in significant ways (such as engaging in commerce), they learn something of each other's language. Most often the dominant group sees less need to borrow much of the other group's language, but both of them usually absorb at least some new words, especially for what the other culture has that is new and useful.[2] For example, Spanish borrowed several thousand words from Arabic while the Moors held part of Spain. Today, that number has diminished, but many words related to science and mathematics, agriculture, political organization and warfare—all areas in which the Moors were especially advanced during the Middle Ages—entered Spanish and are still in use today.

Likewise, Spanish adopted hundreds of terms from a variety of Amerindian languages (and considerably more in the local dialects in regions with a strong indigenous presence). Words as diverse as *huracán* (hurricane), *maíz* (corn), *cacique* (local chief, political boss), *tamal* (tamale), *puma* and *petunia* entered Spanish from indigenous languages of the Caribbean, Mexico, Central America and South America. From Spanish they have traveled to many other languages, including English, as the concepts and the products they name came to be known around the world. Today *salsa*, made from *tomates* and *chile*—both of them first cultivated in the New World and still known by words borrowed from the Aztec language—has replaced *catsup* or *ketchup* as the condiment of choice in the majority of U.S. homes (doubly ironic because *catsup* is also a borrowed word). Since the beginning of the twentieth century, the direction of borrowing has mainly occurred from English to Spanish. English terms in sports, politics, entertainment and technology abound in Spanish, as well as in other languages. Spanish speakers who live in the United States see and hear English every day, even those who do not learn to speak English fluently. Once words have been adapted to fit comfortably into the sound system of Spanish, *grava* (gravel), *troca* (truck) and *espeliar* (spell) are as easy (and logical) for a Spanish speaker to use as the word *salsa* is for an English speaker. Another way languages in contact can change is for native words to alter or expand their meaning. In this way *grados* (first, second, third grades) adds the meaning of "letter grades A, B, C" and *principal* (most important) takes on the meaning of principal of a school. And lastly, native words can be combined in ways that reflect the other language: *ir para atrás* (pronounced "pa'tras") is used for "to go back," rather than the standard *volver* or *regresar*.

So, is peninsular Castilian the "best" Spanish? The people who would agree make several assertions:

1. Peninsular Castilian is best because of its long cultural tradition and the prestige of Spain.
2. Peninsular Castilian is best because it is the language of fine literature and great writers.
3. Peninsular Castilian Spanish is pure; it is not hybridized or filled with unaccepted loan words.

DISCUSSION

Is Peninsular Castilian the Best Spanish?

Agree

Castilian Spanish (in its spoken or its written form) has been the standard variety for years. It is the variety taught in schools in Spain and spoken on national radio and television there. It has been taught as the standard variety of Spanish in the United States for decades. While there are other regional "standards," they simply don't have the same prestige as peninsular Castilian. Some Latin American dialects are stigmatized[3] in certain parts of the United States because of their association with poverty or low levels of education. Castilian Spanish, on the other hand, is universally accepted outside of Spain as an educated, standard variety. This makes it an excellent choice as the dialect to teach in foreign language classes.

In addition, the Spanish government, through its ministries of education and culture, has been very active in promoting the teaching of Spanish in the United States through the support of materials, summer training programs and other opporunties for teachers. Although other regional standards are not denigrated by the Spanish professionals, teachers consciously or unconsciously favor the dialects they have learned in school and professional training.

Disagree

Peninsular Castilian may have tradition going for it, but Latin Americans outnumber Spaniards at least 8 to 1 (roughly 350 million Spanish speakers in Latin America versus 40 million Spaniards). Linguists don't measure Latin American dialects on a "better to-worse" yardstick based on their similarity to the Castilian of Spain. Every region does have its own prestige dialect; what is considered "best" in Argentina should reflect the speech and writing of educated Argentineans; in Colombia, the norms of its educated speakers are an appropriate standard to use when deciding which dialect to teach in the schools, use on radio and television, and so on.

In the United States, the issue is more complex. In the South and West, closer to Latin America, most schools and universities are very comfortable accepting teachers who use the standard variety of any Latin American country, although teachers originally from Latin American countries usually find themselves moving toward a more homogeneous pronunciation (with all their s's and vowels in place) to accommodate their students. On the east coast, Latin American dialects used to find less than universal acceptance, but nowadays the Spanish-language news media, especially television, spread the message that well-educated, well-traveled people are just as likely to speak Latin American dialects as peninsular Castilian.

Is Peninsular Castilian Superior Because It Is the Language of Fine Literature and Great Writers?

Agree

This argument is also heavily influenced by tradition. Certainly, great writing is one mark of a language (in this case, a dialect) that is worth imitating and learning. Spain has undeniably produced some of the world's great writers, especially during its Golden Age: Miguel de Cervantes, Félix Lope de Vega, Francisco Quevedo and Luis de Góngora. In the nineteenth and twentieth centuries, internationally recognized Spanish writers produced great prose and poetry in Castilian: Gustavo Adolfo Béquer, Benito Pérez Galdós, Miguel de Unamuno, Pío Baroja, Federico García Lorca, Camilo José Cela, Carmen Laforet, Juan Benet and many others. Today, Spanish writers such as Ana María Matute, Juan Marsé, Carmen Martin Gaite, Eduardo Mendoza, Rosa Montero, Miguel Delibes and Antonio Munoz Molina are prolific and well received both inside and outside of Spain.

Disagree

Literature is obviously one place to look for the "best" language. But which literature is representative of modern Spanish? Modern Latin American writers are better known in the United States than Spanish ones: Gabriel García Márquez, Isabel Allende, Mario Vargas Llosa, Laura Esquivel, Elena Poniatoska and Carlos Fuentes are very well known and very productive. Latin American poets Octavio Paz, Pablo Neruda and Gabriela Mistral won the Nobel Prize for Literature in the twentieth century, as did novelists Gabriel García Márquez and Miguel Asturias. Still, literature is only one of the many ways in which language is used. Commerce is more important than ever: Americans will interact more with Latin American than with Spanish businessmen. Immigration trends mean that more Americans than ever before will come into contact with speakers of Latin American much more often than peninsular Spanish. Furthermore, it is very difficult to distinguish the *writing* of educated writers of Spanish, no matter where they come from. To heap praise on peninsular Castilian and ignore the language of the other 350 million Spanish speakers is to promote an elitist, anachronistic attitude that all things Spanish are admirable and that Latin American language and culture are second rate.

Can It Be Said That Peninsular Castilian Is Best Because It Is the Purest Form of Spanish?

Agree

The "purity" question is undoubtedly the most emotional component of this issue. In reality, the proponents of peninsular Castilian are not the only ones who argue for purity and fight a valiant battle against the watering down of standards, the wholesale borrowing of English terms and the bastardization of a noble language. Purists—those who plug the leaky dikes of language against the sea of change—may also be speakers of Latin American dialects. They may be teachers or members of the public who were educated in a time or a place where the Spanish language and its speakers "obeyed the rules." The pure (or purer) forms of Spanish were not adulterated with massive borrowings from English. Speakers did not "code switch" (change from one language to another in the middle of a sentence or a phrase). People knew the names of things; their vocabulary was more varied, and richer: it had not become impoverished. One thing Spanish definitely was not—it was not a hybrid like "Tex-Mex," "Spanglish" or "Neuyorican."

Disagree

Opponents ask, "What exactly do you have in mind by *pure*?" Modern peninsular Spanish has many recent loan words. Linguistic innovation is thriving in Spain. Furthermore, borrowing is nothing new in peninsular Spanish. Spanish absorbed hundreds—even thousands—of words from Arabic during the hundred of years of Moorish occupation. What about the French and Italian words that have been incorporated into Spanish beginning in the Middle Ages and continuing through the twentieth century: *jabón* (soap), *chiminea* (fireplace), *servilleta* (napkin), *ópera*, to name only a few? Should we reject the words that Spaniards learned from indigenous Americans in the New World? There are approximately 100 words in common use in Mexican Spanish that come from Nahuatl (*tomate, chocolate, aguacate, guacamole, ejote, elote, petate, cuate, me-*

cate, tamal, mescal, nopal, and on and on). In Andean Spanish, the list includes *puma, llama, papa, ají, condor, pampa* and many others. Today, English is the language from which all dialects of Spanish are borrowing most heavily. Although vocabulary from politics (*el líder*), sports (*un honrón*) and entertainment (*el show*) are prominent in borrowings from English, the most noticeable area today is the field of technology. Sometimes speakers translate concepts literally into Spanish: *el disco duro, la plataforma, el programador, el ratoncito* (hard disk, platform, programmer, mouse). Other times no attempt is made to disguise the English origins of a term: *el sof(t)ware, hacer clic* (software, to click). These borrowed terms are used just as much in peninsular Castilian as in other dialects.

However annoying these new terms may be, it is the question of "hybrid" varieties that causes purists the greatest grief. The hybrid dialects—variously called Tex-Mex, Spanglish or Neuyorican—are usually spoken by bilinguals. Most often they are the children or grandchildren of Latino immigrants who use common English words, adapted phonologically and morphologically, to Spanish in place of common Spanish words,[4] as in *Ayer fui a pagar el bil pero el super no estaba.* (Yesterday I went to pay the *bill* but the *super[intendent]* wasn't there.) Speakers of these dialects also "code switch." Code switching means changing from one language to another between sentences or within the same sentence: *Yesterday I went to pay el bill, pero el super no estaba. Creo que fue al béisbol game. Sabes, su cuñado tiene un season ticket.* (Yesterday I went to pay the bill but the superintendent wasn't there. I think he went to the baseball game. You know, his brother-in-law has a season ticket.) Although it may appear random and haphazard, code switching is governed by rules and fluent code switching requires a speaker to know both languages very well.[5]

In addition to borrowing and code switching, speakers of Spanish from immigrant families sometimes use words or word forms that (1) come from low prestige rural or urban dialects or (2) are characteristic of immature language development. An example of the first is the use of the term *hocico* to mean mouth: *¡Callate el hocico!* (Shut up; quiet your mouth.) In standard Spanish *hocico* is a term that is appropriate only when referring to animals. The expression seems "rustic" or countrified, reflecting, perhaps, the rural origins of the family or the community to educated speakers. The words *naide*, *naiden* and *naides* are alternate pronunciations and low prestige in comparison to the standard *nadie*, used by educated speakers everywhere. In the absence of a formal system of schooling in Spanish or other relatively intense contact with educated dialect norms, non-standard vocabulary, grammar and pronunciation can become established in a U.S. community's Spanish dialect.

An example of immature language development in adult speakers is the use of the form *(yo) sabo*, which is a regularized form. That is, *sabo* follows the pattern of the vast majority of verbs. Although this form is common in children's speech everywhere, in a monolingual environment, children learn that the adult form for the verb *saber* is *(yo) sé* (I know). Where Spanish is less important to achievement in school or where parents are anxious for their children to learn English and believe that Spanish will serve as a home and restricted community language only, child forms are frequently ignored and become a part of a person's idiolect, or personal speech patterns.

You can see that deciding what is the "best" Spanish is not simple. Many of the following questions will ask you to discover what people in your community, including students and teachers, think about what constitutes "good" Spanish or the "best" Spanish. As you carry out these surveys and opinion polls, remember that people are genuinely sensitive about their language. Some people are fiercely proud; others have been told that their variety of language is substandard. Therefore, as you ask questions, be considerate and objective.

QUESTIONS AND ACTIVITIES

1. In Spain and in most Latin American countries, as in the United States, more than one language is commonly spoken in at least some regions. Spain has made Castilian the official language of the country but co-official with the important minority languages in their home regions. How do you feel about the question of official language status for English in the United States? What would it mean to make English the official language of the United States? What advantages and disadvantages would this decision have?

2. Here are a few words borrowed into Spanish from Indian languages: *canoa, huracán, aguacate, tamal, ocorina, tomate, chocolate, jaguar, petunia, cacique*. What kinds of objects or actions did these words refer to? Why do you think the Spanish borrowed these particular words?

What other Spanish words do you know that came from indigenous languages?

3. Look up these pairs of words in a monolingual Spanish dictionary: *piña/ananás*; *aguacate/palta*; *maíz/choclo*; *poroto/frijol*; *esquintle/guagua*. Can you find the place of origin of each of the pair? Can you think of reasons why there are several words for the same referent (object or thing)?

4. Many of the words that Spanish borrowed from Arabic begin with the letters *al* (an article, "the"). For example, *alcalde*, from "al-qadi," which was the title of the local magistrate. With the help of any Spanish/English dictionary, find up to 20 words that begin with *al*. Then find out which ones come from Arabic. (If you don't have a dictionary that gives etymologies or origins of words, use a good online dictionary, such as the dictionary site of the Anaya publishing company (http://www.dicionarios.com). The Spanish definitions will indicate the origin of the words (for example, *ar.* for Arabic). Use the words you find to fill in the following table. What are some of the assumptions you can make about the impact of Moorish culture in Spanish life, based on the number of Arabic words that still survive in the Spanish language?

palabra en español	significado en inglés	categoría
alcalde	mayor	administración pública artesanías y comercio
aljibe	cistern	agricultura casa y muebles ciencia y matemáticas religión

5. Use library resources (preferably in Spanish) to do research on Arabic (1) administration, (2) crafts and commerce, (3) housing and architecture, (4) agriculture or (5) science and mathematics in Spain during the Middle Ages. Imagine that you are a visitor to Moorish Spain sent to learn about their achievements. Write a letter back to your Christian king describing some of the things you observe.

6. Most Americans live in communities where there are at least some Latinos. If you have Latino friends or neighbors, interview them to find out which geographic dialects they can identify. For example, *¿Dónde se habla el castellano? ¿Hay países donde la gente habla un dialecto castellano bastante distinto? ¿Cómo habla la gente allí? ¿Usan diferentes sonidos o palabras?* Be sure to find out where each person is from and the person's approximate age. Adults are much more likely to know about other dialects than young people.

7. What do Latinos in your community think is the "best" Spanish and why? If you live in an area where there are few Latinos, you may be able to connect with a school in another part of the United States to do this survey as a joint project.

8. Have you ever heard someone in the community or a teacher mention something that was an example of "poor" or "bad" Spanish? Fill out this chart as completely as you can. To what extent can you see connections between the age, profession or level of education of the people you interview and their attitudes toward "poor" Spanish? You might want to do this activity as a follow-up to the "best" Spanish survey, above.

edad y sexo	profesión	país de orgigen	educación	ejemplo(s)
40? F	maestra	México	universidad	ir pa'trás, puchar

9. In areas with large Latino populations, discover whether Spanish speakers accept "code switching." To what degree do people accept English loan words? Try to identify 10 or 15 common English loan words used in your community. Ask Spanish speakers to what extent they   accept them. Here's one way you could do it. A few loan words are listed.

palabra o frase mixta	Yo la uso Si/No	Yo la rechazo Si/No	Adulto/ Adolescente
troca bil			
Concha			
fue al grocery			

10. What do you think about loan words and code switching? When you speak to other students or to native speakers of Spanish, do you ever use loan words from English? If you do, what are some of the reasons why? If you are a bilingual speaker, is code switching common in your family?

11. You may be able to find someone who is an adamant "purist" or—on the opposite end of the scale—a vigorous proponent of teaching the predominant local dialect of Spanish, which might be Chicano Spanish, New Mexican, Cuban-American Spanish, Neuyorican or other. Your teacher or an officer in the local Spanish teachers' association or teachers' union may be able to give you the name of an individual. Arrange

a telephone (or e-mail) interview with him or her. Find out this person's views concerning which geographical and social dialect should be taught and why. Summarize what you learned in a short report in Spanish.

VOCABULARY/VOCABULARIO

Nouns/Sustantivos

Castillian (dialect)	el castellano
dialect	el dialecto
geographic differences	la variación geográfica
grammar	la gramática
language	el idioma/la lengua
language, native	la primera lengua, la lengua nativa
linguist	el/la lingüista
linguistics	la lingüística
loan word	el préstamo
the norm, the standard	la norma
prestige	el prestigio
pronunciation	la pronunciación
purist (person)	el/la purista
social differences	la variación social
Spanish	el español, el castellano
Spanish (of Spain)	el español peninsular
Spanish, Latin American	el español latinoamericano
speaker	el/la hablante
speaker, educated	el hablante culto
speaker, native	el hablante nativo
standard Spanish	el español oficial o estándar, el español culto
stereotype	el estereotipo
variety (of language)	una variante
vocabulary	el vocabulario, el léxico
words	las palabras

Verbs/Verbos

to "code switch"	cambiar de código
to criticize	criticar
to loan, borrow	prestar
to pronounce	pronunciar
to research	investigar

Adjectives/Adjetivos

bilingual	bilingüe
cultivated, educated	culto/a
devalued	despreciado/a
hybrid	híbrido/a
mixed	mixto/a
monolingual	monolingüe
pure	puro/a

RESOURCE GUIDE

Books and Articles

Artze, Isis. "Spanglish Is Here to Stay." *Education Digest* (September 2001): 50–55.

Becker, Kristin R. "Spanish/English Bilingual Codeswitching: A Syncretic Model." *Bilingual Review* (January–April 1997): 3–30.

Elias-Olivares, Lucia, ed. *Spanish Language Use and Public Life in the United States.* New York: Mouton, 1985.

Gutierrez, Manuel J. "Simplification, Transfer, and Convergence in Chicano Spanish." *Bilingual Review* (May–August 1994): 111–121.

Lipski, John M. *Latin American Spanish.* London: Longman, 1994.

Lodares Marrodan, Juan. *Gente De Cervantes (Historia Humana del Idioma Español).* Madrid: Taurus, 2001.

Penny, Ralph. *A History of the Spanish Language.* New York: Cambridge University Press, 1991.

Smead, Robert N. "English Loanwords in Chicano Spanish: Characterization and Rationale." *Bilingual Review* (May–August 1998): 113–123.

Stavans, Ilan. "The Gravitas of Spanglish." *Chronicle of Higher Education*, October 13, 2000, pp. B7–B9.

Internet

LANIC Spanish-language newspapers in the continental United States. <http://www.lanic.utexas.edu/la/region/news/>.
II Congreso Internacional de la Lengua Española Instituto Cervantes. <http://cvc.cervantes.es>.

Video

El español de hoy. Videocassette. Princeton, NJ: Films for the Humanities & Sciences, 1999. Color. 32 min.
La Nueva España. Videocassette. Princeton, NJ: Films for the Humanities & Sciences, 1999. Color. 33 min.

Spanish bullfighter Jesús Millán Cambra watches a fighting bull fall during a bull-fight in Valdemorillo, Spain on February 9, 2002. The Valdemorillo bullfight is traditionally the first important bullfight of the Spanish season. (AP Photo/Efe)

Chapter 2

The Bullfight

What would Spain be without bullfights? Does the bullfight represent the "essence" of Spain? Or would it be a "better place" if the bullfight, the *fiesta nacional* (also called the *fiesta brava, fiesta de toros, la corrida de toros*) were prohibited? Few topics can raise hackles faster in Spain than a conversation about bullfights, because—contrary to what many outsiders think—not all Spaniards are in favor of the *corrida de toros*, and not every Spaniard is a fan. Spain has a vocal and active antibullfighting movement (*los antitaurinos*); its adherents are committed and don't mind telling you why.

BACKGROUND

When we hear the word bullfight, most of us think of the *corrida de toros*, an elaborately choreographed and solemn spectacle, with *matadores* (bullfighters) dressed in glittering suits parading before cheering crowds in one of Spain's large bullrings. Nevertheless, the *corrida* is just one of as many as 16 different kinds of bull games known and celebrated in Spain. These *fiestas de toros* range from the most serious and carefully regulated to comic free-for-alls in a town square. Not all of them require bulls. Cows or heifers as well as bull calves are used in some, according to the kind of event. In some kinds of events, the animal lives to see another day.

Organized opposition to bullfights started as early as the sixteenth century. Then it was the Church that opposed the *fiesta brava*. By exposing man to death by the bull, it was too reminiscent of animal fights staged by the pagan Romans. When threats to excommunicate the *toreros* (bullfighters) failed to end the *fiesta de toros*, the Church tried to forbid its clergy from attending the events and to keep towns from staging bullfights on religious feast days or dedicating the bulls to the Virgin Mary. That tactic was just as unsuccessful. Since that time various monarchs have prohibited the bullfight (especially in the eighteenth century) and many individuals and organizations inside and outside of Spain have denounced the *fiestas de toros* as backward, barbaric, and excessively cruel.[1] Even so, the *fiesta de toros* lives on in its many forms.

Although Spain is the undisputed home of *la fiesta brava*, *corridas de toros* also take place in Mexico, Colombia, Venezuela, Ecuador and Peru. In Europe, Portugal and France also permit variations on taurine games.[2] Every major newspaper in Spain has a section devoted to the bulls, and famous bullfighters are followed in the press like movie stars. The best-known bull ranches and their owners are as familiar in Spain as the best-known companies and CEOs in the United States. Occasionally members of the bullfighters' teams or *cuadrillas* achieve national acclaim—although not the superstar status accorded to the *matadores*. Internet sites now compete with taurine magazines and the newspapers for interviews with the *matadores*, their handlers and promoters and offer reviews of bullfights throughout the season, and the true fans (*aficionados*) never tire of trading stories about the best passes (*faenas*) they have witnessed.

Yet, at the same time, a growing number of Spaniards and Latin Americans have organized to protest the blood sport they call the national shame (*la vergüenza nacional*). In May 2000, shortly after the beginning of the Feria de San Isidro, Madrid's bullfighting season, a billboard with a picture of a dying bull appeared on a downtown building. Within two weeks, the city government ordered it to be removed. The antibullfight groups that hung the poster complied but protested the mayor's "blatant act of censorship." After noting that a growing number of people worldwide oppose bullfights, a spokesman for the World Society for the Protection of Animals went on to say, "[a]ny compassionate person who has witnessed a bullfight would find it hard to conclude that it is anything other than a glorified torture show. It is difficult to understand how in the year 2000 such an activity could be celebrated as a national festival."[3]

You can see that this is not a polite disagreement among friends. Let's look at three common questions that one hears when this controversy is discussed.

1. Is the bullfight a barbaric, backward custom, unsuitable for a modern, twenty-first-century nation?
2. Does the bullfight deserve protection because of its deep roots in Spanish culture?
3. Do tourists, rather than genuine followers of Hispanic tradition, provide the economic support that keeps bullfighting alive?

DISCUSSION

Is the Bullfight a Barbaric, Backward Custom, Unsuitable for a Modern, Twenty-First-Century Nation?

Agree

Most Spaniards that want Spain to become "truly European" answer this question affirmatively. For these Spaniards (and Latin Americans) the *corrida* is an embarrassing anachronism, a spectacle that seems more appropriate to medieval than modern times. How can Spain, a country that has joined Europe and often leads in humanitarian and ecological causes, be so barbaric in this respect? Spain is a country that sends its men and women around the world on peacekeeping missions and rescue teams to pull victims from the debris of earthquakes and floods. How can it even contemplate entertaining people with the slaughter of more than 1,500 animals a year in the arena?

The desire for Spain to be more like the rest of Europe and for Spaniards to act and think more like other Europeans is not new; neither is linking the *fiesta brava* with backwardness in comparison to the more rational and enlightened behavior of the northern European countries. For several centuries, Spanish intellectuals have lambasted the *corrida* as barbaric and unbecoming of a nation: "The 'fiesta nacional' is unanimously seen in Europe as the expression of the primitive, savage and violent character of the Spanish people."[4] The opposition to bullfighting in other European countries threatened to delay the entry of Spain and Portugal into the European

Union (then the European Economic Community) in 1985. British, German and Italian animal rights groups were in the lead; France, with a bullfighting tradition of its own, was not in a position to object strongly.

Disagree

It's a bit odd, say the *aficionados* of the bullfight, for other Europeans to call the Spanish barbarians. The English are known for their violence at events like soccer matches; some European countries have banned British fans because of the frequency and ferocity of their hooliganism.

Nevertheless, supporters of the *juegos taurinos* (taurine—or bull—games) admit that their appeal is not to reason but rather to the irrational in mankind. For many *aficionados* the *corrida* is a drama that pits man against elemental nature, and intellect against the brute strength of the bull. They point out that all cattle are eventually killed for food (and the bull is given to charity or its meat is sold, as is any other cow or bull), but the *toro bravo* (the brave bull or the fighting bull) plays a role in something greater. They also remind us that although the bull always dies in a *corrida*, there is no guarantee that the *matador* will emerge unscathed or even alive. Every year scores of bullfighters are injured and several die from injuries suffered in the arena.

The *matador*, with his years of preparation for the ring, his dazzling suit of lights (*traje de luces*) and his ability to control fear in the face of such danger, is both an artist and an athlete. He must stay in training no less strict than that of any Olympic-class runner. Hours of practice and a rigid diet to maintain the important lean and muscular look require dedication as well as an intense desire for fame and *pesetas*.

Ironically, concerns about public health may threaten the future of bullfighting more than political maneuvering and pressure from animal rights organizations. The European Union's rules concerning the testing and disposal of bovine carcasses create additional expenses for bullfight promoters. In the past, the meat from bulls was either sold or given to charities. Today, animals over 30 months of age must be tested for mad cow disease or else the carcasses must be incinerated. The combination of additional costs and lost revenue may cause local fiestas to forego offering *corridas*. Although fighting bulls are raised in open pastures and are, therefore, unlikely to consume contaminated cattle feed that is thought to spread the disease, breeders fear that one questionable test could cause the destruction of entire herds.

Does the Bullfight Deserve Protection Because of Its Deep Roots in Spanish Culture?

Agree

The *corrida* and its related events have roots that extend far back into Spanish history. It is steeped in awe, tradition and the essence of Spanish life. The bull is present in the earliest Spanish art: bisons and bulls figure prominently in the caves of Altamira (about 14,000 B.C.). In pre-Roman times they reappear in the enigmatic statues of the *toros de Guisando* in the province of Ávila. The Roman geographer Strabo compared the shape of a map of the Iberian Peninsula to the hide of a bull. Bullfights have taken place for centuries in the *plaza mayor* of Spain's cities and towns, including the Plaza Mayor of Madrid. When billboards were banned along the highways of Spain's open spaces in the 1990s, a general cry went up to spare the Osborne sherry bulls, two-story black billboard silhouettes of a fighting bull that had come to symbolize Spain to both natives and foreigners, not unlike the way the Statue of Liberty symbolizes the United States. Now, suitably stripped of their advertising and given monument status, the remaining bulls guard the wide and empty landscapes of Spain.

The *fiestas patronales* (festivals for patron saints), celebrated with with their *toros*, are quintessentially Spanish and, apparently, alongside the genuine desire of Spaniards to join Europe, they answer a strong need of Spaniards to reassert their uniqueness. Contrary to expectations, the number of *corridas* and other taurine events actually rose, along with the number of local *fiestas*, after Spain joined the European Community (then the ECC). Many of these events are at the "intermediate" and "local" end of the spectrum[5] and are typical of small communities and open to a much wider range of participants (not just spectators). Although some involve killing the animals, in others the animals are mostly harassed and have plenty of opportunities to butt or toss their tormentors. The famous "Running of the Bulls" in Pamplona is one of these events, in which the participants try to outrun the bulls on their way to the bullring.

The greatest bullfighters have not only inspired newspaper writers, but famous authors as well. Federico García Lorca's "Llanto por Ignacio Sánchez Mejías" is one of the most powerful laments ever published in a modern European language. Ernest Hemingway's "Death in the Afternoon" brought bullfighting to the attention of millions of Americans for the first time. Goya and Picasso, two of Spain's most brilliant artists, and hundreds of lesser ones were fascinated by the *corrida* and were drawn to it again and again as a subject for their work. Clearly there is something in the bullfight that inspires this kind of art and identification. It must touch some strong human emotion that elevates it above the level of organized cruelty to animals.[6]

Disagree

"*Tortura no es cultura*" ("torture isn't culture"), counter opponents of the bullfight. Over the years, the most vocal critics of the bullfight have been the English, other EU countries and the United States, but today Spain has a strong antibullfighting movement. Associations such as ALA (*Alternativa para la Liberación de Animales*) and *Aministi Animal* in Spain and similar organizations in Latin American countries are often affiliated with the Humane Society and/or the World Society for the Protection of Animals (WSPA). In addition to trying to stop bullfights where they are now held, they hope to prevent the spread of bullfights to other countries.

Animal rights groups such as the WSPA use demonstrations, letter and advertising campaigns and educational programs to take their message to the public and to city or national authorities. Several antibullfighting conferences have been held in Mexico City where representatives from Mexico, Colombia, Venezuela, Peru, Ecuador, Bolivia and Spain met to strategize and to raise public consciousness about the issue. The biggest obstacles that *antitaurinos* face are indifference and a generalized feeling that, whether one enjoys attending the *corridas* or not, bullfighting is just part of Hispanic culture.

In addition to protesting cruelty to the bulls, the *antitaurinos* make the case that witnessing cruelty to animals leads to violence in children (or a tolerance for violence). Their efforts have lead to the development of a "humane curriculum" for use in schools and, in Colombia—where there are special bullfights for children[7]—a children's movement to limit and end bullfighting. More recently,

Mexico City passed a rule forbidding children under 18 from attending bullfights. Animal rights organizations were pleased, though skeptical of the commitment to enforce the rule. Still, the ruling sent an alarm through the bullfighting industry.

Do Tourists, Rather Than Genuine Followers of Hispanic Tradition, Provide the Economic Support That Keeps Bullfighting Alive?

Agree

Animal rights organizations point to polls that show that the majority of citizens of countries where bullfighting is permitted show little interest in the sport. Surveys done indicate that 97% of Peruvians and 84% of Mexicans oppose the bullfight (at least when questions were asked that included inflicting pain on the bulls). One of their conclusions is that, since locals do not enthusiastically support bullfights, most of the revenue from bullfights comes from ticket sales to tourists. Furthermore, promoting tourism is one way that the promoters try to sell bullfighting to countries where it has not been practiced or has not been popular.

For example, in 1996 the Costa Rican government announced a decision to spend the equivalent of $1 million to support and promote bullfighting (presumably as a tourist attraction). Costa Rica already had bullfights in which the bull was not killed in the ring. Gerardo Huertas, the WSPA's regional Director for Latin America, stated, "It is totally immoral for a poor country like Costa Rica to spend so much money to promote this cruel spectacle. It is an irresponsible, political decision to appease the powerful Association of Professional Bullfighters, who are supported by Mexico, in an effort to buy the votes of the rural community."[8] An exhibition bullfight with imported Spanish bulls and bullfighters fell flat when a Panamanian organization successfully turned away potential spectators. Only 250 spectators showed up, leaving the promoters $250,000 in the red and subject to a fine levied when one of the bullfighters killed a bull, in violation of Panamanian law. Several years later, another Spanish bullfight firm negotiated rights with the Cuban government to put on a *corrida* with bulls from Mexico and *toreros* drawn from all the countries where the *corrida* is allowed. According to the spokesperson for Empresarios Taurinos, SA, the idea was to "restore a cultural tradition of the island," one that had been suspended by the United States when it took control of Cuba following the War of 1898. The last bullfight in Cuba took place in 1947.[9]

Disagree

If the *corrida* is so unpopular with Spaniards, then why do the numbers of *corridas* and attendance continue to go up? Supporters of the bullfight point out that survey results can vary significantly, depending on how questions are asked. Although it's true that many Spaniards are opposed or indifferent to bullfights, it's one thing to ask people if they like bullfights and another to ask them if they like the idea of torturing animals. According to John Hooper, author of *The New Spaniards*, the only poll that asked Spaniards if they liked the bullfight showed that 35% said yes, about 14% were indifferent and 51% opposed it.[10] The shortage of reliable polls on this topic is curious. In a society almost obsessed with poll taking, the Centro de Investigaciones Sociológicas data bank has no entries for *tauromaquia* (another term for bullfighting), *corrida de toros* or *crueldad* (cruelty), even though its studies have questioned members of the public on issues ranging from voting, work and leisure to genetic engineering and/or horoscopes.

The number of *corridas* definitely seems linked to the resurgence in popularity of local *fiestas patronales* held on or around the day of the town's patron saint. The growing number of *fiestas* around the country may have to do with a need to reconnect to symbols of identity at a time when Spain seems to be rushing toward homogeneity with other European countries in many other respects. Many of these local *fiestas* never had *corridas de toros* or *corridas de novillos* (younger bulls) in the past (in part due to their cost), but the bulls do seem to increase attendance, and municipal governments are anxious to bring people in. And at any rate, whether they attend a *corrida de toros* in one of the main cities, people who journey to their family's home village or go to a *feria* (local festival) on a weekend outing are reasonably likely to take in one of the taurine events. Often these involve giving teenagers and young men a chance to dodge or jump over a young cow, or take part in "caping" a calf or a comic clown *toreo*—what most people consider just innocent fun.

QUESTIONS AND ACTIVITIES

1. Use a well-illustrated guidebook or photographic essay of Spain to find examples of several different kinds of taurine games: *corrida de toros*, *corrida de toros de rejones* (bullfight on horseback), *encierros*, *vaquillas*, *capeas*, and so on. Find out what some of the differences are between the "games" (professional bullfighter/village boys, animal is killed/animal lives, held in an arena/held elsewhere, etc.). Use Douglass' book[11] or the Internet to locate a set of pages that will define several of the different events.

2. All of the cities on the major bullfight circuit in Spain have more than one kind of event involving *ganado* (livestock). In pairs, look for the major *fiesta* at one of the following cities: Valencia, Seville, Madrid, Pamplona or Bilbao. Most of them will have a detailed schedule of events for the *fiesta*. How many of them involve games with bulls (or other cattle)? Each of these will be named to show the Spanish public what kind of event it is. What other events are on the schedule for the *fiesta*?

3. How do these major *fiestas* in Spain compare with the biggest celebration that your city (or nearest large city) holds on a yearly basis? Imagine that you are trying to replicate a Spanish *fiesta* in your city. Pick one of the major *fiestas* you have learned about. If money were no object, what would you have to do to put on a *fiesta* in your town or city? Would there be things that you *couldn't* do in the United States because of federal, state or local laws or specially marked cultural differences?

4. Use old travel magazines or color images from the Internet to make a collage to show different kinds of *fiestas de toros* in Spain. Write a brief description (about a half page, in Spanish) of each kind and bring it to class to display.

5. Watch the segment on the *corrida de toros* in "La Virgen y el *toro*" (El espejo encerrado). Would you classify the narrator and writer, novelist Carlos Fuentes, as a *taurino* or *antitaurino*? Paraphrase three or four statements made by Fuentes to back up your opinion.

6. The "Running of the Bulls" during the *fiesta* of San Fermín in Pamplona is the best-known example of an *encierro* (event when the bulls are driven into the arena or holding pen). Read about the *encierro* and see photos on the Internet. An excellent site is www.sanfermin.com/. You should be able to find a history of the *encierro* at this site (at http://www.sanfermin.com/guia/encierro.html) or another site.

7. If you're lucky enough to go to Pamplona during the San Fermines,

you'd better read some do's and don'ts before you think about running with the bulls. Advice from the experts is at http://www.sanfermin. com/guia/correr.html (or look for another if this link has moved). Summarize the advice they give. Instead of *tú* commands (if the advice is given in this way), use alternate forms such as (*no*) *Hay que*, (*no*) *Debes*, (*no*) *Tienes que* and the infinitive of the verb. If you use *Es mejor que*, *Es importante* or *Es posible que*, don't forget to use the present subjunctive in the subordinate clause.

8. Family table discussion: Role-play one of five members of a family (mother, father, daughter, son and grandfather). They have different opinions about whether the bullfight should be prohibited. Even if they agree in general, they have different reasons why they would like to see it preserved or banned. Get together with your "family" members and decide on roles and points of view. Now, it's 10:00 P.M. and you're all at home for supper. Let's hear your opinions (and reasons).

9. What is the view of religious leaders on the topic of bullfights? What about using animals for medical experiments or as sources of food? The viewpoint of the Catholic Church can be found online at http:// www.zenit.org or an animal rights site such as El Angel de la Web: http://usuarios.tripod.es/arcadenoe/animalesvatic.htm. A statement by Rabbi Ovadya Yosef, one-time chief Rabbi for Israeli Sefardic Jews, appeared in an Associated Press article.[12]

10. Of all the sports in the United States, perhaps only two have aroused anything like the controversy that the bullfight evokes. One is boxing; the other is the American rodeo. Choose one of the two American sports. Compare the ethical implications of this sport to the *corrida de toros*. If you believe that bullfights should be banned, do you have similar beliefs about the two American sports? How much weight should culture be given in allowing rodeos to continue?

VOCABULARY/VOCABULARIO

Nouns/Sustantivos

artist	el/la artista
athlete	el/la atleta
boxing	el boxeo
bull	el toro
bullfight	la corrida de toros, la fiesta nacional, la fiesta brava
bullfighter	el matador, el torero

bullfighter's team	la cuadrilla
bullring	la plaza de toros
cattle, livestock	el ganado
cow	la vaca
fair, local festival	la feria
fan (person)	el/la aficionado/a
festival	la fiesta
festival, patron saint	la fiesta patronal
games	los juegos
nature	la naturaleza
passes (in the bullfight)	las faenas
ritual	el rito, el ritual
rodeo	el rodeo americano
running of the bulls	el encierro
shame	la vergüenza
spectacle, special event	el espectáculo
sport	el deporte
strength	la fortaleza
suit of lights (matador's suit)	el traje de luces
sword	la espada
symbol	el símbolo
torture	la tortura
tradition	la tradición
young bull	el novillo

Idioms/Expresiones

It doesn't matter	No (me) importa

Verbs/Verbos

be enthused about	entusiasmarse (de)
bother, harass	molestar
kill	matar
oppose	oponer, oponerse a

permit, allow	permitir
preserve	preservar, mantener
prohibit, ban	prohibir
run	correr
wound	herir

Adjectives/Adjetivos

antibullfight	antitaurino
barbaric	bárbaro/a
beautiful	hermoso/a
brave, courageous	valiente
crazy, insane	loco/a
cruel	cruel
ethical	ético/a
modern	moderno/a
outdated	anticuado/a
primitive	primitivo/a
pro-bullfight	taurino/a
violent	violento/a
wild, fierce	bravo/a

RESOURCE GUIDE

Books and Articles

Douglass, Carrie B. *Bulls, Bullfighting and Spanish Identities*. Tucson: University of Arizona Press, 1997.

Hooper, John. *The New Spaniards*. New York: Penguin, 1995.

Marvin, Gary. *Bullfight*. Champaign: University of Illinois Press, 1991.

Pink, Sarah. *Women and Bullfighting: Gender, Sex and the Consumption of Tradition* (Mediterranean Series). Oxford: Berg, 1997.

Sanchez, Maria Angeles. *Fiestas de España: Imagen*. Madrid: El País/Aguilar, 1991.

Saura Ramos, Pedro A. *The Cave of Altamira/photographs by Pedro A. Saura Ramos with essays by Matilde Múzquiz Pérez-Seoane [et al.]*. New York: Harry Abrams, 1999.

Shubert, Adrian. *Death & Money in the Afternoon: A History of the Spanish Bullfight*. New York: Oxford University Press, 2000.

Internet

Guía San Fermín/Kukuxumusu. <http://www.sanfermin.com/>.
Portal Taurino. <http://www.portaltaurino.com>.
Toros y Toreros, Señal Colombia. <http://www.torosytoreros.com/>.
World Society for the Protection of Animals. <http://www.wspa.org.uk/newsframe.html>.

Video

Fuentes, Carlos. "La virgen y el *toro*." In *El espejo enterrado* (part 1). Videocassette. [S.l.]: Public Media Video, 1991. Color. 59 min.
———. "The Virgin and the Bull." In *The Buried Mirror* (part 1). Videocassette. [S.l.]: Public Media Video, 1991. Color. 59 min.
Montalban, Ricardo. *El matador*. Videocassette. New York: Gessler Publishing Company, n.d. Color. Ca. 59 min.

Like other Spanish families, members of the royal family often vacation together. Here, on Lanzarote, Canary Islands (December 1999), Spain's King Juan Carlos pushes the wheelchair of his mother, the countess of Barcelona. They are followed (on the left) by Crown Prince Felipe, Princess Elena and her infant son, Felipe, and (on the right) by Queen Sofia. (AP Photo/Ramon de la Rocha)

Chapter 3

The Spanish Monarchy

The current monarch, King Juan Carlos, is very popular with the Spanish public. Surveys show that the king, and the monarchy in general, is as popular today as it was 20 years ago. For example, a survey conducted in November 2000 by the newspaper *El Mundo* indicated that close to 86% of the Spanish public thought well of the king.[1] When asked whether they think the monarchy should continue under Prince Felipe when his father leaves the throne, the Spaniards surveyed gave a similar positive response. Clearly, public opinion toward the monarchy and its future is positive. It hardly seems a controversial issue. Yet there are some Spaniards who believe that Spain should reestablish a republican form of government. For these Spaniards, the Spanish governmental structure, headed by a hereditary monarch rather than an elected head of state or president, is anachronistic and even illegitimate.

BACKGROUND

Juan Carlos Alfonso Victor María de Borbón y Borbón was born not in Spain, but in Rome, Italy in 1938. His grandfather, King Alfonso XIII, had left Spain in 1931 when it became clear that antimonarchist, pro-republican sentiment was sweeping the country. Juan Carlos' father, Don Juan, was not the first in line to succeed Alfonso if the monarchy was ever going to be restored, but fate (a deadly auto accident and the deafness of an older brother) left Juan, the third son, as the heir apparent. Between 1931 and 1936, the new Republic[2] was beset by economic and political crises. Finally, it was challenged by a military rebellion; the ensuing Spanish Civil War resulted in the end of the Republic in 1939. Francisco Franco, the Commander in Chief of the forces that rebelled against the Republic, became *caudillo*, or military leader, of Spain that same year.

Franco dealt very harshly in pursuing those he considered enemies of his regime. Anyone who had sided with the Republic was subject to suspicion and arrest. Thousands of republicans were executed; thousands more were made to do forced labor. Within a few years the Franco regime was well entrenched. Political competition was outlawed: there would be only one party, which came to be called *el Movimiento*, the Movement. Military officers were appointed to many posts in the civilian government, labor unions were "reformed" to eliminate conflict between workers and management and censorship of the press and all media was imposed. Franco gave the Catholic Church, which had supported the rebellion against the Republic (except in the Basque Country), extensive power to supervise private and public morality as well as education. Secret police kept an eye on everyone.

Internationally, Spain was a pariah. Isolated from the rest of the world, purposely left out of the United Nations because Franco had given aid to (and received aid from) Nazi Germany, Spain suffered through more than a decade of poverty and hardship as Franco tried to go it alone. Finally, in 1959, Franco agreed to install a team of technocrats who believed they could improve the economy. Gradually Spain opened up its borders to outsiders and to foreign investment. The decade of the 1960s produced an economic "miracle": tourism expanded rapidly; Spaniards flowed from rural areas to the cities and tourist spots to seek new jobs and eventually to France, Germany and England to find employment in factories, restaurants and hotels in Europe's expanding economy. The standard of living rose for almost all Spaniards.

A decade or so after the civil war, the problem of who would follow Franco became an issue. Spain had no constitution that could guide the devolution of power. In 1947, the Republic was formally abolished and Franco's rubber-stamp *Cortes* (the Spanish parliament) passed a law that restored the monarchy. However, Don Juan, the heir to the throne, was too liberal for Franco's taste. After some years of negotiation, the dictator and the prince agreed that Don

Juan's oldest son, Juan Carlos, would be named Franco's successor. Juan Carlos was already in Spain, where he studied in Spanish military academies, and later, at the insistence of his father, received private tutoring from a team of university professors. He married Princess Sofía of Greece (also living in exile) in 1962. They moved into a relatively modest palace, *el Palacio de la Zarzuela*, in Madrid and began a family. (Juan Carlos and Sofía still live there today.)

Officially named successor to the *caudillo* in 1969, Juan Carlos swore allegiance to Franco's Movimiento Nacional. The young king-in-waiting was not well received by the Spanish public, however. He was awkward in public, and still spoke Spanish with a hint of a French accent from his early years growing up outside of Spain. People saw him as Franco's lackey, and not a very bright one at that. He was the butt of jokes and known by the nickname *Juan el Breve* (Juan the Brief), because few people expected him to last long on the throne. On more than one occasion members of the audience threw tomatoes at the royal couple.

However, Juan Carlos surprised the nation. While carefully fulfilling his duties to Franco, he was also considering how Spain should change once Franco was gone. Ironically, Spain's path to democracy was smoothed when in 1973 the Basque separatist group Euskadi ta Askatasuna (Basque Fatherland and Liberty or ETA) assassinated Admiral Carrero Blanco, Franco's right-hand man and mentor to the future king. After Franco's death in 1975, Juan Carlos assembled a group of political advisors of his own choosing; together they skillfully maneuvered Spain toward dismantling the dictatorship, writing a new constitution and restoring democracy to Spain.

In 1981, three years after the Spanish people ratified the constitution and five years after Franco's death, Spaniards watched in shock as members of a small group of military and Civil Guard officers broke into a televised session of the *Cortes*. Spraying the ceiling with machine gun fire as they entered, they held the nation's elected deputies hostage and demanded reactionary political changes. In Valencia, an armored military unit drove through the streets and trained its guns on public buildings. That night, the king earned the respect of the nation as he spoke on television: as commander of the armed forces, he ordered all military units to return to their barracks and stated that the Spanish democracy had his full support. The coup had been broken and the officers who participated in the conspiracy were later tried and sent to prison. Juan Carlos has rested comfortably on the throne ever since, and most Spanish citizens are happy to see him and his descendents remain there. They cite the following advantages of retaining the monarchy:

1. The institution of the monarchy is a symbol of continuity and unity.
2. Members of the royal family perform the multitude of ceremonial duties that every major government needs to take care of.
3. The royal family is good publicity for Spain and the tourist trade.
4. This royal couple and its children have served the nation very well.

Let's look at the arguments from both sides in more detail.

DISCUSSION

Is the Institution of the Monarchy a Symbol of Continuity and Unity for Modern Spaniards?

Agree

Maintaining continuity has been important in the recent past, especially immediately after the death of Franco and during the Transition (1975 to 1982), when the country was deeply divided over important political issues and many people were genuinely fearful of another civil war. Continuity is important today as well, as a counterbalance to party politics and when issues related to separatism and regional nationalism often crowd the headlines. In the future, when the pace of change may threaten to overwhelm everyone, a figure that anchors people to their common past may be just as valuable. Spain has tried a republican form of government twice in the past, without great success.[3] Several other thriving European democracies are parliamentary monarchies; there's no reason why Spain shouldn't have the same type of system.

Disagree

Many republicans maintain that, continuity or no, the Spanish monarchy is fundamentally illegitimate. The Spanish people were never directly involved in restoring the monarchy; rather, it was

Francisco Franco who decided to name Juan Carlos as his successor. Whatever sentimental comfort and sense of continuity Spaniards derive from the existence of the monarchy and the likeability of Juan Carlos, those feelings should not outweigh the fact that the monarchy was imposed upon the country without legal authority.

Does a Monarchy Have a Legitimate Function in Modern Times?

Agree

Every government needs to take care of duties that are largely ceremonial: receiving diplomats, inaugurating public projects, presiding at many national and international functions, supporting good works, making official visits to foreign countries and sponsoring special projects. European countries that are republics have a prime minister, who takes care of running the country, *in addition to* a president, who does the ceremonial duties. Not only the king, but also Queen Sofía, Prince Felipe and daughters Elena and Cristina are often called upon to officiate or speak at public events. Increasingly, Prince Felipe, who turned 34 in the year 2002, takes on official duties, such as attendance at inaugurations or other official trips. These also give the future monarch an opportunity to become more familiar with the operations of Spanish agencies in such areas as humanitarian aid and nation building abroad.[4]

Disagree

This isn't much of a reason to justify a system of government, say the critics of monarchy. Many large European nations, such as France, Germany and Italy, were once monarchies but now are republics, a more rational system of government. Spain should follow their lead and elect all of its leaders. Today's Spaniards say they approve of the monarchy because they like Juan Carlos. Spain is *Juancarlista* (pro–Juan Carlos) but not *monarquista* (pro-monarchy). Some republicans predict that "unless Felipe does very well, he will have a rough time as king."[5]

Furthermore, as an institution, monarchy is an irrational choice and runs contrary to modern ideas of equality.[6] Why must the Spanish monarch be a man when a woman might be a better choice? Why should the son of just one family in the country be eligible to be the head of state? Why should the oldest male child be chosen over the rest, even he isn't the best suited to govern? Why limit the choice of leaders so drastically and illogically when potentially Spain has 40 million individuals from which to choose its leaders? In addition, a monarchy is expensive to maintain. Even the general public agrees on this point: more than 45% of the same people who overwhelmingly approved of Juan Carlos and his son as Spain's future monarch considered the monarchy "expensive for the Spanish people."[7]

Are the Members of the Royal Family Well Respected and Well Received Outside of Spain?

Agree

The king has addressed the United Nations and enjoys great respect around the world. He speaks out on behalf of democracy and tolerance. In 1995, UNESCO (United Nations Educational, Scientific, and Cultural Organization) awarded Juan Carlos, along with former U.S. President Jimmy Carter, the Felix Houphouet-Boigny Peace Prize, which "honours people, organisations and institutions which have contributed significantly to the promotion, research, safeguarding or maintaining of peace." At the awards ceremony he was praised for leading his country's transition toward democracy. "His courage, intelligence and determination, now legendary, have allowed Spain to become one of the most solid democracies in the world. . . . Father of Spanish democracy, protector of the weak and minorities, he is also one of the pillars of peace in the world."[8]

The royal family make news when they travel on official business or go on vacation abroad; not many people pay attention if the prime minister visits Washington, but a visit from the king and queen makes headlines. The pomp and circumstance of royal weddings has brought favorable attention and thousands of additional tourists to Spain. Several years ago, a group of businessmen from Mallorca, where the royal family has spent part of each summer sailing, made a gift of a new yacht to the king. Their explanation: the tourist business booms when the royals arrive.

Disagree

The republicans question whether good public relations are a valid reason for choosing an antiquated hybrid form of government. Individuals who were pro-republican allowed themselves to be frightened by the attempted right-wing coup in 1981 and have never pressed for reconsideration of a change of governmental structure. The press also shies away from a serious discussion of the republic/monarchy issue, abdicating its responsibility to educate and inform the public.[9] The salary of the king is not open to debate, and even the expenditures of the Royal Household (palace and offices) are not examined; in contrast, the British parliament and the British press debate government outlays to the monarchy. Juan Carlos has occasionally lobbied for specific political issues that are supposed to be off limits to a parliamentary monarch. In addition, a few questions have been asked about the king's relationship to certain individuals with questionable financial records.[10] The Spanish constitution gives the king total immunity from prosecution: the monarch cannot be brought to trial for any reason. Republicans ask, is this right? Does the good publicity derived from an attractive, generally well-behaved royal family outweigh the special privileges it enjoys?

Has the Nation Been, in General, Well Served by This Royal Family?

Agree

Unlike most of his Borbón predecessors and many modern European royals, Juan Carlos, his wife and family have been very conscious of their need to behave responsibly. By comparison with other royal families, they live rather modestly. In 1993, their yearly stipend—on which they paid taxes like ordinary Spaniards—was $85 million, which covered all their personal expenses and a "skimpy" household staff. "Even the yacht he loves to sail is government property, and when the family goes skiing in the Pyrennees, they wait in line to take the lifts like everyone else. Says former British Ambassador Nicholas Gordon Lennox, "He inspires confidence in people, and they feel able to talk to him freely. That is probably why he has always been so very well informed."[11]

The king's children attended ordinary private schools, rather than having private tutors, and graduated from public universities. Both daughters have held jobs; Prince Felipe received a graduate degree in International Relations from Georgetown University in Washington, D.C. and is a commissioned officer in the Spanish armed forces.

Most Spaniards believe that the king played an important role in bringing democracy back to Spain after the death of Franco. Queen Sofía has been an advocate for the arts and charities. The king's strong public support of democracy the night of the attempted coup on February 23, 1981 (often referred to as 23-F in the Spanish press) was crucial to putting down the rebels without bloodshed.[12] It seems ungrateful to even consider rejecting the monarchy, especially while Juan Carlos is on the throne.

Disagree

Those who favor a republic acknowledge that the king played a role in the restoration of democracy (although they differ as to how important his role was) and in putting down the attempted coup. The general public also appears divided on the question of whether a democracy would have eventually developed in Spain without Juan Carlos' support. In the poll cited earlier, somewhat less than 50% thought that democracy would have come about without the intervention of the monarchy, but 8 out of 10 Spaniards believe his role in jumpstarting the process was critical to its success.[13] Still, the republicans say, just because today's monarch is doing a good job, there's no guarantee that his successor will be suitable. While it's possible to vote out an elected president who doesn't do his job well, getting rid of a monarch is much more difficult. The country could be stuck with an incompetent or misbehaving king or queen for years. What if Felipe, the future king, seriously embarrassed the nation or committed a grave crime? Unlike the U.S. Constitution, the Spanish constitution has no mechanism for removing the monarch, and there are no laws in place to declare him incompetent if he were severely ill or insane and resisted abdication. Does this make any sense?

The Spanish media still treats the royal family with kid gloves. Their jaunts around the country and the royal grandchildren make pleasant reading in Spain's celebrity-conscious press,[14] but the king and queen are never seriously scrutinized. As one of Europe's most eligible bachelors, Prince Felipe, however, gets more press coverage than he wants. Questions about the Prince's love life and choice of a future mate abound. Will he/won't he marry soon? (He doesn't seem to be in a hurry.) May he/may he not marry a commoner? (A royal decree dating from 1776 forbids it, but legal experts believe the decree does not apply, since the current constitution abrogated all others.) Does he/does he not have to have the permission of the king and the *Cortes* to marry? (Yes, if he wants to inherit the throne; it's in the constitution.) Should he/should he not be allowed to pick his own wife? (Most of the public and political leaders think if he can be trusted with the kingship he ought be able to make an acceptable choice in a wife.)[15]

Nevertheless, to many people, the royal family seems to spend as much time on its yachts and on the ski slopes as on serious work for the nation. Spaniards should have an open and honest debate about the system and then let the people decide.

QUESTIONS AND ACTIVITIES

1. Make a list of activities that a president of the United States performs and a similar list of activities for the Spanish monarch. (These are enumerated in the Spanish constitution of 1978. See http://www. DocuWeb.ca/SiSpain/Politics or http://www.lanzadera.com/monarquia /"Funciones y competencias"). What are the similarities? What are the differences?

2. Find out how to correctly address the king and the queen and to refer to the members of the royal family in writing. Find out what the official title of Prince Felipe is. See the appropriate articles of the Spanish constitution or http://www.lanzadera.com/monarquia/.

3. One of the most important obligations of the king and queen in a traditional monarchy was to produce an heir (especially a male heir). Why was this so important? Is it as important today as in earlier centuries? Why or why not?

4. Imagine that you are the secretary to the king, the queen or Prince Felipe (choose one). Make up a list of activities for the next two days for one of these royals. Be sure to include both official duties and personal activities. Compare your list with the lists of other students. Use the Website of the Royal Household for ideas (http://www.casareal. es).

5. You work for a Spanish news magazine. The editor wants a story on public opinion. Write five questions to ask the ordinary man or woman on the street to find out what the average Spaniard thinks about the current royal family. Interview your fellow students and record their responses. With the assistance of your instructor, decide in advance if you should use *tú* or *usted* in your questions.

6. Write three questions to discover if average people believe that Spain should continue to be a monarchy in the future. Then do a man/

woman-on-the-street interview in class. In order to ensure a wide range of opinions, your teacher may want the interviewees to draw lots for three roles: a person opposed to the monarchy, an indifferent person or a strong supporter of the monarchy. Be sure to ask those you interview to explain the reasons behind their answers. See who can be the most convincing in their roles. Once again, you should decide whether *tú* or *usted* is the most appropriate form of address for this interview.

7. Celebrity gossip magazines have a long history in Spain (where political and social views contrary to the Franco regime were not allowed) and they are still popular. Look at recent issues of magazines such as *¡Hola!* or *People en Español* for stories on the royal family. What aspects of life as a member of the royal family are emphasized? Read one of the stories. How does the life of this member of the royal family compare with a corresponding member of the U.S. president or vice president's family?

8. Do additional research on Queen Sofía. In what activities or causes has she taken an important public role? In what ways has she exerted influence on the king? If you could do a story on her for your school newspaper, what questions would you want to ask her? (Be sure to address her correctly.)

9. One of the most important reasons the Spanish public approves of the king and queen is their good behavior and comparatively modest style of living. Imagine that you are the royal parents. Write a list of do's and don'ts for the future king to keep him in good graces with the Spanish public. You should use the *tú* form since you will be writing as if you were the parent writing to your child; for example, *Compórtate bien en los lugares públicos. No fumes.* Review the affirmative and negative *tú* commands if you need to.

10. Sources say that Queen Sofía has had some definite opinions about the characteristics of the future wife of her son, Felipe. Write down a list of 6 to 10 characteristics that you think would be important in a future queen of Spain. Use *Es importante que tu esposa sea (subjunctive)* . . . */Es necesario que ella . . . + subjunctive*, etc. Trade papers with a classmate. Take the part of Felipe, agreeing or disagreeing with her advice: *Sí creo que es importante que mi esposa sea . . . /No creo que sea tan importante que ella sea . . .* or *Estoy completamente de acuerdo, Mamá. Pero es necesario que ella también sepa/tenga/conozca. . . .*

11. You have been invited to speak on a Spanish television program about Americans' opinions of monarchy in general and the Spanish royal family in particular. Many points of view will be represented. You should be able to provide at least two supporting arguments for your opinion. Prepare to role-play the television scene with your classmates

and your teacher (or another student) serving as moderator. If your school has a video camera, make this more authentic by taping the "program."

VOCABULARY/VOCABULARIO

Nouns/Sustantivos

crown	la corona
firstborn	el primogénito
His/Her/Your Majesty	Su Majestad
king	el Rey
monarch	el/la monarca
monarchists (pl.)	los/las monarquistas
monarchs (pl.)	los reyes
monarchy	la monarquía
prince	el Infante, el príncipe
princess	la Infanta, la princesa
queen	la Reina
the Republic	la República
republicans	los republicanos
right(s) of the firstborn	la primogeniatura
royal family	la Familia Real
Royal Household (palace and all of its offices)	la Casa Real
succession to the throne	la sucesión al trono

Verbs/Verbos

abdicate	abdicar
award a prize/present an award	presentar un premio
behave well/poorly	comportarse bien/mal
crown	coronar
elect	eligir
have an appointment	tener una cita, tener un compromiso
make an appointment	hacer una cita
marry, get married	casarse

open, inaugurate	inaugurar (un hospital, una base naval, etc.)
pass a law	promulgar una ley
renounce, relinquish	renunciar
run for (an office)	postularse para (la presidencia, etc.)
run for office, become a candidate	hacerse candidato
vote	votar

Adjectives/Adjetivos

prepared	preparado/a, capacitado/a
royal	real

RESOURCE GUIDE

Books and Articles

Acuna, Ramon Luis, and Alfageme, M. "Juan Carlos I: The Democratic King." *UNESCO Courier* 48(11) (November 1995): 32–34.

Alfageme, Maite. "La sucesión pendiente." *Epoca*, January 12, 1998, pp. 10–14.

Borras Betriu, Rafael. *Los ultimos borbones: de Don Alfonso XIII al príncipe Felipe.* Barcelona: Flor de Viento, 1999.

"Entre el amor y el deber." *People en Español* 4(7) (September 2001): 45.

"Felipe, el soltero de oro." *Epoca*, February 2, 1998, pp. 10–15.

Hooper, John. *The New Spaniards.* New York: Penguin, 1995.

"La boda que unió a España: Cristina e Iñaki empezaron su vida matrimonial con muy buenos augurios." *People en Español* (Añual 1997): 29–30.

Latona, Robert. "Juan Carlos." *Europe* (October 1993): 18–19.

Martínez, Sanjuana. "Voces en España en favor de la República: Que la figura del rey deje de ser tabú." *Proceso*, May 10, 1998, pp. 46–50.

Powell, Charles T. *Juan Carlos of Spain: Self-Made Monarch.* Basingstoke, UK: Macmillan, 1996.

Richardson, Bill. *Spanish Studies: An Introduction.* London: Arnold, 2001.

Satrustegui, Joaquin *¿Qué es la monarquía?* Barcelona: La Gaya Ciencia, Distribuciones de Enlace, 1976.

Serrano Balasch, Ramón. *89 republicanos y el rey.* Barcelona: Plaza y Janes, 1998.

"Su majestad la nariz." *People en Español* (November 1998): 42–43.

Williams, Mark. *The Story of Spain*. Malaga: Santana Books, 2000.

Internet

Constitución Española. Congreso de los Diputados. <http://www.congreso.es/funciones/constitucion/indice.htm>.

Datos de Opinion. Bulletin of the Centro de Investigaciones Sociológicas (CIS) *Boletín* #20. <http://www.cis.es/boletin/>.

"Felipe de Borbón y Grecia." *¡Hola!* <http://www.hola.com/perfiles/felipeborbon/>.

¡Hola! Realeza y personalidades. <http://www.hola.com/casasreales/>.

"La boda de la Infanta (princesa) Cristina." *El Mundo: Revista* 104. <http://www.el-mundo.es/larevista/num104/textos/boda.html>.

Monarchies of Europe/Monarquías de Europa. <http://www.lanzadera.com/monarquia>.

Página Oficial de Su Majestad el Rey. <http://www.casareal.es>.

Resources for Spain. Society for Spanish and Portuguese Historical Studies. <http://www.ukans.edu/iberia/ssphs/spainresources.html>.

Sí Spain. <http://www.sispain.org>.

"Valoración de la Monarquía." *25 años sin Franco, El Mundo*, special supplement. <http://www.elmundo.es/noticias/2000/graficos/noviembre/semana3/monarquia.html>.

Portrait of Christopher Columbus. From H. F. Helmolt, ed., *History of the World* (New York: Dodd, Mead and Company, 1902). No known portraits of Columbus were made during his lifetime or by persons who could have known him. Verbal descriptions of the explorer by family members and acquaintances differ in some details. Most agree that he was taller than average, with a rather long face, long (and possibly aquiline) nose and a ruddy complexion. (Perry-Castaneda Library, University of Texas at Austin)

Chapter 4

Columbus and the "New" World

October 12 is celebrated in many communities in the Western Hemisphere. Italian Americans celebrate it as Columbus Day, in honor of their compatriot. Latin Americans call the same day *el Día de la Raza* or *el Día de la Hispanidad* (the Day of Hispanic Peoples) to mark the arrival of Hispanic culture and the blending of traditions that is the trademark of Latin American civilization. Most indigenous peoples don't consider it a day to celebrate at all. It's not unusual for one person or historical event to evoke different responses from different audiences. Nevertheless, the negative reactions to Christopher Columbus and what he stands for surprised planners on both sides of the Atlantic as they began preparations for an elaborate celebration of the five hundredth anniversary of Columbus' arrival in the New World in 1992.[1] The *quintocentenario* (quincentennial) inspired a flood of articles and an examination of the man, the times and the effect of the European conquest of the Americas.

BACKGROUND

On a still morning in August of 1492, Christopher Columbus (*Cristóbal Colón*) departed from the Spanish port of Palos, not far from the Portuguese border, in his flagship, the *Santa Maria*. A total of 90 sailors in three small vessels made up the expedition that would change the history of the world. That morning represented the culmination of years of dreaming and waiting in the antechambers of the royal palaces of Europe's Atlantic powers, Portugal and Spain.

Columbus had arrived in Lisbon in 1476 at the age of 25. There he found work as a mapmaker and traveled with Genoese merchants to destinations north and south. A voyage in 1477 took him to England and Iceland. It is possible that he even traveled to Greenland. What seems certain is that stories he heard about lands farther to the west ignited his imagination and set in motion a dream that only grew in intensity as the years went by.[2]

Lisbon was a city teeming with mariners, adventurers and learned men, from whom Columbus acquired practical knowledge and books about geography. After marrying Filipa Moniz Perestrello, a woman from an aristocratic Portuguese family, Columbus spent several years on the island of Madeira, in the Atlantic some 600 miles southwest of the Portuguese capital. There his brother-in-law Bartolomé Moniz, also known as Bartomeu Perestrello, served as governor. Columbus—not much of a businessman—spent much time observing the winds and currents. In 1482 or 1483 he made a long voyage with a Portuguese fleet as far as the equator along the African coast, where the Portuguese were looking for gold and establishing colonial outposts as they pressed south, searching for a route to the East Indies. Once again, Columbus' imagination was fired by the possibilities of discovery of riches that could be reached by a new sea route. In addition, Columbus obtained valuable experience in tropical latitudes, which improved his navigational skills.[3]

The lure of profits to be made from expensive spices and the wealth of China spurred increasing interest in exploration in Western Europe. The stories of Marco Polo had circulated widely. By the 1470s, learned men all over Europe believed that the earth was round. None, however, had acted on this belief by setting out westward into the Atlantic Ocean to reach a destination in Asia; that was what set Columbus apart. To realize his dream, however, Columbus needed the backing and patronage of a sovereign prince. Probably with the help of his wife's family, in 1484 he was granted an audience with the king of Portugal, John II, who listened, considered and then rejected Columbus' proposal.

Columbus shifted his gaze to Spain. Newly widowed, he had in-laws in the city of Huelva and acquaintances in nearby Palos. He found additional friends in the Franciscan monastery of La Rábida, among them scholars of astronomy and a confessor to the Spanish queen, Isabel of Castile. Nevertheless, almost a decade went by before the Italian navigator and mapmaker would be able to convince the Catholic Kings to sponsor his voyage. Other projects occupied the monarchs: politically important marriages of their children Isabel, Juan and Juana, and the conclusion of the Reconquest, the centuries-long campaign to recover lands lost to the Moors in the eighth century. After the siege and eventual surrender of the city of Granada were accomplished in 1492, the monarchs could turn their attention to the insistent petitions of the Italian navigator. The possibility of finding wealth to underwrite a crusade to liberate the Holy City of Jerusalem interested Fernando. Isabel was equally moved by the prospect of bringing millions of new souls to the Church. In the end, it would be Castile that sponsored the voyage. Columbus was given enough to contract three small ships capable of an oceangoing voyage and outfit them with crew and supplies for a trip of several months.

Columbus found crew members well suited for a long and difficult journey. In Palos he contracted with the highly regarded sailors, Martín Alonzo Pinzón and his brother, Vicente Yáñez Pinzón, to captain two of the ships, the *Pinta* and the *Nina*, respectively. Columbus, a good navigator with no actual experience as a sailor, would captain the flagship, the somewhat larger *Santa María*. Once the crew was completed and the ships were outfitted for the voyage, they set sail for the Canary Islands to take on fresh water and fresh food supplies and then headed west.

The voyage took longer than Columbus had predicted, partly because the winds subsided for several days, but principally because the explorer had seriously underestimated the circumference of the earth and, therefore, the distance he would need to travel. His faith in his own vision, however, never seems to have failed him. Finally, in the moonlight of the predawn hours of October 12, one of Martín Alonzo Pinzón's crew sighted land at a location in the islands now called the Bahamas.[4] Daylight showed that the unimpressive island was home to a few people who lived in simple huts and wore no clothing. They were members of the Lucayan Tainos, the most northern of numerous groups of the Taino people, who occupied the Bahamas, the Greater and the Lesser Antilles. Columbus noted in his log that the Lucayan Tainos were docile and would be easy to turn into good servants and Christians.[5] He picked six of them to take aboard to begin training as interpreters. Moving on in the direction of other islands indicated by the natives he met, Columbus repeatedly asked about gold, which they possessed in small amounts in the form of jewelry. Always the Spaniards were told that the source of the metal that interested them was farther away.

Continuing on, the small fleet arrived at Cuba on October 28 and explored the coast for six weeks, with disappointing results. Still looking for gold and Asia, the Spaniards headed toward another island, which the Cubans assured them was a place where much gold would be found. Martín Alonzo Pinzón, who had been unhappy with Columbus' dallying, became separated from the other ships (although it is more likely that he deliberately set out on a different course). Pinzón and the *Pinta* were gone for nearly two months. The Indians Columbus and his men encountered were more suspicious of the strangers and even showed weapons. They explained that they feared a predatory tribe from other islands, called the Canibs or Caribs.[6] Columbus eventually moved on to Bohio, to which he gave the name of Española (Hispaniola),[7] where he found a somewhat more advanced people. During exploration of the coast, the *Santa Maria* was badly damaged on rocks near the shore. Having developed good relations with one of the local *caciques* (chiefs) and convinced that a gold field lay close by, Columbus decided to build a fortress at a location called Navidad, where he would leave part of the crew with some of the ship's guns, provisions and seed for a year. By chance, as he was departing, Pinzón's ship appeared on the horizon. With the remaining two ships and men, Columbus and Pinzón headed for Spain to take back the news of the admiral's discovery.

After a harrowing storm during which their ships were separated, Columbus and Pinzón reached the port of Palos on the same day. The monarchs received Columbus about a week later in Barcelona. The explorer took with him the odds and ends of gold that he had located, exotic birds and a few natives to show to his patrons. Fernando and Isabel treated him with great honors and they were eager to talk about a follow-up expedition.

When he returned to Hispaniola somewhat more than a year later, Columbus took with him 17 ships and 1,200 men, among them a number of skilled farmers, as well as animals, plants and seeds to begin the serious job of establishing a self-sufficient outpost. After a few weeks of exploring the Lesser Antilles and sighting Puerto Rico

(Borinquén in the Taino language), Columbus arrived at Navidad on the island of Hispaniola, only to find that not one man had survived the year.

The fortress had been burned to the ground and the site was littered with human remains. Gradually, the story emerged as Columbus questioned the Tainos: Spaniards had quarreled among themselves. Many wanted to be free to look for gold as much as they pleased. Spanish renegades took Taino women. Finally, a native *cacique* (chief) attacked the fort and other Tainos hunted down and killed the rest of the Europeans. The good and "docile" natives had had enough.

The massacre at Navidad marked a turning point in the history of relations between Europeans and [American Indians]. Columbus realized this immediately. . . . He understood that the myth of the good savage was over and that the colonization of the new lands would henceforth be a long, hard struggle. The time of discovery, of peaceful exploration of the islands and the seas, was also over. The happiness and magic of the meeting between the 2 worlds had ended at Navidad.[8]

Columbus began the work of setting up a colony. He put subordinates in charge of various operations and then left on another voyage of exploration. When he returned five months later, Hispaniola was again in turmoil. Indians were carrying on a guerrilla war against the Spaniards. Finally, in an effort to quell the native revolt, Columbus and his brother Bartolomé set out with troops to teach the Indians a lesson. Although they encountered a force of at least several thousand, the Spanish routed them with their firearms, crossbows and horses, which terrified the Indians. Nevertheless, it took 10 months to entirely subdue the Indian population. The Spanish forces also captured hundreds of natives. Columbus proposed to sell them in Spain to offset some of the losses incurred by the second voyage, since little gold had been found. He also began to tax the Indians, forcing each adult male to produce enough gold to fill a small flask every three months. However, there wasn't enough gold to meet the taxes. Columbus' tax scheme backfired: Indians disappeared into the forest to plan another uprising.[9]

In the meantime, in Spain, Columbus' critics among those who returned from Hispaniola had the ear of the monarchs. On the explorer's return, the king and queen were clearly intent on discovering when they could expect to get some payback on their investment. It was becoming well known that Columbus was an arrogant, hard-headed and ineffective administrator and had exceeded his authority on the island. Furthermore, the queen was opposed to enslaving the native people, even if they had been captured in war.

Although he completed two more voyages, the admiral's fortunes did not improve. Stubbornly clinging to the belief that China or perhaps the Indies lay just a bit farther away, he continued to explore the Caribbean coastlines and islands but did not do any significant exploration of the interior. Several massacres of Taino communities took place during the period of his third voyage. Columbus refused to accept the authority of a representative sent by the king and queen to serve as an administrator of Hispaniola. He was arrested and sent to Spain in chains. Reinstated, he returned for a final voyage. This time, he explored the coast of Central America, but lost all of his ships and was forced to spend a wretched year shipwrecked on the island of Jamaica. Eventually he returned to Spain, where he made repeated unsuccessful requests to the king for the portion due to him from the discoveries he had made. Columbus died, still believing he had explored the outer fringes of the Indies—or China, or Japan—in 1506.

The voyages of Columbus opened a new chapter in the history of the world, a period of exploration that would eventually bring to light two new continents and a new ocean, millions of human beings whose existence was undreamed of, a flood of silver and gold, and oddities such as rubber, tobacco, cocoa and *chicle* (the tree sap from which chewing gum is made). Valuable new edible plants from the Americas, such as potatoes, tomatoes, *chiles* and corn, would transform the diet of people not only in Europe but also around the world.[10] For all this he has been hailed as a visionary and perhaps the greatest explorer of all time. Should he also be blamed for the hundreds of years of exploitation and discrimination that his expeditions inaugurated in the New World? Should the descendants of indigenous and African peoples blame him for the enslavement of their ancestors? Let's look at some of the questions in this debate:

1. Should Christopher Columbus get the credit for "discovering" the New World?

2. Did Columbus set the pattern for a program of genocide in the New World?

3. Should we celebrate the "discovery" of the New World, knowing that it also cut short forever the autonomous development of the pre-Columbian world?

DISCUSSION

Should Christopher Columbus Get the Credit for "Discovering" the New World?

Agree

Leaving aside the question of whether or not one can "discover" a hemisphere already inhabited by 50 to 90 million people, most modern scholars accept the fact that Columbus was the first European to cross the ocean, land in the New World, return and make the news well known. Columbus not only had the idea of crossing the Atlantic Ocean to reach land on the other side, but also carried it through. Others, in spite of the generally accepted notion that the world was more or less round, had not taken the step to use that knowledge in the adventure of discovery.

It seems certain that Columbus' great idea came to him over a long period of time, study and observation, which he accumulated through reading and conversations with mariners and scholars. He was also a keen observer of the stars, winds, currents and behavior of birds during voyages that he made as a passenger on commercial ventures north, south and west from his base in Lisbon. From these sources he concluded that the ocean was not nearly as wide as predicted by Ptolemy, the widely read geographer of ancient Greece. Columbus believed that the world, in other words, was a much smaller place than had been assumed. Little by little, he built up his argument for a westward voyage to reach the East—probably of not much more than a month with steady winds. The Italian navigator was bolstered by his faith in his own providential role in bringing Christendom to the other half of mankind. He also had the stubbornness to match such a grandiose vision and so he was completely confident in the correctness of his project. With this assurance, he was able not only to endure the disappointment of failure at the court in Lisbon and nearly another decade of waiting for approval of his project in Spain, but also the lengthy ocean crossing and disappointing material rewards of his voyages.

A fellow Italian, Paolo Toscanelli—scholar, physician and astronomer as well as mapmaker—had suggested traveling west across the Atlantic Ocean as the shortest route to China and the Spice Islands of the east in 1474. In his response to questions from a member of the court in Lisbon, Toscanelli even drew a map that showed the route he recommended. However, Toscanelli's letter reached Lisbon too late; the Portuguese crown had already committed its resources to looking for a passage to the Indies around Africa. Columbus apparently gained access to Toscanelli's letter and map though family connections, but biographer Gianni Granzotto believes that by this time, Columbus had already formulated his own plan and his erudite countryman's reasoning only served to confirm his own.[11]

Disagree

The strongest alternative candidate for the European discoverer of the New World is Leif Erikkson. The Viking explorer not only "found" what today is the Atlantic coast of Canada, but Vikings actually established settlements there hundreds of years before Columbus' first voyage. Archaeologists have documented one of these, L'Anse aux Meadows, in Newfoundland. Furthermore, the accounts of Eric the Red and his son Leif were relayed to Iceland in the form of the Vinland Sagas. It is quite possible that Columbus heard of these exploits during his voyage to the north in 1477. Those who give credit to Columbus point out, however, that the Newfoundland settlements were abandoned and were not relieved by new settlers, as was the case with the Spanish colonists, who soon built towns and established a regular trade with the mother country. Neither do the Vikings appear to have been aware that what they had found was more than an extension of the northern islands that they had colonized earlier. Unlike the story of Columbus' discovery, which within only a few weeks had traveled to Paris and Rome, the Viking tales were buried in folklore and myth.[12]

Others say that co-credit, at least, should go to Martín Alonzo Pinzón, the skilled captain from Palos and rival of Columbus. It was a sailor on Pinzón's ship, the *Pinta*, who first saw land in the moonlight before dawn on October 12, 1492. Pinzón was also the first to relay news of the discovery to the Spanish monarchs in February 1493. The news arrived from Bayonne, France, where Pinzón's *Pinta* finally landed after his ship and Columbus' were separated during a fierce Atlantic storm near the Azores, and where Columbus was detained for a short time. However, Fernando and Isabel refused to receive Pinzón, saying that they would hear the story of the voyage to the Indies only from the admiral himself. Pinzón returned to Spain, arriving only a few hours behind Columbus, whose ship had been repaired in Lisbon. Pinzón slipped away from the *Pinta*, went ashore and died at his home not far from Palos several days later.

Another tantalizing candidate for discoverer of the New World comes from the story of the "unknown helmsman." He was the only survivor of the crew of a ship that had been caught in a storm that pushed it to other lands beyond the Atlantic Ocean, where they saw unfamiliar people and exotic plants. Later, the vessel drifted back toward Europe. The helmsman—in the tattered remains of his ship—arrived at the very town, Porto Santo, where Columbus was living at the time. According to the story, Columbus put the poor man up at his house, where he drew a map for the navigator and then died. This tale was reported but discounted by the first chronicler of the discovery, Fernández de Oviedo.[13] However, it was picked up, made the subject of a poem by Garcilaso de la Vega and perpetuated by the enemies of the Columbus family after the admiral's death.

Did Columbus Set the Pattern for a Program of Genocide in the New World?

Agree

Taino culture was virtually obliterated within two generations after the arrival of Columbus. When the Tainos began to become rebellious, he tried to put them down with arms, captured many and forced others to look for gold. His tactics were followed by more vicious methods. In 1502, a new governor, Nicolás de Ovando, arrived with 2,500 colonists from Spain. To protect them from harassment by the natives, he struck first. To forestall a possible rebellion in the southeast, he ordered 600 or 700 Taino men rounded up; they were herded into an enclosure and all were killed. A year later, when some 80 chiefs from the southwestern region of the island had gathered in the house of the female *cacique* Anacaona, Ovando ordered the house set ablaze.[14] The same governor instituted the *encomienda*, a form of coerced labor. Whole communities were obliged to work for six months at a time in the gold fields. Their numbers declined quickly due to overwork, malnourishment and

disease. The early chronicler of the Spanish conquest, Fray Bartolomé de Las Casas, estimated that only 10% of the Tainos survived
their turn of work in the gold fields. This kind of wanton disregard
for human life, inflicted by one racial or cultural group upon another, has only one name—genocide. The Spaniards murdered and
abused the Tainos and used them up until they were gone, and then
brought in African slaves to do the backbreaking work of mining
and agricultural labor on the islands.[15]

Although the term had not been invented yet, Spain's political
enemies, especially the English and the Dutch, would have gladly
called the result of the Spanish conquest genocide. Las Casas' *Brev-
íssima relación de la destrucción de las Indias* (*Very Brief Relation
of the Destruction of the Indies*), written in 1542–1543, was translated and published throughout Europe after its first printing in Seville in 1552. This tract, with its horrific descriptions of the
treatment of the Indians during the conquest and subsequent colonial rule, became one of the important sources for the *Leyenda Negra* (Black Legend),[16] the body of anti-Spanish literature propagated
by Spain's adversaries. The *Leyenda Negra* lived on long after the
colonial empire ceased to exist, in the opinions of northern Europeans and North Americans toward Spaniards and the people of the
Latin American republics.

Disagree

The use of the term genocide in this instance is misleading and
prejudicial. The Spaniards were motivated by their lust for gold.
Their mistreatment and exploitation of the native peoples of Hispaniola did not result from a conscious attempt to wipe out a group
of people but an unfortunate side effect of their primary motivation:
to find gold any way they could. In modern military jargon, the loss
of Native American life was acute "collateral damage."

However, many indigenous people in the Antilles died of disease,
as elsewhere, when native populations came into contact with European maladies. In Mexico, Central America and South America,
estimates of the population decline in indigenous communities is as
high as 90% in some areas, most of it due to disease. Many of these
victims of the conquest were not even in contact with Europeans;
the epidemics outpaced the advance of the Spanish and the Portuguese into the interior of the Americas. For example, modern scholars believe that Huayna Capac, the father of the last Inca, died of

one of these "new" diseases, leaving the Inca empire divided, open to civil war and an easier target for eventual conquest by *conquistador* Francisco Pizarro.

Europeans in the fifteenth and sixteenth centuries were nearly as ignorant of how these diseases were spread as the native peoples who fell victim to them. With the exception of smallpox and the plague, which still caused major epidemics, diseases such as measles, mumps and scarlet fever had reached a rough equilibrium in the European population by this time; while some Europeans died from these latter diseases, each and every one of them were deadly to the Native Americans, who had no immunity or natural defenses against them. With no understanding of the bacterial and viral causes of disease, Spaniards were no more aware of how to protect the natives from European infections than they were to protect themselves from an equally deadly scourge that the Native Americans seem to have inflicted on them: syphilis. Although it is not absolutely certain that syphilis did not already exist in the Old World, the evidence for the rapid spread of this serious—even lethal—sexually transmitted disease in Europe shortly after the discovery of the Antilles is certain. Within two years of the return of Columbus' first crew, the new disease (or perhaps a more virulent variety caused by the same bacterium) had showed up in Italy and was spreading to France; within 10 years it had spread to all corners of Europe.

In addition to losses caused by disease, the numbers of Tainos declined as they were absorbed into the growing Spanish population of the island. Intermarriage of Europeans and native women was common. The Spanish census of Hispaniola in 1514 showed that some 40% of Spanish men had Taino wives.[17] As was the case during the early phase of the conquest in other parts of the New World, the children of these marriages would have been accepted as Spaniards and counted as such. The later introduction of African slaves also contributed to the dilution of the Taino ethnic element in the Antillean population. A small number of people who recognize themselves as Tainos survive in Puerto Rico, where interest in the Taino past continues to grow.

Finally, other Hispanists point out that Spain, alone of all the European powers, actually questioned the morality of its use of forced labor, imposition of European religion and enslavement of Native Americans. These questions were debated for decades in Spain in the highest religious and academic circles. Queen Isabel had demanded that the slaves that Columbus had sold on returning from his second voyage be freed and repatriated to their homeland. Ultimately, however, the demands of the Spanish colonists for workers for their mines, farms and workshops outweighed the moral arguments of the clergymen and intellectuals.

Should We Celebrate the "Discovery" of the New World, Knowing That It Also Cut Short Forever the Autonomous Development of the Pre-Columbian World?

Agree

Some people believe that Columbus has become the target of "politically correct" critiques of American history and people who seek to "glorify primitivism":

It was Columbus' discovery for Western Europe that led to the influx of ideas and people on which this nation was founded—and on which it still rests. The opening of America brought the ideas and achievements of Aristotle, Galileo, Newton, and the thousands of thinkers, writers, and inventors who followed. Prior to 1492, what is now the United States was sparsely inhabited, unused, and undeveloped. The inhabitants were primarily hunter-gatherers, wandering across the land, living from hand-to-mouth and from day-to-day. There was virtually no change, no growth for thousands of years. With rare exception, life was nasty, brutish, and short: there was no wheel, no written language, no division of labor, little agriculture and scant permanent settlement; but there were endless, bloody wars. Whatever the problems it brought, the vilified Western culture also brought enormous, undreamed-of benefits, without which most of today's Indians would be infinitely poorer or not even alive. Columbus should be honored, for in so doing, we honor Western civilization.[18]

Others simply point to the inevitability of the European and indigenous "encounter." The countries of Western Europe, particularly the Spanish and the Portuguese, were in a race not only for riches, but to spread the Christian faith. New developments were pushing Europe toward an explosion of curiosity about the world they lived in. Imagine what the reaction to the news of Columbus' voyage must have been in England or France. Consider the astonishment that must have followed when it became clear that beyond Columbus' "Indies" lay another enormous ocean and the Asian continent farther still. The discovery by Columbus in 1492 not only brought Western civilization to the New World; in many ways, it gave impetus to the scientific and cultural revolution that built much of what we now think of as the modern world.

Latin American historian John Chastain agrees that Iberians (or Columbus) should not be singled out for special blame for their role in history. "The Iberian invaders of America were personally no more sinful than most. They came to America seeking success in the terms dictated by their society: riches, the privilege of being served by others, and a claim to religious righteousness. It makes little sense for us to judge their moral quality as human beings because they merely lived the logic of the world as they understood it, just as we do."[19]

Disagree

On the other hand, Chastain also states, "Latin America was born in blood and fire, in conquest and slavery. . . . It is precisely conquest and its sequel, colonization, that created the central conflict of Latin American history."[20] We can never really escape the fact that the inhabitants of the New World started out on very uneven terms with the Europeans and that the political and economic dependency that colonialism fostered has been difficult to shake off.

October 12 has become a day of protest for indigenous peoples in Latin America. In 1992, the five hundredth anniversary of the arrival of Colón brought out indigenous groups in virtually all of the Western Hemisphere countries. "With the sword and the cross, they took everything from us," said Adrian Esquina Lixco, a Pipil chief from El Salvador on the eve of the quincentennial.[21] The persecution of Native Americans was not limited to the early years of the conquest. A group from El Salvador planed a march on October 12, 1992 to commemorate a peasant revolt in 1932, when the military government killed approximately 30,000 people, many of whom were indigenous. As a result of the terror, many of the indigenous people abandoned their traditional language and dress. Columbus Day demonstrations have continued across the continent since then, often protesting the failure of contemporary governments to address concerns of indigenous groups. In Chile, as in several other countries, continuing discrimination, lack of adequate political representation and title to ancestral lands are major issues.[22]

It is impossible to know what might have come from New World cultures if they had been able to develop autonomously. Agriculture had developed independently in the New World, giving rise to important food crops, especially in Mesoamerica and the Andean region. Metallurgy was advanced, though not to the stage of discovery of iron. The Mayan culture had developed a system of written glyphs. Mayan timekeeping, in the form of annual and cyclical calendars, was more precise than European calendars of the same era, and the Mayans developed the concept of zero, a key to sophisticated mathematical calculations. Complex religious and political hierarchies had developed in several regions.

Possibly the most important obstacle to the technological development of the New World was the lack of large animals, such as cattle or horses, that were capable of pulling loads. Some pre-Colombian cultures were familiar with the wheel but, lacking animals that could make wheeled vehicles truly useful, had not exploited it. The lack of written languages that could be easily adapted to syllabic or phonetic symbols meant that innovations and information traveled slowly. The arrival of the Portuguese and the Spaniards (followed by the English, Dutch and French) ended the 10,000 or more years of autonomous cultural development of the Native Americans. We will simply never know what they might have done with another 500 years.

QUESTIONS AND ACTIVITIES

1. Imagine the scene between Columbus and the Spanish monarchs when he met them in Barcelona to explain what he had accomplished on his first voyage. Write a script and act it out.

2. Columbus described the indigenous peoples of the islands he visited on his first voyage as docile and easy to turn into servants. What do you infer about his attitude toward the Tainos from this description? Columbus also repeatedly stated in his diary that the Taino people had no religion of their own. Is this likely? Why would he be prone to misinterpret or overlook their religious beliefs?

3. If you have already studied the Aztecs or the Incas, how did Colombus' first encounters with Native Americans compare with Cortés' and Pizarro's experiences? What had the Spanish conquerors learned in the 40 or 50 years after Columbus' first contacts that enabled them to conquer these new empires so rapidly? Why were the Aztecs and the Incas uninformed about the arrival of the newcomers?

4. Use the Internet to search for information about Taino culture at the time of Colombus' arrival. Search for Taino and Arawak (the larger linguistic group to which the Tainos belonged). What can you learn about their religious beliefs, villages and way of life?

5. Hatuey was a Taino chieftan who fled to Cuba. What became of his attempt to resist the Spaniards? How is he remembered by Cubans today? What reasons can you think of to explain why the Tainos generally put up little resistance to the Spanish soldiers and colonists?

6. Several villages in the highlands of Puerto Rico are home to some of the descendents of the original Taino people of Boriquén (or Borikín) and others live in the continental United States. Use the Internet to locate more information about contemporary Tainos.

7. Some indigenous groups are demanding that they receive payments for land that was taken from them (or that the land be returned to the tribe). Under what circumstances, if any, do you believe a national government should compensate Native Americans for their lost lands? Have Native Americans in your state or province been successful in obtaining title to lands that were taken away from them or another form of compensation?

8. What is your opinion concerning the central question of this chapter: Should we hold Christopher Columbus responsible for the fate of the indigenous peoples of the Americas? Why or why not?

VOCABULARY/VOCABULARIO

Nouns/Sustantivos

admiral	el almirante
arms, fire	las armas de fuego
arms, weapons	las armas
artifacts	los artefactos
beliefs	las creencias
canoe	la canoa
the Catholic Kings	los Reyes Católicos
coast	la costa
colonist	el colono
explorer	el explorador
five hundredth anniversary	quintocentenario
gold	el oro

horse	el caballo
inhabitant	el/la habitante
iron	el hierro
island	la isla
land, earth	la tierra
native people	los indígenas (m.), los nativos
navigator	el navegador
ocean	el océano
port	el puerto
religion	la religión
sailing vessel	la nave (f.)
sailor	el marinero
sea	el mar
servant	el sirviente
slave	el esclavo
town	el pueblo
village	la aldea
worker, laborer	el obrero

Verbs/Verbos

attack	atacar
capture	capturar
conquer	conquistar, vencer
disembark	desembarcar
explore	explorar
fish	pescar
force	forzar, obligar
greet	saludar, recibir
grow (food)	cultivar
look for, seek	buscar
pay	pagar
sail, navigate	navegar
set sail	zarpar
trick, deceive	engañar
work	trabajar, labrar

Adjectives/Adjetivos

advanced	avanzado/a
brave	valiente
docile, meek	dócil
peaceful	pacífico/a
primitive	primitivo/a
round	redondo/a
simple	sencillo/a

RESOURCE GUIDE

Books and Articles

Bigelow, Bill, Barbara Miner, and Bob Peterson, eds. *Rethinking Columbus: Teaching about the 500th Anniversary of Columbus's Arrival in America.* Milwaukee, WI: Rethinking Schools in collaboration with the Network of Educators on the Americas, 1991.

Chastain, John Charles. *Born in Blood and Fire: A Concise History of Latin America.* New York: W.W. Norton, 2001.

Crosby, Alfred W. *The Columbian Exchange: Biological and Cultural Consequences of 1492.* Westport, CT: Greenwood Press, 1972.

———. *The Columbian Voyages, the Columbian Exchange, and Their Historians.* Washington, DC: American Historical Association, 1987.

Davidson, Miles H. *Columbus Then and Now.* Norman: University of Oklahoma Press, 1997.

Donghi, Tulio Halperin. "Backward Looks and Forward Glimpses from a Quincentennial Vantage Point." *Journal of Latin American Studies* 24 (1992): 219–234.

Fernández de Oviedo y Valdés, Gonzalo. *Los viajes de Colón*; nota preliminar por Jaime Delgado. Madrid: Ediciones Atlas, 1944.

Fuentes, Carlos. *El espejo enterrado.* Mexico: Fondo de Cultura Economica, 1992.

———. *The Buried Mirror: Reflections on Spain and the New World.* Boston: Houghton Mifflin, 1992.

Gibson, Charles. *The Black Legend: Anti-Spanish Attitudes in the Old World and the New.* New York: Knopf, 1971.

Granzotto, Gianni. *Christopher Columbus.* Garden City, NY: Doubleday, 1985.

Josephy, Alvin M., and Frederick E. Hoxie, eds. *America in 1492: The*

World of the Indian Peoples before the Arrival of Columbus. New York: Knopf, 1992.

Keegan, W.F. "Landfall." *Archaeology* 45(1) (January 1992): 44–50.

———. "Destruction of the Taino." *Archaeology* 45(1) (January 1992): 51–56.

Lester, Paul Martin. "Looks Are Deceiving: The Portraits of Christopher Columbus." *Visual Anthropology* 5 (1993): 211–227.

Rogozinski, Jan. *A Brief History of the Caribbean: From the Arawak and the Carib to the Present.* 2nd ed. New York: Facts on File, 1999.

Rouse, Irving. *The Tainos: Rise and Decline of the People Who Greeted Columbus.* New Haven, CT: Yale University Press, 1992.

Wilson, Samuel M., ed. *Indigenous People of the Caribbean.* Gainesville: University of Flordia Press, 1997.

Winsberg, Morton D. "Five Hundred Years after the Old World Discovered the New World." *Social Studies* 83(5) (September/October 1992): 216–219.

Yewell, John, Chris Dodge, and Jan DeSirey, eds. *Confronting Columbus: An Anthology.* Jefferson, NC: McFarland & Co., 1992.

Internet

El Boricua: A Monthly Bilingual Cultural Publication for Puerto Ricans. <http://www.elboricua.com/history.html>.

"The First Voyage" (Martín Alonzo Pinzón). <http://www.mariner.org/age/firstvoyage.html>.

Jatibonicu Taino Tribal Nation of Borikén. <http://www.taino-tribe.org/jatiboni.html>.

La Voz del Pueblo Taino/The Voice of the Taino People. <http://www.indigenouspeople.org/natlit/uctp/lavoz.htm>.

Presencia Taina. <http://www.PresenciaTaina.org/>.

Taino Ancestral Legacy Keepers. <http://www.indio.net/talk/Taino/edu/>.

Video

Columbus Didn't Discover Us. Videocassette. Wendell, MA: Turning Tide Productions, 1992. Color. 24 min.

Columbus and the Age of Discovery. Videocassette. Princeton, NJ: Films for the Humanities & Sciences, 1991. Color. Seven videocassettes, 58 min. each.

Chapter 5

Alcohol, Tobacco, Drugs and *La Vida Loca*

To Americans and Northern Europeans of the nineteenth and twentieth centuries, brought up in the puritanical Protestant tradition—and even to the Catholic French—Spaniards and Latin Americans seemed exotic and impulsive. On the one hand Spaniards were prone to acts of individual heroism and cared little for their own safety in battle or in the face of the bull; on the other they were considered indolent and inefficient. They were also highly individualistic and—paradoxically—subject to worrying about *qué dirán*, or community opinion (literally, what will they say?). But on one thing visitors of other nations agreed: Spaniards knew how to *live for the day*. The *fiesta*; the *siesta*; the evenings spent roaming from one bar to another enjoying the company of friends; afternoon or evening *tertulias* (discussing your favorite topic with a group of friends); the *sobremesa* (conversations carried on after dinner) with a cognac and good cigar . . . yes, this was the good life.

Yet this was also a lifestyle that carried with it a number of risks. As we have become more aware of the perils of heavy use of tobacco, alcohol and drugs, indulgence in risky behavior has come under more scrutiny in most countries, including Spain. Some people, both inside Spain and out, are asking if Spain is suffering from a culture of excess.

BACKGROUND

In his book *The New Spaniards*, John Hooper devotes an entire chapter to what he terms the "Cult of Excess," beginning with something as apparently innocuous as coffee drinking. Writing about the popular double roasted, extra-strong *torrefacto* (dark roasted coffee, similar to *espresso*), Hooper states, "The Spaniards' addiction to *torrefacto* is all of a piece with a nation in which there is very little that is bland, gentle or reassuringly soft. . . . [The relatively peaceful political] transition has not prevented—and in some respects may have actively promoted—indulgence in excess of a different, though scarcely less destructive, kind."[1]

The use of tobacco was for centuries encouraged by the Spanish government, which had a state monopoly. (The University of Seville is now centered in the city's old cigarette factory, which was the setting for the novel and opera *Carmen*.) For generations Spaniards bought their cigarettes, cigars and postage stamps at a neighborhood institution, the *estanco* (tobacco shop), licensed by the Spanish government. The bureaucracy of the Franco regime made no attempt to discourage the use of alcohol and tobacco. Although authorities ignored small qualities of cannabis, penalties for the sale of any illegal drugs could be harsh. As the Franco era came to a close, the use of drugs began to increase, along with the desire to enjoy an uncensored lifestyle and increased contact with tourists, travel and U.S. and European media. Soon Spaniards were not only some of Europe's heaviest consumers of alcohol and tobacco, but of marijuana, cocaine and heroin as well.

In the past, Spaniards, especially men, were apt to indulge rather heavily in alcohol and tobacco. Few women drank in public and fewer smoked. However, drinking behavior in particular was subject to strong social controls, even for men: everyone frowned on public intoxication, with the possible exception of drinking during *fiestas*. Today, however, these social controls have come unraveled, especially among adolescents, young adults, and women.

It has taken the Spanish public and government several decades to begin to take seriously the level of all kinds of drug use within the country. What may have begun to change the mood of government and civic leaders is the awareness that, while the use of all these addictive substances has leveled off or is decreasing among adults, there is evidence that their use is increasing every year among

Spain's youth. The costs to society, both in expenditures for health and increased crime and destruction to property, are mounting. Here are some questions we might ask about this issue:

1. Does Spanish culture glorify excess?
2. Is alcohol, drug and tobacco abuse on the rise in Spain?
3. Should more stringent laws be put in place to discourage abuse of addictive substances?

DISCUSSION

Does Spanish Culture Glorify Excess?

Agree

Yes, and it's nothing new, but a kind of wild streak that has run through Spanish culture for centuries, some would argue. One has only to look at Goya's paintings of *Carnaval* to see the irrational abandon on the faces of the revelers. *Carnaval* celebrations were suppressed during several periods of Spanish history, including during the Franco regime, because they were considered too dangerous or too licentious. Only since the Transition has *Carnaval* reappeared, most noticeably in Cadiz and in the Canary Islands.

The *fiestas* for which Spain is justly famous are occasions not only for the release of social and personal tensions, but also for conspicuous consumption of food, materials and human effort. The *Fallas* of Valencia, celebrated during March, literally consume a year's worth of money and effort from the city's *barrios* (neighborhoods). The *barrios* compete with each other to produce the biggest and best gigantic paper maché figures the size of Rose Parade floats, all of which are burned in a blaze of glory on the last day of the fiesta honoring St. Joseph. (The carpenters, whose special patron is St. Joseph, are said to have originated the *Fallas* by burning the sawdust from their workshops in a kind of material and spiritual shop cleaning.)

The best known of all of Spain's big blowouts is the *fiesta* of San Fermín, which takes place in Pamplona in July. Like almost all Spanish *fiestas*, this one honors a patron saint, but the religious significance of the *fiesta* has been eclipsed by the revelry that accompanies the bullfights, and especially the dangerous *encierros* (running with the bulls through the streets to the bullring). For a week, the city is the scene of prodigious drinking and celebrating virtually 24 hours a day until the *fiesta* ends on July 14. In all justice, it is true that today as many foreigners as Spaniards—and perhaps more—attend the *fiesta*, which has attracted the world's attention since the days of Ernest Hemingway, who made it known to American readers in *The Sun Also Rises*. Spain's fascination with death (such as in the bullring or in the *encierro*) is an example of glorification of risky behavior.

A much newer example of Spanish excess in the pursuit of just plain fun is *La Tomatina*, which takes place in the main square of Buñol, Valencia on the last Wednesday in August. Although it also occurs at the end of a religious *fiesta*, its origins are purely secular, even if there's no single version of how it got started. According to some it began around 1945, when participants in the traditional parade of giant and comical figures tangled with some local boys who were within easy reach of a fruit and vegetable stand. The same clash was repeated the next year, and soon lobbing tomatoes became a custom, in spite of the opposition of the police and the city fathers. Banned for several years during the 1950s, the *Tomatina* returned due to its popular support from the town's citizens. Nowadays 20,000 to 30,000 people do battle with 90,000 pounds of ripe tomatoes for a brief hour or two of sloshing good fun in the blazing sun and then retreat to wash off in the nearby river. The city, too, gets a good hosing down and then reopens the next day. Organized and publicized by Buñol's *ayuntamiento* (city government), the *Tomatina* is now the biggest event of the year and has made the town known around the world.

Disagree

All this is just Iberian exuberance, and really not more excessive than the *fiesta* tradition of other Southern European countries of Catholic tradition, such as Italy or Southern France. This is a lifestyle that has developed over several centuries, and certainly not the recent invention of some kind of permissive, consumer and tourism-orientated culture. Even under Franco, chanting *fútbol* fans would clog the streets sometimes for hours celebrating a particularly gratifying victory.

While it's true that Spain has more bars than France, England and

Germany combined, the bar is more than just a place to consume alcohol. Spaniards stop by the bar to have coffee on the way to work and again at mid-morning. Bars also function as restaurants, where one can buy a simple lunch; some of them have a restaurant upstairs or in the back. In the late afternoon they are the place where Spaniards and tourists stop for *tapas* or *pinchos* (both are small servings of food) and a glass of wine or beer with friends. The bar is a center of social activity.

Visitors to Spain are inevitably awed by their hosts' late-night staying power, and Spaniards have long been known for their late hours. Supper at 10:00 P.M. is the norm, because the Spanish work-day ends around 8:00 P.M. for many workers due to the two-hour mid-day break. Today, however, with more money to spend than a few decades ago, Spaniards are able to extend their bar hopping until the wee hours of the morning on any given day. Remember that not just drinking, but eating and enjoying the company of friends, are the primary goals of most of the adult Spaniards who go out, whether it is on the weekend or a workday night.

It's possible that the long life span, as well as lower cancer and heart attack rates of Spaniards (compared to Northern Europeans and Americans) may be due not just to their diet (as has been suggested by several studies) but also to their ability to really let loose on occasion. And the Spanish diet includes wine, which is an essential ingredient in nearly all *fiestas* and lunch or supper for many Spaniards.

Is Alcohol, Drug and Tobacco Abuse on the Rise in Spain?

Agree

The issue of drugs and—more recently—alcohol is fairly high on the list of concerns of average Spaniards. There's no question that the use of drugs is higher at the turn of the century than it was a generation earlier. Among Western European countries, Spain is first, second or third on the list of consumption of all of the common addictive substances. What is not so clear is how much it is increasing and in which subpopulations.

Spain ranks third among European countries in per capita consumption of alcohol. Among teenagers, tobacco and alcohol are the most popular drugs. Studies reported by the Ministry of the Interior reveal that more than half of teenagers used alcohol during the month before the survey and about 1 in 3 had used tobacco, with more girls than boys admitting to smoking and drinking.[2] The increase in smoking among young women in recent years is as troubling to Spanish health authorities as to public health officials in the United States. The illegal drug used most often by Spanish teenagers is cannabis (marijuana and its cousin, hashish, which has traditionally been smuggled into Spain from North Africa). Spanish experts consider much of this activity experimental, but note that around the age of 14 or 15, experimental use of alcohol and tobacco often develops into a lifetime habit. By the time they are in college, more than 40% of Spanish students are confirmed smokers. The same study showed that roughly 2 in 10 had experimented with cocaine and designer drugs like Ecstasy. Officials also worry about the tendency toward *policonsumo*, or consumption of more than one addictive substance. Smokers are more likely to use alcohol and cannabis, too, than nonsmokers, for example.

Alcohol in Spain, as well as in the United States, is an important contributor to violent death and serious disease. Spanish medical experts estimate that 13,000 deaths a year can be attributed to alcohol: 46% of homicides, 25% of suicides and fatal accidental injuries, 40% of automobile deaths plus deaths due to tumors and cancers and chronic diseases, at a cost of billions to the national economy.[3] Use of alcohol (customarily at least one drink during the last month) has risen to 76% of teenagers between the ages of 14 and 18.[4]

Disagree

Although few well-informed people can disagree with the statistics provided by the national and international agencies that assess these questions, there is room to speculate on whether they are cause for special alarm. Surveys and studies have provided evidence that leads to conflicting—or at least uncertain—conclusions. Studies done by the *Centro de Investigaciones Sociales* (Center for Social Research or CIS) do show that consistently, after terrorism and unemployment, Spaniards identify drugs and alcoholism as an important problem facing the country. When questioned about their predictions for the future, a substantial majority of ordinary Spaniards interviewed for a CIS survey done in 1997 believed that the consumption of alcohol and drugs (of all kinds) would increase or stay the same in the next five years, that is, through 2002. Four out of 10 people in the same survey, however, believed that smoking would decrease.[5]

Spain still has many smokers. Although antismoking campaigns are more visible now, many smokers are not convinced that smoking will seriously harm their health. In an article published in the *Los Angeles Times*, a 60-year-old Spanish smoker with a 45-year habit said that it was fashionable to be against smoking now. He went on to say that he wouldn't be surprised if it turned out that experts would decide that smoking is good for your health, just as they decided that olive oil was good for you.[6] This kind of wishful thinking on the part of consumers has brought some Spanish health authorities to attack the source of the problem: the tobacco industry. At least one autonomous community, Andalusia, initiated a lawsuit similar to ones brought by states in the United States to recover damages for health care costs incurred in the care of patients with tobacco-related diseases such as lung, mouth and throat cancer and emphysema. Public health officials also hope to convince the European Union to end its subsidies to tobacco farmers in Spain.

There are some signs that habitual alcohol consumption has hit a plateau since the 1980s. Fewer adult Spaniards abused alcohol in 2000 than in 1997. The number of young people who say they never drink has shown a small increase (10%). The same survey, conducted by the Interior Ministry's *Plan Nacional Sobre Drogas* (National Drug Plan), indicated that the number of Spanish teenagers who admitted to using alcohol, cocaine, amphetamines and hallucinogenic drugs had dropped, compared to a similar survey done two years earlier. Nevertheless, drinking among teenage girls has increased during the same period. Approximately 50% of girls between 15 and 19 said that they drank during the month before the survey.[7]

Should More Stringent Laws Be Put in Place to Discourage Abuse of Addictive Substances?

Agree

Critics say that Spanish society has become too permissive. The autonomous communities now set the age limits for purchase of alcohol and tobacco (raised from 16 to 18 years), but at the turn of the century these were widely ignored. Teenagers and young adults go out, especially on weekend nights, and come in very late. Of teenagers who go out, more than 50% come home after 2:00 A.M. on weekends and nearly 10% don't return until after daybreak. The frequency and lateness of partying increases with age into young adulthood: about one-half of all 18-year-olds go out every weekend night year round.

Late hours, though not for young people, have been a constant of social life in Spain, at least in the large cities. One of the most pleasant Spanish customs, for Spaniards and visitors alike, has been making the rounds of *mesones* (traditional taverns) and bars to have *tapas* and wine with friends before a late dinner, perhaps a movie or concert and then a visit to one or two other places, particularly in the summer to see and be seen at the *terrazas* (cafes with outdoor tables). Now, however, some bars never close; the last customers straggle home at 7:00 or 8:00 in the morning.

Making the rounds of bars is too expensive for teenagers, and underage customers are discouraged. High school and college-age people gather in the *plazas* to drink, smoke and socialize. Often the goal is to get drunk as quickly as possible—a relatively new phenomenon in Spain, where traditionally public drunkenness was looked upon as genuinely shameful. The alcohol of choice for these gatherings is large bottles of beer or "kits" of big bottles of soft drinks and alcohol purchased in food stores and gasoline stations. The big bottles have given their name to these street gatherings: the *botellón* (big bottle). Hundreds of young people—even thousands— have been coming together several nights a week in a plaza or several blocks, blocking traffic, making lots of noise for the neighbors and leaving behind a huge mess to be cleaned up the next day.[8] Officials estimate that in Madrid alone 300,000 young people hit the streets and head for a *botellón* on any given weekend night.[9]

Addiction to the "hard" drugs—cocaine and heroin—causes concern among the Spanish public as well. In the years after the end of the Franco era, many Spaniards clamored for an end to the restrictions they associated with the dictatorship. As a result, the Socialist government decriminalized personal drug use. Eventually, drugs became a public, not just a private, indulgence. Heroin addiction— and with it, AIDS infection—reached alarming proportions. Under pressure from the public and the conservative *Partido Popular* (Popular or People's Party), in 1992 a law banned drug use in parks or streets and gave the police powers to enter homes without a search warrant if they suspected that drug use was going on inside.

As other countries have also discovered, the appetite for drugs in Spain brought increased criminal activity and corruption of police and other public officials. By the turn of the twenty-first century, Spain had achieved the dubious honor of being one of Europe's gateways for the importation of cocaine and heroin. In large part this is due to its proximity to North Africa, a major conduit for hashish and heroin, and to its Atlantic ports plus its cultural ties to Latin American producer countries, such as Colombia. However, the free and easy climate for public drug use in the 1980s may have brought drug crime rings into Spain earlier than might have been the case otherwise, and conservative politicians used this as ammunition in their political campaigns.[10]

Disagree

Not surprisingly, people like the smoker quoted in the *Los Angeles Times* article above believe there are already too many restrictions on small liberties, such as the right to smoke when and where you please. Nevertheless, polls conducted in 1995 by CIS found that roughly three-fourths of the Spanish public favored restrictions on smoking in public places and other unspecified measures to reduce consumption. Younger people, however, were less likely to agree with restrictions and a more recent informal survey revealed that no-smoking regulations were observed less than half the time in Spanish workplaces.[11]

Others point out that education may be at least as important as legal restrictions on smoking and cigarette sales. A pilot program in 16 Barcelona schools funded by the European Union succeeded in lowering the rate of new smokers aged 12 to 16 by 50%. These promising results led the Barcelona school authorities to extend the program to all public schools by the end of 2003. (Teachers in the pilot program schools also benefited. One hundred twenty teachers participated in smoking cessation programs and 75% of them were still "smoke free" after 6 months.[12]) In addition to placing a minimum age on purchasing tobacco, health officials propose restricting access to tobacco by raising the price of cigarettes and prohibiting the advertisement of tobacco products.

Many Spaniards, like other Europeans, are not convinced that harsh laws are successful in reducing drug, alcohol or tobacco abuse. They point out that the call for restrictive laws for youth is hypocritical, given the fact that their parents have provided them with models of tobacco and alcohol consumption and taught them lack of consideration for others, and that the laws proposed by the *Partido Popular* government will be the most restrictive in the European Union. Others point out that there are few alternatives for recreation for youth and that high prices for drinks in bars drive young consumers of legal age out into the streets, too. Socialist Party leaders accused the *Partido Popular* administration of relying on punitive, anti-youth measures. The Socialists promised to tackle the problem of disorder and alcohol abuse by addressing the broader issues of education, jobs, housing and ethical and cultural formation as well as the free time and social outlets for young people. They pledged to create a Ministry for Youth, a cabinet-level government office, if they receive the majority in the 2004 elections.[13]

In spite of these reservations, public opinion seems to have swung in favor of a less permissive policy toward public intoxication and drug use in recent years. Tired of the noise, trash and vandalism that the *movida* (roughly, "the happening") generates each weekend, the public also complains about the cost of cleaning up the weekend mess, estimated to run over $1 million a year in Madrid alone.[14] Drug treatment clinics have been forced to close their doors in some towns due to the opposition of neighbors to the presence of addicts. Under pressure from neighborhood associations, the city governments of both Madrid and Seville moved to ban the nighttime consumption of alcohol in the streets in 2002. How this policy will square with Spain's long tradition of *fiesta* and late-night hours is uncertain. But in 2001, Barcelona was one of only two major Spanish cities that avoided the problem of large weekend gatherings of drunken youths, and Barcelona, critics point out, is located in one of only two autonomous communities that had already instituted nighttime controls on the consumption of alcohol in the streets.

The problems of drug, alcohol and tobacco use and addiction are not limited to Spain, of course. In general, until recently there were fewer inhibitions concerning the use of alcohol in Latin America than in Spain. Once considered a plague of rich nations, addiction to cocaine has become a serious health and public safety issue in many countries of Latin America. Because the market is flooded with drugs in Colombia, Central America and Mexico, they are more widely affordable than ever before. Other addictive substances such as paint and glue are abused by large numbers of poor children, especially the *niños abandonados* (abandoned or street children) living in urban areas.

QUESTIONS AND ACTIVITIES

1. Why do countries like Spain and the United States subsidize farmers to grow tobacco at the same time their health departments try to convince the public not to smoke? How would you address this contradiction if you were in a position of authority, for example in the Department of Agriculture?

2. Should governments try to dissuade people from drinking or from smoking if their behavior causes no direct harm to others? Where does the power or the obligation of the government to protect individuals end?

3. Should advertising of tobacco products be curtailed in Spain as it has been in the United States? Why?

4. Experts believe that teenagers are especially susceptible to tobacco advertising. Do you agree or disagree? Explain your opinion.

5. Do you believe that rules and regulations or education are more effective in dissuading young people from starting to use alcohol, tobacco or illegal drugs? How effective are parents in influencing teenagers' experimentation with addictive substances?

6. The legal age for purchase of alcoholic beverages in Spain has been regulated by the autonomous communities. Recently the national government proposed raising the legal age to 18. Some U.S. states prohibit the sale of alcohol to anyone under 21. Which age limit do you support and why? Or do you think all age limits should be abolished? Explain your reasons.

7. Role play a situation in which a married couple with two teenage children wants to discourage them from going out to meet their friends in a plaza downtown. How will the teenagers respond? What alternatives can the parents offer?

VOCABULARY/VOCABULARIO

Nouns/Sustantivos

after-dinner conversation	la sobremesa
afternoon break	la siesta

appetizers, bar food	las tapas, los pinchos
autonomous community	la comunidad autónoma
big bottle (drinking in the street)	el botellón
bullfight	la corrida de toros
Carnival, Mardi Gras	el Carnaval
city government	el ayuntamiento
consuming more than one thing at a time	el policonsumo
corralling the bulls	el encierro
extra dark roasted coffee	el torrefacto
Fallas (burning of giant figures)	las Fallas
festival	la fiesta
fiesta of San Fermin	los San Fermines
fiesta of the tomato	La Tomatina
gatherings to talk	las tertulias
"happening," what's going on	la movida, la marcha
neighborhood	el barrio
party	la fiesta
Popular (People's) Party	el PP (Partido Popular)
public opinion (what will people say)	el qué dirán
Socialist Party	el PSOE (Partido Socialista), los socialistas
tobacco store	el estanco

Verbs/Verbos

abuse	abusar
drink	beber
get drunk	emborracharse
smoke	fumar
take drink	tomar
take drugs	drogarse

RESOURCE GUIDE

Books and Articles

Hooper, John. *The New Spaniards.* New York: Penguin, 1995.
Jordan, Barry, and Rikki Morgan-Tamosunas, eds. *Contemporary Spanish Cultural Studies.* New York: Oxford University Press, 2000.
Richardson, Bill. *Spanish Studies: An Introduction.* London: Oxford University Press, 2001.

Internet

Ayuntamiento de Buñol. <http://www.lahoya.net/ayuntamiento/>.
Centro de Investigaciones Sociológicas. *Boletín.* <http://www.cis.es/boletin/index.html>.
Drogas. *El Mundo.* <http://www.elmundo.es/especiales/2001/09/sociedad/drogas/autodefinido.html>.
Guía de San Fermin. <http://www.sanfermin.com>.
La Tomatina, Buñol, Valencia. <http://www.donquijote.org/spain/fiestas/tomatina.asp>.
Medspain. <http://www.medspain.com>.
Ministerio del Interior. *Plan Nacional Sobre Drogas.* <http://www.mir.es/pnd/noticias/index.htm>
Ministerio del Interior. *Plan Nacional de Drogas.* <http://www.sindrogas.es>.
The Tomatina de Buñol. <http://www.lahoya.net/tomatina/menuing.html>.

Deforestation is blamed for the collapse of this mountain slope in the district of Huachinango, state of Puebla, Mexico in 1999. Although the village in the foreground was spared, the deforested mountainside collapsed on and buried the community of Acalma, killing all but 30 of the 150–200 residents. (AP Photo/Damian Dovarganes)

Chapter 6

The Environment

Global warming; floods and droughts; premature extinction of species of plants and animals; destruction of ancient forests; pollution of the air, streams, ground water and oceans—these issues concern citizens of Latin America and Spain as well as the United States. What are the best ways to deal with these problems in each country? Can the needs of the human population for food, living space and jobs be met without destroying the environment in Spain and Latin America? Are environmentalists exaggerating the magnitude of the problem?

BACKGROUND

Held back by disease and limits on food supply, the human population of the earth grew slowly until the middle of the nineteenth century. The Industrial Revolution was followed by improvements in science and medicine. These, along with the "Green Revolution," which developed higher-yielding food crops and promoted the use of artificial fertilizers and insecticides, contributed to an unprecedented growth of the human population. While no one can argue with the desirability of lower infant and maternal mortality, better nutrition and longer life expectancy, the fact is that these developments have lead to an astonishing rate of growth in the numbers of human beings who must compete for the same resources.[1] Already several large countries in Latin America, such as Mexico and Peru, must import basic foods to meet the needs of their people.

Although population growth in the industrial West has slowed in the last half-century, in parts of the developing world the human population continues to grow at rates that will cause the national population to double every 20 or 30 years. In spite of its slower population growth, the industrialized world—led by the United States—consumes most of the energy and other natural resources, such as wood, minerals, fish and meat. Therefore, the consumption patterns of the developed nations contribute just as much, if not more, to the destruction of the environment as the increasing population of less-developed countries. In many areas in Latin America, "natural" resources are disappearing at an alarming rate. Each *year*, Ecuador loses 4% of its forests. The Mexican government estimates that Mexico has lost 59% of its forests in the last 20 years and at least 1.482 million acres are lost yearly, much of that to illegal tree harvesting.[2] Mangroves that protect coastal areas from erosion, serve as hatcheries and safe havens for large numbers of marine and bird species and clean the water in tropical areas are disappearing due to their cutting and overuse as shrimp breeding areas. In other parts of Latin America, surface water and groundwater have been polluted by careless oil producers who have dumped toxic by-products into inadequate slush pits, sickening and killing plants, animals and human beings in the area.

In Spain, mining has caused similar results. Many of the beaches that are the mainstay of Spanish tourism must be closed from time to time because of pollution, mostly caused by urban development and inadequate sewage treatment. "Desertification" threatens other parts of Spain, where there are no longer any trees to hold the topsoil and control runoff after the heavy rains that come every few years.

Human, animal and plant species are closely linked in any given natural environment. For example, the tall, slow-growing Brazil nut tree, which grows widely dispersed in the Amazonian rainforests of Peru and Brazil, depends on only one animal to pollinate its flowers and another to spread its seed, which is enclosed in very thick, hard pods about the size of a softball. These creatures are a particular species of bat (which pollinates the Brazil nut flowers) and the *paca*, a large rodent that is capable of gnawing through the pod to reach the seeds. A few of the seeds end up on the forest floor and possibly germinate miles away, thus ensuring the dispersion as well as the propagation of the species.

The Brazil nut tree provides shade, protection and habitat for many other species of plants and animals, but if the *paca* populations were to die out, the only other animal capable of opening the seedpods is man. Fortunately, men are interested in collecting Brazil nuts for food and for income,[3] but they are probably not nearly as effective in dispersing them through the rainforest as the rodent. No other insect or mammal—not even man—will pollinate the flowers. Brazil nut trees grow too slowly to consider planting them in a "plantation," so this industry, which provides a livelihood for people living in the rainforest, in effect relies on a bat and a lowly rodent to continue spreading the seeds that will grow into other trees over the space of many human generations.

Ecologists say that we have no choice but to take steps now to stop further destruction of the environment, which provides a home and food not only for several thousand endangered animal species but, ultimately, for the human race. However, not everyone agrees with the urgency of the problem or where and how to address it. Here are some of the statements heard in this debate.

1. We must take steps immediately to stop global warming.
2. Economic growth is incompatible with environmental protection.
3. Environmentally sensitive areas need special protection, including national and international agreements, coupled with their effective enforcement.
4. The developed world must pay a proportionally greater share of the costs of halting environmental destruction and repairing the damage already done.

DISCUSSION

Do We Need to Take Immediate Steps to Stop Global Warming?

Agree

Everything on earth belongs to a single, unified ecosystem; what we do to it now has the potential to haunt our grandchildren. Our forefathers could not have foreseen the environmental changes that have taken place in the last 200 years. Even in the 1950s few people could have imagined the impact that inventions like the automobile and air-conditioning would have on our demand for energy.

The so-called greenhouse gases[4] (*gases invernaderos*), especially carbon dioxide (produced by combustion of fossil fuels such as coal, oil and natural gas) reduce the radiation of heat from the earth's atmosphere back into space. Scientists know that the average temperature of the atmosphere rose several degrees during the twentieth century, a seemingly small amount, but enough to cause glaciers and the polar ice caps to retreat. This small amount of warming could produce a chain reaction: higher sea levels, important changes in global weather patterns, growth in the size of deserts and shifts in areas suitable for agriculture.

The world needs to wake up now, say environmentalists. Cutting back on the production of greenhouse gases, including carbon dioxide, is one important step that should be taken immediately. We must reduce our consumption of fossil fuels, such as petroleum, natural gas and coal, and concentrate on developing and using renewable sources of energy.

The cutting of forests—many of them in Latin America—ends their role as "carbon sinks," where carbon dioxide is processed and taken out of the atmosphere. The burning of forests to open new grazing land is particularly harmful since it not only produces carbon dioxide but also simultaneously eliminates the trees that can remove it from the air.

The greatest part of the forest in Latin America that is being logged or burned is in the rainforests. These once covered the lowlands of most of the tropical zone, which stretches from southern Mexico to the middle of Paraguay. The soil in rainforests—especially in the Amazon basin—is often poor and not well suited to either intensive farming or grazing, yet the destruction of rainforest land continues at a horrendous pace. At the current rate of cutting, Ecuador's forests will disappear entirely within a generation, due to a combination of logging, grazing, oil exploration and subsistence farming. The destruction is similar, if not quite as rapid, in all of the tropical forests of Latin America.

Desertification—the loss of productive farm or pastureland due to drought and erosion—is claiming thousands of acres in Mexico and southern Spain each year. In Europe, ecologists predict that dry summers will occur much more frequently in the southern tier of the continent (Portugal, Spain, Italy and Greece) due to global warming.[5] Already, as a result of drier summers, forest fires have become increasingly common in Spain and harder to control.

Disagree

Opponents reject this apocalyptic vision of the earth's future. They note that we can't be sure that the small rise in temperature that has occurred during this century is due to human activity. There have been even larger fluctuations in average global temperatures in the past, long before man had the capacity to influence nature on any but the most local scale.

Nevertheless, the signatories to the Kyoto Protocols, an agreement signed in Kyoto, Japan in 1997, set a goal of cutting greenhouse gas emissions to 5% below 1990 levels by 2010. To accomplish this, countries would have to use a combination of taxes and regulation, in addition to subsidies for "green technologies." Business, especially in the United States, opposed these targets as being unrealistic and much too costly, since existing equipment would have to be upgraded or replaced. The private sector says that in some cases businesses would have to shut down and thousands of jobs would be lost.

Many of the less developed nations also objected to the strict standards of the Kyoto agreement. Eager to take advantage of global markets, countries such as India and China and a number of Latin American countries felt it was unfair to make poorer countries meet the same standards for greenhouse emissions. They argue that they needed to grow and to industrialize in order to provide a better standard of living for their people. Burdened by debts to foreign banks and international agencies and pressured to meet their payments, Third World governments frequently believe they have little choice but to favor earning hard cash over saving wilderness areas that bring in little direct income.

In spite of private sector concerns about the costs of environmental protection, a Clinton administration official reminded a U.S.-based Latin American trade group that "[A] modern state cannot ignore environmental issues. Countries must carefully husband their resources for maximum benefit not only for today, but for tomorrow; not only for the elite, but for all their citizens—so that development truly improves peoples' lives and economic growth is sustainable over time."[6] The Bush administration, however, opposed the Kyoto agreement as exacting too harsh a price on U.S. business and in its place proposed voluntary goals for reducing carbon dioxide emissions.

Is Economic Growth Compatible with Environmental Protection?

Agree

"Growth per se is not to be blamed for environmental degradation," says one group of experts, "but, in some respects, rapid growth appears to make the problem worse. When the sources of environmental problems—underpriced resources (forests, water or air), weak institutions and unclear property rights—are not addressed adequately, rapid [economic] growth seems to aggravate them."[7]

Taking care of the environment—even improving it—does not mean condemning developing countries to even more poverty or reducing developed countries to a preindustrial state. With respect to developing regions, such as Latin America, a growing number of environmentalists and development organizations say that sustainable development is the best solution.[8] Sustainable development (*desarrollo sostenible*) is a relatively new concept and one that has received much attention from scientists and members of the development agencies. Sustainable development refers to economic activities that feed and employ the population while not causing irreparable damage to the ecological system. This kind of development sustains both the human population and the environment over the long term.

The term "sustainable development" was adopted to describe the challenge of taking the new environmental values we had popularized, and incorporating them into the traditional social and economic values that have always governed public policy and our daily behavior. We cannot simply switch to basing all our actions on purely environmental values. Every day, six billion people wake up with real needs for food, energy and materials. The challenge for sustainability is to provide for those needs in ways that reduce negative impact on the environment. But any changes made must also be socially acceptable and technically and economically feasible. It is not always easy to balance environmental, social and economic priorities. Compromise and cooperation with the involvement of government, industry, academia and the environmental movement are required to achieve sustainability.[9]

What counts as sustainable development depends on the environment: in some places no amount of cutting of trees should be allowed, while in others selective cutting might produce lumber for local building or sale, poles for fences and small branches for firewood or charcoal. In numerous areas grazing has pushed "fragile lands" to the brink of desertification, while in other environments grazing by certain kinds of animals (llamas or alpacas, for example, in the Andean highlands) will not cause damage, and the animals also provide wool and meat for the local population. Still, some critics say that sustainable development alone will not produce lasting benefits; others believe that there are faster ways to promote environmental awareness in environmentally sensitive areas.

"Sustainable business" goes a step beyond a simple sustainable development project. Studies[10] show that families and communities need to see immediate benefits for themselves (as well as long-term potential benefits) before they accept the changes to accepted practices that are required. However, advisors also need to develop a long-term marketing strategy so that the sales for the products will not dry up once a funding agency moves on to another project and local people are left on their own. Examples of sustainable business practices are the promotion of the use of "green" products and agreements with major companies to buy coffee (or cacao, etc.) that is produced under conditions that do not destroy the environment or subject workers to inhumane or unsafe working conditions.[11]

Ecotourism is another way that developing countries may be able to combine protecting the environment and creating jobs that will have a lasting, positive effect on the economy. Responsible tour operators not only provide tourists with a vacation away from it all, but also educate them about the ecosystems that they are visiting. The interest of outsiders can be helpful in convincing local people that the plants and animals of their environment could be much more valuable to them as a long-term, renewable resource than as a way to make immediate cash. Indigenous groups have begun to develop ecotourism projects of their own where they not only show visitors the plant and animal life but also their own culture (to the extent they want outsiders to intrude on their daily life). For countries that pioneered in the development of national parks and wild-life preservation, such as Costa Rica, the income generated by nature tourism has become a significant part of the national economy.[12]

However, others maintain that evidence shows that a greater concern about the environment comes after—not before—gains in standard of living and per capita income. Most of the people in this camp are free market advocates; they believe that the shortest and surest path to protecting biodiversity and natural resources is to focus on economic growth, and expect local concern for the environment to follow.[13] Finally, there are people who are convinced that environmentalists advocate a return to a primitive, communal existence and the rejection of modern life altogether, along with its benefits to health, comfort and well-being. Some religious conservatives oppose the environmental movement because in their view it runs contrary to Judeo-Christian beliefs, placing man within and subject to the environment rather than above it as its divinely appointed master and steward.[14]

Disagree

Economic expansion comes at an unsustainable cost to the environment, say some conservationists. As an example, they might cite the case of olive oil production in Spain. Olive oil, a profitable export commodity, comes from groves in southern Spain, mostly Andalucía. The European Union subsidizes olive oil production as a way to boost the economies of the weaker southern European nations, particularly Portugal, Spain, Italy and Greece. Environmentalists say the subsidies encourage growers to use irrigation in the *olivares* (olive groves) in order to increase their production per acre. However, water supplies are already inadequate. The tilled soil of irrigated groves is also subject to wind and water erosion, which environmentalists say causes a yearly loss of 80 million metric tons of irreplaceable topsoil in olive-growing areas in Andalucía. Bird habitats are lost as more of the brushy Mediterranean forest (*bosque mediterráneo*) is cleared to plant new groves.[15]

In some cases, the creative use of simple and inexpensive technologies can overcome obstacles without causing environmental damage. One particularly interesting example is the use of nets on the arid northern Chilean coast, where rain is extremely infrequent but where a fog, called the *camanchaca*, blows in off the cold Pacific waters during much of the year. The nets, called *atrapanieblas* (fog trappers), intercept the microscopic droplets of fog, which eventually run down the nets into tubing and reservoirs. During the heaviest fogs, the array of nets can collect thousands of gallons of fresh water a day and enough to supply drinking water and water for bathing, washing and gardening in a few coastal towns. Expansion of the system could lead to the installation of a fish processing plant, which would benefit the area economically as well. The technology is inexpensive, requires few special skills to install or maintain and has been successfully exported to other parts of the world with similar geographic conditions. This is an example of a technological innovation that can be applied to achieve sustainable development.

Nevertheless, small successes like this one pale by comparison with the damage wreaked upon the environment by big business. Big energy companies and our insatiable demand for oil to fuel inefficient automobiles are responsible for an incalculable amount of damage to the environment, including areas that are extremely sensitive. Economic concerns—higher profits for industry, jobs for workers—inevitably outweigh environmental concerns. In Ecuador, plans to lay an oil pipeline from the Amazonian oil fields to the Pacific coast brought the government and environmentalists to blows. The route chosen for the pipeline ran right through the Mindo-Nambillo reserve, a cloud forest region with more than 450 species of birds, 43 of which are endangered. Not far from Quito in the Andes, the area's residents derive their living from ecotourism, which also could be endangered if spills ruin the forest. Environmentalists fear not only breaks in the pipeline from earthquakes and landslides but also the inevitable damage to the reserve that will come with access roads and squatters who try to start farms in the virgin forest. However, the construction of the pipeline was predicted to bring 52,000 jobs for Ecuadorians and $2.6 billion in foreign investment in the next three years.[16] Given the state of the economy, the need for the new pipeline couldn't be denied, although the dispute over the route continued until foreign environmentalists were deported and several Ecuadorians were jailed.

Do Environmentally Sensitive Areas Need Special Protection, Including International Agreements?

Agree

Animals and plants in danger of premature extinction[17] can never be replaced. Overexploitation, loss of habitat and pollution can create conditions from which some species cannot recover. The threat to certain mammal and bird species is well known (the quetzal, jaguar, river otter, river dolphin and certain kinds of monkeys and parrots, to name only a few), but species of amphibians, reptiles, insects and plants are also on the recently extinct or endangered lists. Many of these species are endemic to parts of Latin America; that is, they exist only in a single, restricted area and nowhere else. If the local population becomes extinct, that species will disappear forever. Spain also has several bird and mammal species that are restricted to the Iberian Peninsula today.

Even when other populations exist farther away, the loss of one or more species locally affects the biodiversity of the area and the balance of the ecosystem is altered, sometimes with serious negative consequences. When species are lost prematurely—reducing the biodiversity (*biodiversidad*) of an area—we not only lose interesting and often beautiful plants and animals, we are eliminating species that may have beneficial effects that we are not yet aware of.

Less than 1/2 of one percent of the planet's 265,000 species of higher plants has been exhaustively analyzed for their chemical composition and medicinal properties. . . . From that 1/2 of one percent comes some 25 percent of all prescription pharmaceuticals that have been developed to date.[18]

Many environmentalists believe that one of the most effective ways to protect fragile environments is to create special preserves where the harvesting of plants and animals is carefully controlled (if allowed at all). In these parks or preserves new incursions from agriculture, logging, mining, industry or urban growth are not allowed. Under encouragement and pressure from environmentalists inside and outside of Latin America, the number and extent of protected areas has grown in the last several decades. Costa Rica has been a leader in the development of national parks that serve as protected areas for wildlife, as well as in the movement to "bank" "carbon credits" from industrialized nations. Non-governmental organizations (NGOs), such as the World Wildlife Fund, Conservation International on an international scale and many national organizations in Latin America and Spain raise money to purchase land in sensitive areas.

Indigenous groups in Latin American countries have been especially concerned about preserving the environment, and some have worked hard to protect or regain their ancestral rights to land in order to husband it—to preserve not only the wildlife, but also their own culture. Ecotourism[19] has recently brought many visitors from the outside to experience the varied environments of Latin America. After some negative experiences with tour operators that kept most of the profits and did not employ local community members, more indigenous groups have begun to organize their own ecotourism operations, often with the assistance of government agencies or NGOs.

What has been done so far is still not enough, say critics. Endangered species are still hunted and trapped for sale as pets, and smuggled out of the country under awful conditions that result in the death of more animals than arrive alive at their destinations. International treaties[20] have not been very effective in eliminating this trade; enforcement is not always easy and consumers in the United States, Europe and other wealthy countries are willing to pay high prices for exotic pets.

Spain also has its environmental problems. The *CIA Fact Book* lists the following current issues: pollution of the Mediterranean Sea from raw sewage and effluents from the offshore production of oil and gas; water quality and quantity nationwide; air pollution; deforestation; desertification.[21] Every year some of Spain's beaches have to be closed due to pollution. The result is a significant loss of revenue to local businesses as well as damage to the littoral environment.

Industrial accidents also threaten the environment. In 1998, the collapse of a dam holding toxic mining wastes (*residuos tóxicos*) flooded an area 50 by 80 kilometers (roughly the size of Washington, D.C.). Thousands of tons of toxic overflow crept toward the Doñana National Park in southern Spain, an area of wetlands where an estimated 6 million migratory birds stop on their way to winter in Africa. Species of lynx, otters and eagles, all endangered in Europe, also live within the reserve's boundaries. The public was outraged. Fortunately, the toxic mud stopped just short of the boundaries of Doñana; nevertheless, the spill set off an ecological catastrophe of unprecedented costs in Spain. By the end of the year 2000, the Spanish government had already spent some 23 billion pesetas on cleanup and measures to protect against intrusions of contaminated mud and water.[22] Even so, much more work remained to be done to repair damage to the agricultural and wild environment, and many mineworkers left without employment.

Disagree

Supply and demand is what it's all about, say the critics of regulation and special protection. They believe it will never be possible to regulate away environmental problems. Developing nations, which include all of the Latin American and Caribbean countries, need economic growth to feed and provide jobs for their citizens. Strict environmental controls raise the cost of doing business in these countries and discourage both foreign investment and national companies. If you make the rules too strict, entire industries and tens of thousands of jobs will be lost.

For example, the relatively new shrimp export business in Ecuador grew from earnings of $31 million in 1979 to $185 million in 1983 and $539 million in 1994. By that time, the industry employed 260,000 people in its ponds, hatcheries, processing plants and other facilities; shrimp farming became an economic mainstay for the country. Ecuador furnishes nearly 10 percent of the U.S. supply, and shrimp is the third-leading export after oil (petroleum) and bananas. Ecuador cannot simply close down the shrimp industry; doing so would be a recipe for economic disaster.[23]

Recently, politically conservative writers and politicians, often at odds with environmentalists over issues of regulation, have put their weight behind conservation efforts that buy land to protect it from logging, draining or other modification. They believe that preservation, rather than regulation, will be a more effective solution to protecting wild species and biodiversity.[24]

Should the Developed Nations of the World Pay a Greater Share of the Costs of Halting Environmental Destruction and Repairing the Damage?

Agree

Not surprisingly, the less developed nations (*los países en desarrollo*) favor this position. They believe it is unfair for them to bear the same level of costs to control the global effects of environmental change or to clean up damage to their own countries. Most of the injury to the environment, they say, came in response to the highly industrialized countries' voracious appetite for consumer goods, which multinational companies were willing to provide at any cost to the environment. Therefore, the "developed" countries should help to foot the bill for the cost of cleaning up the damage. The peoples of underdeveloped nations should not have to pay for expensive new technologies needed now because their richer neighbors set such a bad example, polluted so much, or stripped less developed nations of their natural resources in the past.

In this view, Latin America, like many former colonies of Western European nations, have been victims of centuries of "dependency," first as subjects of an overseas colonial empire and later as countries dependent on the economic and political winds and whims of Europe and North America. Whatever bad environmental habits Latin Americans picked up (such as exploiting the land to the maximum), they did primarily in response to the demands for raw materials from Europe and the United States. Furthermore, the industrialized countries are much better able to pay for new measures to prevent new damage or to correct old insults against the environment (such as oil seepage).

Disagree

"Be reasonable," says the industrialized North. U.S. labor leaders fear that companies will move and take their jobs to less developed countries if environmental laws are not uniformly enforced, but businesses often point to rising costs to the consumer of environmental controls. On the other hand, advocates of free trade insist that the economic benefits of fewer—not more—controls on business will raise the environmental bar higher and faster than adding new layers of red tape.

In the meantime, by means of direct support and through international agencies and technological assistance, the governments of several industrialized nations have been willing to help the underdeveloped South. Spain has been quite active in funding environmental programs and sustainable development projects, especially in Latin America. The European Union, as well as Canada and the United States, NGOs based in these countries and the World Bank, have been especially active in promoting sustainable development projects as well as funding research in effective solutions to environmental problems. Furthermore, a consensus is growing among environmentalists and economists that common ground can and must be found. Daniel Esty, an American economist, has proposed an International Environmental Organization (IEO) modeled on the lines of the world trade agreements.

[The IEO] might initially focus on defining general environmental principles to guide the world community. For example, universal acceptance and application of the polluter-pays principle—forcing governments, industry and individuals alike to bear the full costs of the environmental burdens they impose on society—would create powerful incentives for pollution prevention and environmental care, consistent with the long-term interest of the public in a healthy environment and ongoing economic growth.[25]

QUESTIONS AND ACTIVITIES

1. Role-play: you (and your group members) are leaders of an ecotourism tour. Use the Audubon Society's *Guía Etica Para Viajes Ambientalmente Responsables,* http://www.audubon.org/ (especially http://www. audubon.org/market/no/ethic/indexspan.htm) to prepare a shorter version to explain the rules of ethical ecotourism to your group of tourists. (As an alternative, after reading the *guía,* the other members of the class can prepare questions about what they may and may not do. For example, may the tourists feed any of the birds or other wild animals they will see? Can they do any individual exploring off the marked paths?)

2. Both national and international groups are trying to avert damage to the environment, plant and animal species. Use the website of the World Wildlife Fund to read about endangered species in Spain or Mexico. Describe the habitat of the animal. What has put the species in danger of premature extinction? What is being done to try to help it survive?

3. Because of the value of petroleum and forest products, conflicts of interest between governments, business and ecologists will continue to occur. Use a site such as Rainforest Action to identify one of these conflicts and read about it. Then search an online newspaper from the same country to look for opposing views. Who are the interested parties? What does each of them want? What does each of them have to lose? Where would you stand on this issue? Why?

4. A weekly television news program has arranged for a panel discussion with representatives of environmental groups, business and the government to discuss the conflict in #3. Each side should prepare a statement and several questions for the other groups to answer. (Give the questions to your "opponents" in advance so that they can prepare reasonable

answers to your questions.) Your teacher or another student can serve as moderator.

5. The Kyoto Protocol provoked a controversy in the United States concerning the reality of global warming and the contribution of modern, industrialized culture to the measure and projected change in temperature. Useful search terms for a search of news and web pages are climate change (*cambio climático*) and global warming (*efecto invernadero, calentamiento del planeta/calentimiento mundial*).

6. Imagine that you work in the U.S. embassy of a Latin American country. Your job is to prepare the U.S. ambassador for a meeting with a coalition of local environmental groups who are concerned about a U.S. company's timber operations in the temperate rainforest in Chile. Discover what has been happening on both sides and write an executive summary (a short summary of both positions, approximately a half page for each side) on the conflict for the ambassador.

7. Do you believe that pollution and emission of greenhouse gasses will be better controlled by mandatory requirements or voluntary standards? If the Kyoto Protocols were to go into effect in the United States, how would they affect businesses in your state? Why do you think the European Union decided to ratify the Kyoto agreement when the United States did not?

8. What areas or cities in Spain attract the largest number of tourists? What have been some of the benefits to the nation? What problems has tourism created in Spain? Are there any that specifically affect the quality or the sustainability of the environment? How is tourism affected by ecological deterioration or catastrophes such as the Doñana spill? Useful search terms include *turismo, ecoturismo, medio ambiente, daño ambiental*.

VOCABULARY/VOCABULARIO

Nouns/Sustantivos

animals, endangered	los animales en peligro de extinción
countries, developing	los países en vías de desarrollo
countries, underdeveloped	los países subdesarrollados
damage	el daño
demand	la demanda

development	el desarrollo
development, sustainable	el desarrollo sostenible
ecotourism	el ecoturismo
environment	el medio ambiente
forest	el bosque
growth	el crecimiento, la expansión económica
indigenous (people)	los indígenas
laws	las leyes
NGOs (non-governmental organizations)	las ONGs (o ene ges)
pollution	la polución, la contaminación
rainforest	el bosque tropical, la selva
tourism	el turismo
waste, toxic	los desechos tóxicos, los residuos tóxicos

Verbs/Verbos

cut	cortar
destroy	destruir
develop	desarrollar
exploit, use	explotar
grow (larger, taller)	crecer
preserve	preservar
protect	proteger
support	apoyar
take advantage of	aprovecharse (de)
take care of	cuidar

Adjectives/Adjetivos

environmental	ambiental
toxic	tóxico/a

RECOMMENDED SOURCES

Books and Articles

Barrero, Antonio. "Espacios naturales protegidos . . . superficialmente." *Revista Ecosistemas* No. 18, 1996. <http://www.ucm.es/info/ecosistemas/espacios.htm>.

Bonta, Marcia. "A Jungle Haven in Peru."*Americas* (January–February 1987): 8–13

Browder, John O., ed. *Fragile Lands of Latin America: Strategies for Sustainable Development.* Boulder, CO: Westview Press, 1989.

Jones, Benjamin. "Saving Doñana Nature Reserve." *Europe* (October 1998): 43–46.

Gardner, Gary. "Religion and the Quest for a Sustainable World." *Humanist* (March–April 2003): 10–15.

Huber, Peter W. *Hard Green: Saving the Environment from the Environmentalists: A Conservative Manifesto.* New York: Basic Books, 1999.

Kaplan, Marion, and Stephanie Maze. "Iberia's Vintage River." *National Geographic* (October 1984): 460–513.

Lindsay, James M. "Global Warming Heats Up." *Brookings Review* (Fall 2001): 26–29.

Mooney, Michael J. "Come the Camanchaca." *Americas* (July–August 1995): 30–37.

Schuster, Angela M. H. "On the Healer's Path: A Journey through the Maya Rain Forest." *Archaeology* (July–August 2001): 34–38.

Serageldin, Ismail, and Andrew Steer, eds. *Making Development Sustainable: From Concepts to Action.* Washington, DC: World Bank, 1994.

Shute, Nancy et al. "The Weather Turns Wild: Global Warming Could Cause Droughts, Disease, and Political Upheaval." *U.S. News and World Report*, February 5, 2001, pp. 40–44.

Thomas, Vinod, and Tamara Belt. "Growth and the Environment: Allies or Foes?" *Journal of Social, Political and Economic Studies* 22(3) (1997): 327–334.

Young, Kenneth R., and Blanca Leon. "Nature on the Rebound." *Americas* (English Edition) (February 1999): 30.

Internet

Ecosistemas: Revista de ecología y medio ambiente (Spain). <http://www.aeet.org/ecosistemas/>.

Intergovernmental Panel on Climate Change (IPCC). <http://www.ipcc. ch/>.
Planeta.com (ecotourism and ecology). <http://www.planeta.com>.
Rainforest Action Network. <http://www.ran.org/>.
Sustainable Business.com. <http://sustainablebusiness.com/>.
United Nations World Summit on Sustainable Development (2002). <http://www.johannesburgsummit.org/>.
World Wildlife Fund. <http://www.wwf.org.mx/> (Mexico), <http:// www.wwf.es/>(Spain).

Video

"ACEER [Amazon Center for Environmental Education and Research] Useful Plant Trail Video Guide." Videocassette. Port Royal, S.C.: Environmental Media Corporation, 1995. Color. 30 min.
"Manu: Peru's Hidden Rain Forest." Videocassette. Burbank, CA: PBS Home Video, 1997. Color. 60 min.
The Natural World of Latin America (11-part series). Videocassette. Televisión Española, Films for the Humanities. Princeton, NJ: Films for the Humanities, 1996. Color. 26–29 min.
"Population Explosion and Industrialization." Videocassette. [*Latin American Lifestyles* series]. Melville, NY: Video Knowledge, Inc., 1977. Color. 21 + 21 min. (English narration, Spanish narration).

Chapter 7

Population

The world welcomed its 6 billionth inhabitant in 1999. How many people will be around in the year 2050, when you are a grandparent? United Nations demographers provide us with estimates that range from a low of 7.9 billion, a middle figure of somewhat more than 9 billion, to a high of 10.9 billion. Until recently, population growth has been steady in Spain but dramatic in Latin America. Cities have seen very high rates of growth in both areas. What have been the causes and the effects of changes in the rates of population growth and the rapid urbanization experienced on both sides of the Atlantic? Have measures taken to control population growth been successful? What groups oppose measures to control population growth, and why?

BACKGROUND

Almost everyone knows that Mexico City is one of the largest cities in the world. With a population estimated at more than 20 million, Mexico bulges at its ever-expanding seams. During the decade of the 1990s, more than 1,000 new immigrants arrived *every day*, and the city is home to approximately 20% of the nation's entire population. The "megacities" of Buenos Aires, Santiago and Lima are home to over 40% of their nations' respective populations. Spain has its large cities too, although only Madrid, at 5.1 million inhabitants, rivals the largest Latin American urban centers.[1] Ma-

Mexico City (shown here), along with many other capitals, is one of the *primate* cities in Latin America. Primate cities have a disproportionate share of the national population, employment and Gross National Product—some of them as much as 50% or more—and continue to attract rural immigrants looking for employment and educational opportunities. (AP Photo/Victor R. Caivano)

drid, along with Barcelona, Seville and Valencia, dominates Spain in terms of population and influence in industry, commerce and culture.

It's not just the largest cities that are growing: smaller urban areas too are experiencing fast rates of growth in Latin America. At the same time, Spain and some of the Hispanic countries are undergoing negative population growth in their rural areas, and overall the birthrate in Spain rivals that of Italy for the lowest in Europe. These changes in size and location of populations will necessitate changes in social policies in every nation. According to the report of the United Nations International Conference on Population and Development, held in 1994,

The majority of the world's countries are converging towards a pattern of low birth and death rates, but since those countries are proceeding at different speeds, the emerging picture is that of a world facing increasingly diverse demographic situations. In terms of national averages, during the period 1985–1990, fertility ranged from an estimated 8.5 children per woman in Rwanda [Africa] to 1.3 children per woman in Italy. [During the same period] expectation of life at birth, an indicator of mortality conditions, ranged from an estimated 41 years in Sierra Leone [Africa] to 78.3 years in Japan.[2]

Life expectancy in Latin America is closer to developed countries and infant mortality is lower than other, less developed countries. This puts most Latin American nations between the other two groups in nearly every demographic category. Let's look at some of the assertions concerning population growth and see how they play out in Hispanic countries.

1. Nations can no longer afford the rates of population growth that were common in the twentieth century, particularly in developing countries.
2. The best way to slow or stop the increase in population is through the use of contraceptives.
3. Governmental and/or supragovernmental bodies (such as international agencies) should work to develop plans to anticipate and address changes in population, create programs to redistribute the population, and so on.

DISCUSSION

Do Current Rates of Population Growth Threaten the Environment and Hispanic Countries' Ability to Adequately Feed Their Inhabitants?

Agree

Those in favor of a continued effort in population control, including organizations such as Population Connection (formerly known as Zero Population Growth), Population Action International and the United Nations Population Fund, point out that severe damage to the environment has already occurred to the world's wilderness, our water and air supplies and agricultural lands because of population pressure. Air quality in many of the world's large cities is intolerable. In the majority of Latin American countries, weak environmental regulations have slowed the changeover to lead-free gasoline; old and inefficient bus, truck and automobile motors pump tons of soot particles into the air each day. Although many city residents in Spain and Latin America use public transportation, a growing middle class in both regions has been more capable of and interested in buying automobiles. As a consequence, private cars now clog the streets of Spanish and Latin American cities. The pollution created by cars and industry blanket most Latin American cities with smog, contributing to increased health risks in the cities and ozone depletion worldwide.

The rapid growth of the cities has also created a crisis in water supply and water quality in most Hispanic countries. In Latin America, construction of adequate water treatment plants must wait in line for scarce funds or foreign assistance. Polluted rivers create polluted coastlines, not only spreading disease, but in some cases ruining economically vital fishing industries and the potential for tourism. The population has grown much too fast for governments to keep up.

In rural areas, especially in Latin America, larger populations have pushed farmlands further and further into "marginal" areas where the land is not well suited to agriculture. Steep slopes are more subject to erosion; forest that is cleared for agriculture no longer holds back the land during rainy season, resulting in increased runoff and landslides. Tropical forests that are cleared for agriculture are frequently shallow and are quickly exhausted, leading to a new round of clearing and environmental damage. Already several countries have had to import some of their basic foods, in part because productive land is disappearing.

In Spain, as we shall see, growth of the population per se is not adversely affecting the environment in agricultural areas. However, population has put pressure on natural areas. In this case, the problem stems not so much from growth of the Spanish population (which is negative aside from the effects of immigration). Rather, tourism from within Spain, and from outside as well, has increased dramatically and many national parks and coastal areas are filled to capacity with campers, hikers and weekend or summer visitors.[3]

Disagree

Those who disagree accuse the other side of vastly overstating the problem. This group proposes the use of genetically modified plants, or higher technology, including fertilizers, insecticides and herbicides, to increase yields and feed more people, thus enabling the earth to support a larger population. The first generation of applied scientific agricultural research after World War II was termed the "Green Revolution" and had important effects in many areas of the world. Environmentalists, however, point out that intensive agriculture that relies on the use of fertilizers and equipment is often out of the reach of small farmers, who lack capital and technical expertise. Therefore, intensive agriculture is most often used in the commercial production of export crops. Development plans have often favored this approach because exports bring needed foreign exchange into the economy. Although it provides employment for a segment of the population, intensive commercial agriculture in Latin America frequently does not have much of an effect on the ability of the land to feed the national population.

The advocates of "sustainable development" take a much less aggressive approach. They say that intelligent use of modern or traditional technologies, scientific knowledge and ingenuity and careful attention to involving local farmers in planning and implementing changes can maintain or increase the "carrying capacity" of agricultural lands. Advocates of sustainable development (*desarrollo sostenible*) point out that current populations (and possibly somewhat larger ones) can be better fed in certain instances by adapting traditional forms of land management, such as terracing (in the Andes, for example), raised fields and the use of *arroyos* (dry stream beds) in arid regions.[4] Most advocates of sustainable agriculture would make judicious use of artificial fertilizers and, in some instances, careful introduction of new breeds of plants or animals that could increase yields without exhausting or eroding the soil or displacing local plants and animals. This debate is far from settled. Proponents of the second wave of the Green Revolution say that greater attention to building infrastructure (for example, transportation), markets, finance and the elimination of corruption would improve the amount of food produced and delivered to local markets.[5]

In response to its negative growth rate, Spain has seen a sharp increase in immigration, both legal and illegal. Some Latin American countries have already become exporters of workers (for example Ecuador, the Dominican Republic and Colombia to Spain and the same countries plus Mexico and Central America to the United States). While unskilled workers form a large percentage of emigrants, more than ever, well-educated younger people leave their home countries to look for better opportunities abroad.

Are Contraceptives the Best Way to Slow or Stop the Increase in Population?

Agree

Most individuals and countries favor voluntary methods to regulate population growth. The majority of Latin American countries have some sort of family planning programs (*control de natalidad, planificación familiar*), some of which have contributed to dramatic reductions in fertility rates (average number of children per woman) in recent decades.

For example, Mexico's fertility rate dropped from 6.8 in 1960 to 2.8 in 1995. The country's innovative family planning program, begun in the 1970s, includes mobile health teams and clinics to serve the needs of rural areas, Indian populations and pregnant teenagers. Puppet theaters address family planning issues by overcoming widespread rural illiteracy. Integrating traditional Indian medicine into the rural health clinics has also been successful with indigenous peoples. Midwives, who most often assist in births in rural areas, have received training not only in improving sanitation during delivery but also discussion of family planning. Local *curanderos* (traditional healers), who are now incorporated into rural health care centers, also discuss family planning options with the people they treat. Overall, by the end of the twentieth century, the percentage of sexually active Mexican women aged 15–49 who use birth control was about 53%.[6] The intrauterine device (IUD) is a popular form of birth control in many localities and is often used by women who want to space out births. Increasing the time between pregnancies is important to both families and communities, since the survival rate of newborn children and their older siblings, as well as their mother's, increases when pregnancies are spaced at intervals longer than two years.[7]

A few Latin American countries and Spain have legalized abortion (*aborto*), although in most countries there are restrictions (endangerment of the mother's life or health, rape, or fetal malformation). A few more permit abortion only with approval of a court or the husband. Some countries—such as Chile, Colombia, El Salvador, Honduras and the Dominican Republic[8]—do not permit legal abortion under any circumstances. Nevertheless, the number of abortions is high, especially in Latin America, due to the lack of sex education and the limited access to contraceptives. A large number of abortions are illegal; some medical groups estimate that as many as 6 million illegal abortions are performed each year in Latin America.

Advocates of family planning blame social conservatives, including the Catholic Church, for opposing publicizing contraceptive use and discouraging sex education. Health experts in Peru say that up to 60% of pregnancies in their country are unwanted and half of these are terminated. Although there are no legal barriers to abortion in Peru, the high cost (approximately $300) and limited access to safe abortions leaves many poor women in Peru, as elsewhere, with few options. Between 20 and 30% of all maternal deaths each year are attributed to unsafe, illegal abortions.[9]

Disagree

The population issue raises especially difficult questions for the Catholic Church in Latin America. Writing about the entire world population, an author in a widely read Catholic periodical states:

A full 96 percent of the annual population increase occurs in developing countries, including most of those places where overcrowding and resource depletion are already a grave problem. . . . Christians must take as one of their highest priorities the alleviation of hunger and illiteracy in the developing nations. Over 1 billion people on the planet enter the new century unable to read or even to sign their names. Over 35,000 children die needlessly every day.[10]

In spite of its traditional concern for the world's poor, however, the Catholic Church has not altered its stance on population control issues because nearly all programs that involve limiting family size also promote the use of at least some form of artificial contraception. Although it offers family planning advice using "natural" methods, the Catholic Church does not accept the use of any form of contraceptives. Most other religious denominations do not oppose artificial contraceptives (anticonceptivos). Abortion and sterilization, however, are less widely accepted and some other religious groups disagree with their use in family planning as well.

The admonitions of the Catholic Church have not been especially effective in this area. In spite of the fact that 90 to 95% of the population of Hispanic countries say they are Catholic, the use of modern methods of birth control by married women in Hispanic

South America averages around 45%, in Central America and Mexico 53% and in Spain 70%, the same percentage as for the United States.[11] According to Engender Health, sterilization is the most common form of birth control worldwide and is expected to be used more frequently in Latin America and the Caribbean in the future. Already in several Latin American countries. including Puerto Rico and the Dominican Republic, sterilization (tubal ligation or vasectomy, especially the former) is a common form of contraception after the birth of several children,[12] and more poor women would use modern contraceptives if they were easily available and affordable.

Promoting the reproductive health and rights of young people remains a controversial topic in most countries because it involves sensitive issues of sexuality and parental rights and duties. Sex education in schools is extremely limited. Churches have become more active in educating and counseling adolescents about sexuality in ways that are compatible with their religious views. In recent decades the literature of the Catholic Church has moved away from characterizing premarital sex as sinful and moved toward stressing the importance of commitment in relationships and the role of sex as a bond between loving couples.[13]

The United States is also an important participant in the debate on population control and family planning methods, since our government funds a variety of public health programs in developing countries through the United States Agency for International Development (USAID). In the 1960s the United States became the largest donor to international family planning assistance. In 1984 the Reagan administration announced a cutoff of funds to organizations that had any involvement with offering or counseling for abortion or advocating changes in anti-abortion laws.[14] This rule was rescinded by the Clinton administration in 1993, but the restriction was put back in place by President George W. Bush in 2001.[15]

Is Planning Needed to Anticipate and Address Changes in Population and to Create Programs to Redistribute the Population?

Agree

As a result of improved sanitation and the development of effective medicines, such as antibiotics, in the second half of the twentieth century more children survived to reproductive age. They produced even more children, dramatically pushing up population growth rates—and as a consequence, the world's population. In the 1980s and 1990s a drop in growth rates occurred due to the spread of birth control and family planning. In the twenty-first century the combined result of this demographic whiplash will be a larger *total* population worldwide but a smaller *proportion* of young people and a larger *proportion* of older people (the elderly "baby boomers" and their senior citizen children) in most every country. This shift in the makeup of the population will have important consequences for the nations of the world. Until recently, the challenge for many nations of Latin America has been to find ways to educate and provide work for young people. In 25 years, many nations will be struggling to care for their growing elderly population.

This is already happening in Europe. With less than 1.2 children per woman of childbearing age, Spain rivals Italy for the lowest fertility rate in Western Europe and must already dedicate an important share of its budget to pensions for the elderly (*la tercera edad*). As the proportion of younger people shrinks, there will be a proportionately smaller work force to generate tax revenue to pay for the elderly. After decades of trying to address the needs of younger people for education and employment, many countries find themselves short of professionals and facilities—for example, doctors and hospitals—to provide services for the elderly.

In countries like Spain, where the birthrate is not high enough to sustain the population at its present level, "negative growth" also means there are not enough Spanish workers to fill the available jobs. Alarm is growing in some quarters: people fear a loss of national identity as more immigrants enter the country; others are concerned that negative attitudes toward foreigners will increase. Several European countries have adopted policies intended to encourage higher birthrates.

Anxiety about low birthrates is not entirely new in Spain. In the aftermath of the Civil War (1936–1939), the Franco government tried to boost the disappointing national birthrate by offering prizes for the largest family in each province; the winning couples often boasted 15 children or more. In the end, it was not this symbolism but a much-improved economy that gave more couples the confidence to have larger families. Before it began to decline, the fertility rate in 1970 was 2.86 children per woman nationwide and more than 3 in southern Spain. Nowadays, young families want more tangible help than a medal from the government; they want subsidized day care, assistance with educational expenses, and regulations that would help women have more flexible working hours. Without it, couples that want to have children must postpone starting a family or they may decide that raising a family is not a realistic option. The low birthrate doesn't reflect a dislike of children: over 90% of married women have at least one child; but more and more of them have only one. In addition, most Spanish women give birth to their first child between the ages of 30 and 39.[16]

Increased consumerism (creating a "need" for higher incomes) and rising prices for housing developed alongside of increases in educational opportunities for women, the incorporation of more women into employment outside the home and lack of alternative childcare and/or flexibility of work schedules for female employees. All of these have had an effect on the ability of families to plan and care for children, especially among the lower and middle classes. Young women in Spain have criticized the government for whining about the low birthrate while not helping women find ways to afford to care for their children and their families, now that many families rely on the female partner's income to help make ends meet. In addition, the educational level of women is an especially important factor in virtually every country around the world. A researcher noted that in Spain,

main factors having an effect on the decision to have children [were] level of education, marriage, and religious belief. For example, while the mean birth rate in illiterate women in Spain is 3.19, it is 1.37 in women who have completed secondary-school education, and only 0.77 in women with a university degree.[17]

The effect of education, even basic literacy, on fertility rates in less developed countries is equally profound. In countries with high female illiteracy, birthrates are very high; they decline as more women have access to schooling.

In the developing countries of Latin America, the high birthrates (and high infant mortality rates) that were common in rural areas have begun to decline as more people moved to the cities, where health facilities are somewhat easier to access. In addition, the cash economy of the city (rather than subsistence farming) makes it even harder to care for and house families with numerous children.

Disagree

Opponents of family planning programs, for the most part Catholic Church hierarchy and lay organizations, believe that governments should stay out of the business of influencing the size of families. Frequently they oppose governmental involvement in any kind of family planning program, and with good reason, they say. In 1997, the world press picked up a story that Peruvian government clinics were coercing women (and some men) into agreeing to sterilization. The women affected were almost always poor, lived mostly in rural areas and had several children. Clinic personnel were accused of demeaning their lower-class patients and using tactics such as threatening to stop food assistance for other children in the family or refusing to let the women go home from the hospital without submitting to the sterilization procedure (a tubal ligation).

Allegations differed as to the total number of women affected, but several women were said to have died as a result of the sterilizations. Although supportive of programs that would liberalize access to birth control and family planning services, feminist journals were among the first to denounce the abusive practices of the Peruvian clinics. After the Ministry of Health stepped in to improve the program, a follow-up investigation found no evidence that new patients had been coerced, but the clinics still needed to improve their information about sterilizations and explanation of choices.[18]

Opposition to government guidelines on family size has come not only from the Catholic Church and political conservatives, but also from many indigenous communities and organizations in Latin America. A report of the United Nations International Conference on Population and Development in 1994 summarized their concerns:

Indigenous people have a distinct and important perspective on population and development relationships, frequently quite different from those of the populations with which they interrelate within national boundaries. In some regions of the world, indigenous people, after long periods of population loss, are experiencing steady and in some places rapid population growth resulting from declining mortality, although morbidity and mortality are generally still much higher than for other sections of the national population. In other regions, however, they are still experiencing a steady population decline as a result of contact with external diseases, loss of land and resources, ecological destruction, displacement, resettlement and disruption of their families, communities and social systems.[19]

Sterilizations performed without the patients' informed consent, like those described in Peru, have been frequently denounced in indigenous communities[20] as a violation of human rights and have led indigenous groups to accuse governments of indulging in a form of genocide. The United Nations has urged all its members to follow guidelines concerning representation of indigenous groups in matters of policy—such as public health and population programs—that affect them, but compliance with these guidelines varies widely. ·

Finally, some critics of birth control and population control programs imply that the availability of contraception has contributed to the decay of the family and the increase in societal problems. By removing the element of personal responsibility from sexual relations and enabling women to limit the number of children, say these opponents, women are encouraged to work outside the home, leaving existing children with inadequate adult supervision, and men are less likely to take responsibility for their families. Rising crime rates, drug addiction and broken homes are the result.

QUESTIONS AND ACTIVITIES

1. Use *National Geographic* and other magazines to learn more about one major Spanish city (such as Madrid, Bilbao, Barcelona) or Latin American urban area (such as Buenos Aires, Caracas, Santiago, Lima, Mexico City or Bogotá). What are some of the reasons tourists might visit this city or urban area? Why would people from towns and smaller cities in the same country move to that particular city or urban area to live? Make a list of similarities and differences.

2. Imagine that you are a person of high school age in a developing country, such as Chile. You want to leave your small village and go to the capital city, Santiago. With another classmate, prepare a conversation between you and a teacher or other older friend. Explore the advantages and disadvantages of leaving home and going to the city.

3. What do your friends and family know about global population trends? What do they believe about the desirability of family planning programs in other countries? Develop a short list of questions (a version in English and in Spanish). Do a survey of at least five people and write a report of the survey and results in Spanish.

4. Has your region experienced population growth? What effects has growth had on the local environment (for example, the amount of green space, agricultural land, traffic, etc.)? If your area has experienced a decline in population, what have been the effects?

5. Do you believe that sex education encourages young people to have sex? Do you think that, if contraceptives were not easily available in the United States, fewer adolescents would engage in sex? Provide your reasons for both answers.

6. If you were the minister of health in one of the Latin American countries where abortion is currently illegal, would you favor legalization of abortion to reduce a high maternal death rate? Explain your reasons.

7. In general, women with higher levels of education have fewer children. What are some reasons that might explain this trend? What are other factors that influence the number of children per family?

8. Imagine that you and several classmates have been given the task of anticipating the needs of a small city in Spain as its population ages. Brainstorm a list of all the things, services and kinds of workers that will be required to provide for the needs of an older population (all the way from more places that sell take-out food to gerontologists).

9. If your school policy permits it, establish an e-mail or chat connection with a group of elderly Spaniards. Find out (1) what services are available to retired people in their community and (2) who pays for them (government or their own savings). One organization you might try is *SeñorSenda* (http://www.sendasenior.com).

10. Look for articles in the Spanish press on the birthrate (*tasa de natalidad*) or family size (*familia numerosa*). What concerns do writers express about the national birthrate and its effects on the nation?

11. How does Spain compare to other European nations in helping families with children? Summarize your findings in a report in Spanish. Do you think government assistance would boost Spain's extremely low birthrate? Explain your opinion. A good article to use is "El 'lujo' de tener hijos," which appeared in the May 27, 2001 edition of *El País*.

VOCABULARY/VOCABULARIO

Nouns/Sustantivos

abortion	el aborto
adolescents	los adolescentes
advantage	la ventaja
agriculture	la agricultura
average	el promedio
birth	el nacimiento
birthrate	la tasa de natalidad

care	el cuidado
children	los hijos
city	la ciudad
contraception	el control de natalidad
contraceptives	los anticonceptivos
control	el control
death	la muerte
death, infant	la mortalidad infantil
death, maternal	la mortalidad materna
death rate	la taza de mortalidad
decline, loss	el decrecimiento
development	el desarrollo
development, sustainable	el desarrollo sostenible
disadvantage	la desventaja
elderly, old people	los viejos, la tercera edad
environment	el medio ambiente
family, large	la familia numerosa
growth	el crecimiento
health	la salud
immigrants	los inmigrantes
life expectancy	la esperanza de vida
parents	los padres
planning	la planificación
planning, family	la planificación familiar
pollution	la polución, la contaminación
population	la población
population, rural	la población rural
population, urban	la población urbana
problems, economic	los problemas económicos
problems, social	los problemas sociales
residents	los residentes
responsibility	la responsabilidad
retired people	los jubilados
services	los servicios

smog	la contaminación atmosférica
trends	las tendencias
values	los valores
worker, unskilled	el jornalero, el obrero
young people	los jóvenes

Verbs/Verbos

be born	nacer
control	controlar
decide	tomar una decisión
decrease (in size)	decrecer
develop	desarrollar
die	morir
emigrate, move to	emigrar
grow (in size)	crecer
have sex	tener relaciones sexuales
legalize	legalizar
move (to a place)	mudarse (a)
support a family	mantener a una familia
take care of	cuidar (a)

RESOURCE GUIDE

Books and Articles

Bailey, Ronald. "Billions Served: An Interview with Norman Borlaug." *Reason*, April 1, 2000, pp. 30–37.

Bosch, Xavier. "Spain's Birth Rate Drops to an All-Time Low." *Lancet*, January 8, 2000, p. 26.

Browder, John O. *Fragile Lands of Latin America: Strategies for Sustainable Development*. Boulder, CO: Westview Press, 1989.

"Cada año hacen en Latinoamérica 6 millones abortos clandestinos." Efe News Services, November 3, 1999, online, LexisNexis™ Academic, accessed July 15, 2001.

Corell, Mavi, and Gabriela Canas. "El 'lujo' de tener hijos." *El País*, May 27, 2001, accessed July 13, 2001, <http://www.elpais.es>.

Drinan, Robert F. "Church Grapples with Crowded Planet." *National Catholic Reporter*, December 3, 1999, p. 18.

Evans, Imogen. "What Do You Do, Partner?" *The Lancet*, July 27, 1996, pp. 211–212.

Gilbert, Alan, "Viva the City." *Geographical Magazine* (June 1994): 17–20.

Guimarães, Roberto. "The Environment, Population, and Urbanization." In Richard Hillman, ed., *Understanding Contemporary Latin America*. 2nd ed. Boulder, CO: Lynne Rienner, 2001, pp. 197–227.

"Indigenas [de] México Denuncian Campaña Masiva [de] Esterilización [en] Chiapas." Efe News Services, December 9, 1999, online, LexisNexis™ Academic, accessed July 23, 2001.

McDevitt, Thomas et al. *Trends in Adolescent Fertility and Contraceptive Use in the Developing World*. Washington, DC: U.S. Bureau of the Census, 1996.

"Not as Different as They Look." *The Economist*, September 26, 1992, p. 46.

Richardson, Bill. *Spanish Studies: An Introduction*. New York: Oxford University Press, 2001.

"Seremos 30 millones." *Expansión* (Madrid), May 17, 2001, LexisNexis™ Academic, accessed July 23, 2001.

"Terrible crimen la anticoncepción: Norberto Rivera." *El Nacional* [Mexico, D.F.], May 25, 1997, LexisNexis™ Academic, accessed July 15, 2001.

Internet

Creando vida. <http://www.creandovida.cl/principal.htm>.

Ecosistemas: Revista de Ecología y medio ambiente. <http://www.ucm.es/info/ecosistemas/>.

Engender Health. <http://www.engenderhealth.org>.

"Etica Sexual." Creando vida. <http://www.creandovida.cl/vientos/capitulo1/9b.htm>.

Mujer/Fempress: Revista Mensual Latinoamricana. <http://www.fempress.cl>.

Population Reference Bureau. <http://www.prb.org>.

"Programme of Action International Conference on Population and Development." Chapter 6, Part 1, February 29, 1999. July 20, 2001. <http://www.agora21.org/cipd/frame05.html>.

United Nations Population Fund. <http://www.unfpa.org>.

United States Agency for International Development. <http://www.usaid.gov>.

Chapter 8

Gender

In the wake of scandals involving the last term of President Alberto Fujimori, Lourdes Flores, lawyer and conservative politician, came close to getting into the runoff election for the presidency of Peru. If she had done so, she would have stood a good chance of being the first female elected to the presidency of a Latin American nation in her own right. (Others such Violeta Chamorro and Mireya Moscoso have been widows of former presidents or of popular reformers.) Flores' candidacy raised some interesting questions in Peru, where—as in many places in the Hispanic world—women politicians are considered more trustworthy and honest than men and more concerned about family and women's issues, but also less independent. Questions arise about whether women are "tough" enough to engage in the rough and tumble of political life at the highest levels or make the life-and-death decisions that a president might have to make. Will women ever be considered the full equal of men? Should they even want to be?

BACKGROUND

Machismo is the Spanish name for a particular set of values or attitudes about what boys and men should be and do. *Machismo* is the product of a patriarchal society, that is, one in which males have a disproportionate amount of power and authority. Historically, Spain, like other Mediterranean countries, had a strong patriarchal

Female workers outside a *maquiladora* (foreign-owned assembly plant) in Juarez, Mexico in 1999. *Maquiladoras* generally pay higher wages to their women employees than many other employers, but are not without their critics. (AP Photo/ Thomas Herbert)

social system. The *machismo* we see played out in the lives of people today is derived from this set of traditional attitudes about men and women and their proper roles in the family and in society.

The word *machismo* is derived from *macho*, the Spanish term for the male (*la hembra* is the female). *El macho* can be used to refer to both humans and animals: *el macho de la rana* (the male frog). However, the term *machismo* is relatively new. Apparently it was coined in the 1940s when newspaper writers and the public began to refer to Mexico's president, Manuel ávila Camacho, as "Macho Camacho." From there, *machismo* came to serve as a handy term for the concept of maleness that had developed in Hispanic societies.

In the *machista* framework, men dominate. They are strong and independent, while women are subordinate and submissive. Men refrain from showing emotion; women are expected to have tender feelings. Men have great sexual freedom; women and girls must remain pure and faithful. Men live their lives in the public arena; women's domain is the house and the family circle. Men are expected to provide for and protect their families; women give the emotional support and perform the household duties. In only one respect are women "superior" to men in this schema: they are more spiritual. For this reason they are entrusted with the religious upbringing of children as well as caring for their physical needs. Men may be indifferent to religion and, sometimes, too much interest in the Church or in religious activities is considered emasculating.

Few individuals fit this description of the traditional male or female in each and every detail. There are many fathers who encourage their daughters to excel; there are women who live very independent lives. However, in many families in both Spain and Latin America, the values that underlie the distinct gender roles have been taught by word and by example for many generations, so they still have great influence today. Men or women who break the mold generally pay some sort of price, which may range from bemusement or mild disapproval to outright hostility.

Contact with other cultures produced changes in the twentieth century. Media, in the form of books and magazines and especially television and movies, have introduced Hispanic men and women to a wider range of possibilities, but cultural change often occurs slowly and unevenly. In the seventeenth century, the brilliant young poetess Juana de Asbaje y Ramírez retreated to a nunnery and became Sor Juana Inés de la Cruz in order to have the freedom to indulge in intellectual pursuits that were not considered proper for a woman in the society of colonial Mexico. She struggled to assert that women were the intellectual equals of men and that they did not deserve to be held back because of their sex. Her complaint[1] against men who try to seduce women and then criticize them for being "too easy" rings just as true for many modern Hispanic women as it did for her generation.

Today, there are many more opportunities and more freedom for women, but girls and women still face obstacles, especially in the developing countries of Latin America. In Spain, already somewhat more women than men now attend universities and upper-class women in Latin America now take a college education for granted. However, as you move down the social class ladder, girls are less and less likely to have an equal opportunity for schooling as boys.

Machismo also has a profound effect on family life and the division of labor. Men are not expected to help with housework or to be involved with the day-to-day care of children. To do so would be "womanly" and certainly not "manly."[2] Rarely do men pitch in to do the dishes or wash the clothes. A man expects dinner to be ready when he comes home from work and breakfast to be made in the morning. However, a woman who works outside the home hardly ever has someone to do the same for her (unless it is a daughter). Latin American sociologists call this *la Doble Jornada*, the Double Workday.

Another consequence of *machismo* is a high level of tolerance in the society for physical, sexual and psychological abuse of women and girls. Since men—in the *machista* framework—are naturally superior to women and should be dominant, they feel free to punish them or control them as they wish. As in other societies, domestic abuse occurs at all social levels, but poverty and low levels of education increase the likelihood that a woman will suffer some kind of abuse at the hands of a husband, father or other male. The instance of violence against women is alarmingly high in most Latin American countries and in Spain as well. Finally, *machismo* spawned the *mujeriego* or Don Juan, the man who feels a need to prove his attractiveness to women and his ability to seduce them, and in doing so humiliate their boyfriends, husbands or other family members. This side of the traditional male personality has given rise to some of the most famous characters of Spanish literature since the Golden

Age and continues to be a source of inspiration for writers and film-makers, although today most often as a target of ridicule.

In both Spain and in Latin American countries, women have been active in promoting rights and speaking for the need for protection against abuse. On the other hand, not everyone believes that current laws and practices need changing. Here are some of the statements that feminists would make concerning the issue of women's rights.

1. Each country needs to develop legislation delineating women's rights and outlawing abuse. In addition, law enforcement personnel and judges must be re-educated to recognize violence against women and support the effort to bring it to an end.
2. Education must be made a high priority in efforts to improve the status of women.
3. Men must learn to share responsibilities and authority in the family and must show more respect for women outside the home.

DISCUSSION

Does Each Country Need to Develop Legislation Delineating Women's Rights and Outlawing Abuse? In Addition, Should Law Enforcement Personnel and Judges Be Re-educated to Recognize Violence against Women and Support the Effort to Bring It to an End?

Agree

There is an old *refrán*, or saying, in Spanish: "la mujer en casa con la pierna quebrada" (The woman should be in the house, with a broken leg.) This represented a kind of ideal scenario for the traditional man: his wife would be at home, unable to wander about freely. While the *refrán* may seem laughable to many of us, there are still men who do not want their wives to leave home without them. Some of them worry about the Don Juans who have designs on their spouse and access to her; the prospect of infidelity creates intolerable jealousy. "Too much freedom" for women is often blamed for the anger that abusers feel toward their victims; a woman who disobeys also "provokes" violence.

Until recently in many Hispanic countries, the legal rights of men and women within marriage were very unequal. During the Franco era in Spain, for example, women needed their husbands' permission to sell property or leave the country. In case of marital separation, the father automatically had custody of the children. The legacy of these kinds of patriarchal legal systems is hard to erase. Spain, now a very modern nation in almost all respects, still has a high number of cases of spousal and partner abuse. Even more disturbing is the number of women who are killed by estranged husbands. Spain has made good progress in educating women about their rights and in passing legislation against domestic violence; educating boys and men is a more difficult task. A recent survey showed that virtually everyone (96%) agreed that physical abuse against women was totally unacceptable. However, fewer people said they would be willing to report a man who frequently hit his wife. The difference in educational level was important: among those who had graduated from high school or college, the proportion who would report abuse was three-fourths of those interviewed. Among those with only a primary school level of education the proportion was two-thirds, and among those with no schooling the proportion was only about one-half. It is encouraging to note that more than three-fourths of all respondents thought that the government should get involved more in the effort to curb domestic violence.[3]

Non-governmental organizations (NGOs) and a Women's Office in the Ministry of Work and Labor Affairs (*Instituto de la Mujer*) in Spain and in Latin American countries work to eliminate discrimination and laws that make it difficult for women to obtain and keep jobs and to train women for better jobs. Considerable progress has been made in formulating suggested legislation; less in getting it passed and enforced. For example, the United Nations reports that

world wide, all but 26 countries have signed Convention on the Elimination of All Forms of Discrimination against Women, making it the second most widely ratified human rights treaty. . . . However, physical and sexual abuse affect millions of girls and women worldwide [and] yet [they] are known to be seriously under-reported.[4]

The police and the judicial system are often part of the problem. They often look away or side with the man who has struck his wife or who has beaten his daughter for running away because they, too, believe that men have a right to control women in this fashion. Part of the solution must involve educating and supervising law enforcement. This will be a long process, but progress is being made. Projects sponsored by UNIFEM (the United Nations Development Fund for Women), some of them in place since 1995, have brought together professionals in legislative matters, law enforcement and the judiciary for workshops and information on women's rights. In several countries, including Colombia, the revision of constitutions gave women's organizations an opportunity to lobby successfully for new rights (in marriage, reproductive decisions and freedom from abuse, for example).[5]

Disagree

The continued popularity of Mexican *rancheras* (a type of traditional song), such as "*Yo soy el Rey*" (I am the King) indicate that the man who brags about his power over women, his aggressiveness and his ability to hold liquor is a figure that still holds at least sentimental appeal for a large segment of the Mexican public.[6] Nevertheless, this picture of the *macho* is a stereotype and does not accurately reflect the wide range of behavior and attitudes displayed by men in Hispanic societies. Age, social class and personal circumstances, as well as individual personality, make a difference in male behavior and attitudes toward helping with child care, family chores and women's freedom. According to informal surveys, younger Spanish men are much more willing to share household responsibilities than their fathers, although tedious tasks, such as cleaning and ironing, almost always fall to women.

For others, feminism has brought with it a series of consequences and negative effects, as much for women themselves as for their families and society as a whole. In the opinion of this group, "radical feminists" have preached a view of women's rights that were anti-family. They say that radical feminism has undermined many of the positive aspects of womanhood in both Spain and Latin America: the satisfactions of motherhood and the close bonds between man and wife.[7] Numerous individuals who hold this opinion are fervent Catholics who identify feminism with pro-abortion views. They accuse feminists and health organizations of using the incidence of rape and incest to promote acceptance of abortion and of exaggerating statistics on maternal deaths due to illegal abortions to advance their cause.[8]

Many Latin American women have, in fact, been reluctant to embrace the same demands espoused by feminists in North America because they view "equality" as a double-edged sword. They did not want to abandon family and motherhood in order to obtain equality in all matters. Furthermore, working-class women have had to be concerned with issues of family survival and have often been most concerned with obtaining better working conditions, salaries and job security for workers of both sexes rather than risk driving a wedge between working men and women.

Would Putting a High Priority on Education Significantly Benefit Women?

Agree

In developed countries, by the end of the last century, educational levels were roughly the same for girls and boys. In some countries the number of young women attending college was higher than for men, although in certain fields male students far outnumbered females, and vice versa. In developing countries, the picture is not as bright for girls and women. Women generally have lower levels of education than men. Both parents and the public often view education as less important for girls because it is assumed that their lives will be centered on the family.

Educational opportunities for girls and women vary widely from country to country in Latin America, and it can be misleading to generalize. The situation is worse for females in countries with large indigenous populations, such as Guatemala and Bolivia. In Bolivia, the rate of illiteracy in adolescent and young women is twice that of boys and men; nearly 40% of Bolivian women over the age of 25 are illiterate. Most of these are indigenous women. In Guatemala in 1994 the illiteracy rate for women was nearly 50%. However, some countries, such as Uruguay and Argentina, have literacy rates comparable to those in Spain, France and Italy.[9] In Chile, illiteracy is uncommon; however, while girls have a higher overall educational level than boys (10.1 years of schooling versus 8.9 for boys), at university level male students outnumber females 6 to 4.[10] Clearly young Chilean women lack either motivation or enough opportunities for educational advancement.

Educational opportunity has a clear relationship to opportunity for employment and leadership in the community, which bring women improved self-esteem and status in the eyes of others. The United Nations' *World's Women 2000* report notes that "Despite calls for gender equality, women are significantly under-represented in governments, political parties and at the United Nations."[11] If women are to be able to join the ranks of leaders in the twenty-first century, the education of girls and young women must be one of Latin America's highest priorities during the first several decades.

There are other good reasons to devote extra money and energy into female education. Infant mortality and maternal death rates are highest in countries with low levels of female literacy. Use of modern methods of birth control (for example, birth control pills) is generally linked to improvements in female literacy in the adult population. The ability to plan the number of children a family wants and can support impacts the level of health for both mothers and children. The level of education of females is one of the most significant indicators of social well-being in developing nations.

Disagree

Those who would argue directly against increasing educational opportunities for women are generally confined to the working classes. Families who are impoverished need the help of all members of the family to contribute to the family income. Marriage for girls in middle- and upper-class families is usually delayed, but in working-class families many girls marry while in their early or mid-teens. It is difficult for parents to see much benefit in sacrificing to keep girls in school if they expect that girls will marry early and become a part of another family. Older daughters frequently drop out of school to care for their younger siblings or work alongside other family members in a family business or trade in what is called the "informal sector" (i.e., selling food or small items on the street, making clothes, handcrafts, knitting and so on). In rural areas, girls have many chores, from helping to cook and wash to watching the family's livestock.

While it has provided educational opportunities for women for centuries through its schools, the Catholic Church has put its high-status positions out of the reach of women. Liberal Catholic theologians around the world are calling for changes that would include not only allowing women to study for the priesthood but to be eligible for the post of bishop and archbishop. In Madrid in 2001 the twenty-first Congress of the John XXIII Association of Theologians stated that it was vital that the Church no longer discriminate against women, who account for 60% of practicing Catholics. In the same meeting, speakers labeled the Church "male-centered" and "*machista*" (male chauvinist).[12]

Independent organizations offer other ways of improving opportunities and the status of women besides directly increasing governmental budgets for education. An example is Women's World Banking, a non-profit organization that supports women entrepreneurs in 35 countries. Their branch in Chile, Finanzas Internacionales y Nacionales para la Mujer (FINAM), offers financial help and advice to new and established businesses, including very small businesses run by women (micro entrepreneurs) as well as workshops, networking and technical advice. Similar organizations exist in other countries. Some specialize in working with women in rural areas or, like FINCA (the Foundation for International Community Assistance), providing small loans, especially to women, who form the largest portion of the world's poor and who traditionally have less access to credit.

Should Men Have to Share Responsibilities and Authority in the Family and Show More Respect for Women Outside the Home?

Agree

An equitable sharing of household responsibilities and authority within the household is not only fair, but it provides a model for the healthy development of children, say proponents. Especially when women work outside of the home, it should be unthinkable that husbands refuse to help out with cooking, housework or child care. Why should men feel free to go out again after supper to be "with the boys" while the wife is expected to take care of the children at home? Both fathers and mothers deserve time to be with friends or to enjoy some other activities outside the home. Although people seldom disapprove when men go out, a wife who leaves for an evening class or to attend a meeting of an organization may be criticized by her husband's family (or her own) and by neighbors and friends because she is neglecting her family.

Others point out that democracy and equality for men and women must begin in the home. It is useless to legislate equality in the public sphere if inside the family girls must do all of the domestic work and take orders from their brothers as if they were the family authority. Children learn gender roles by observing their parents and older relatives. If women want a more equal society outside the home, they must teach equality inside the home as well. Latin American sociologists have noted that it is not just men but also women—mothers, aunts and grandmothers—who teach boys to be domineering. Women often subtly favor male children over female children as well. Even at an early age, boys are waited on by their mothers and sisters and chided if they act timid or cry "like a girl." This early training easily translates to the world outside the home, where men then expect women to wait on them at the office and where they have difficulty taking directions from women or accepting them as equals on the job or in public. Many men still don't understand why many women are annoyed when they toss off a *piropo*, a comment meant to express admiration for a woman passing by.

Disagree

Crude remarks are definitely disrespectful, but a clever or even poetic *piropo* is meant to please both the giver and the receiver, say defenders of the art. A Cuban newspaper called *Juventud Rebelde* admitted that the aggressiveness of present-day *piropos* is proof that the *machista* model still survives in Cuban society and indicates that some "cave men" still view women as sexual objects. However, the writer of the article called for a revival of the "beautiful and delicate" *piropo* and recommended that when courting young ladies, it was good to be prepared with "a nice phrase, subtle dialog and attractive conversation."[13]

Some women who are familiar with both Anglo-American and Hispanic culture agree.

It would be a shame if in Spain, the *piropo*, which is really a bit of gallantry and a compliment to a woman, would be lost and things reached a state like that in the U.S., where men are afraid to express their emotions toward women for fear of being accused of sexual harassment.[14]

Women, moreover, aren't the only ones who receive *piropos*. The verb *piropear* can mean merely to give a (public) compliment: sports heroes, movie stars and others can be the receiver of a *piropo*. The

Spanish newspaper *El País* reported that on a walk through down-town Madrid, the heir to the Spanish throne, Prince Felipe, was greeted by shouts of *"¡Guapo, guapo!"* (good looker, handsome guy!) and *"¡Viva la madre que te parió!"* (Long live the mother who gave birth to you!),[15] both classic *piropos* when addressed to women.

It isn't easy to find a serious published defense of the Hispanic male's reluctance to take an equal share of housework or child care, but surveys show that men are reluctant to give up the idea that these are woman's work, not man's. In a study done in Spain among adolescents from ages 14–18, 42% of male adolescents thought that women should shoulder most of the responsibility (88% of girls and 58% of boys thought that household tasks should be shared equally). At the same time, about one-third of the boys thought that the father should be the authority in the family (only one-twelfth of the girls did).[16]

Ironically, in parts of the Hispanic world, women have great authority inside the four walls of their homes. The sharp division of male and female space and authority in Spain, especially in the south, is well known. Writing about an Andalucian town, anthropologists Brogger and Gilmore note that

[w]omen dominate family life both physically and morally; they make the important conjugal decisions, and represent the ultimate authority in the eyes of their children in all matters relating to family life. But outside the house, it is vastly different. Women undergo an amazing transformation once they set foot outside their own houses. Strength gives way to weakness, control to submission: loud, commanding voices diminish to whispers.[17]

Spanish and Latin American literature also has had some strong female figures. A few of them, such as Bernarda Alba and Doña Barbara, ascended to the level of tyrants in their sphere of influence. In newer Hispanic fiction, assertive women are much more common, especially in the stories and novels of women writers.

QUESTIONS AND ACTIVITIES

1. Do you believe brothers and sisters should do the same household chores as they grow up? Why? Does equality in the household lead to more

equal treatment of men and women on the job? Explain why or why not.

2. What are some arguments against complete equality for men and women in certain careers, such as the military, law enforcement, fire-fighting, construction, and so on? Where do you stand on this issue? Why?

3. In numerous Latin American countries, women did not win the right to vote until after World War II. In Spain, women were first allowed to vote in the 1930s, during the Second Republic. What reasons can you think of that might have been made for not granting women an equal right to elect political leaders and vote on important issues?

4. Is it important for both sexes to have equal rights before the law? Think of as many ways as you can that either women or men would be penalized if they did not have the same rights as the other sex.

5. Do you think that a woman would make a good president? If they were equally qualified in terms of knowledge and experience, would you vote for a man or for a woman for president? Explain why. Do you think your answer would be different if you lived in Spain or Latin America?

6. Why, in your opinion, are the salaries for men and women who do the same job often higher for men? Is this just?

7. The European Union, of which Spain is a member, has instituted a version of affirmative action giving specific advantages to the underrepresented sex in employment in fields where one sex has traditionally been dominant.[18] In other words, if a man and a woman, equally qualified for the position, applied for the same job, and if men had traditionally dominated that field, the woman would be given preference in hiring. Do you think this is a good policy? Explain your reasoning.

8. Write a report on the life of Sor Juana Inés de la Cruz. A good place to begin your research is *Ten Notable Women of Latin America*.

9. View the film *Yo, la peor de todas* (I, the worst of all). Write a report comparing opportunities for Latin American women today with those open to women in Sor Juana's time. Do you think she would approve of the changes? Would she be satisfied with them? Explain your point of view.

VOCABULARY/VOCABULARIO

Nouns/Sustantivos

authorities	las autoridades (la policía)
authority (abstract)	la autoridad

civil rights	los derechos civiles
compliment	el piropo
"double workday"	la doble jornada
educational level	el nivel educativo
equality	la igualdad
home	el hogar, la casa
household chores	las tareas domésticas
human rights	los derechos humanos
husband	el esposo, el marido
jealousy	los celos
judge	el/la juez
judicial system	el sistema judicial
machismo	el machismo
male	el varón, el macho
opportunity	la oportunidad
physical, sexual and/or psychological abuse	el abuso físico, sexual y/o psicológico
police (individuals)	el/los policías
police force	la policía
respect	el respeto
responsibility	la responsabilidad
sexism	el sexismo
teenagers	los/las adolescentes
wife	la esposa
young people	los/las jóvenes

Verbs/Verbos

be jealous	tener celos
become angry	ponerse enojado
clean	limpiar
cook	cocinar, cocer
defend (oneself)	defender(se)
develop	desarrollar(se)
earn (money)	ganar (dinero, un sueldo)

fight	pelear
go out with friends	salir con los amigos
hit	golpear, pegar
leave	salir, abandonar
obey	obedecer
order	mandar
take care of children	cuidar a los niños
take charge of	encargarse (de)

Adjectives/Adjetivos

dependent	dependiente
dominant, dominating	dominante
independent	independiente
jealous	celoso/a
respectful	repetuoso/a
strong	fuerte
vulnerable	vulnerable
womanizing	mujeriego

RESOURCE GUIDE

Books and Articles

Agosín, Marjorie. *A Dream of Light & Shadow: Portraits of Latin American Women Writers.* Albuquerque: University of New Mexico Press, 1995.

Andrade, A. Rolando. "Jose Alfredo Jimenez: A Cultural Dilemma." *Studies in Latin American Popular Culture* 16 (1997): 147–161.

Ashby, Ruth, and Deborah Gore Ohrn. *Herstory: Women Who Changed the World.* New York: Viking, 1995.

Brogger, Jan, and David D. Gilmore. "The Matrifocal Family in Iberia: Spain and Portugal Compared." *Ethnology* (Winter 1997): 13–30.

Drezin, Jenny, ed. *Picturing a Life Free of Violence: Media and Communications Strategies to End Violence Against Women.* New York: UNIFEM and the Media Materials Clearinghouse of the Johns Hopkins Center for Communication Programs, 2001. Also available in pdf format: see <http://www.unifem.undp.org/resour.htm>.

García Pinto, Magdalena. *Women Writers of Latin America: Intimate Histories*. Austin: University of Texas Press, 1991.

Gilmore, David D. *Manhood in the Making: Cultural Concepts of Masculinity*. New Haven, CT: Yale University Press, 1990.

Gutmann, Matthew C. *The Meanings of Macho: Being a Man in Mexico City*. Berkeley: University of California Press, 1996.

Henderson, James D., and Linda Roddy Henderson. *Ten Notable Women of Latin America*. Chicago: Nelson-Hall, 1978.

Hooper, John. *The New Spaniards*. New York: Penguin, 1995.

Htun, Mala. "Women in Latin America: Unequal Progress toward Equality." Originally published in *Current History* (March 1999). Reprinted in Paul Goodwin, comp., *Global Studies: Latin America*. 10th ed. Guilford, CT: McGraw-Hill/Dushkin, 2003, pp. 146–150.

Jaquette, Jane S., ed. *The Women's Movement in Latin America*. Boulder, CO: Westview Press, 1994.

Jones, Anny Brooksbank. *Women in Contemporary Spain*. New York: Manchester University Press, 1997.

Juana Inés de la Cruz, Sister. *Poems, Protest, and a Dream: Selected Writings*. Margaret Sayers Peden, trans. New York: Penguin Books, 1997.

———. *A Sor Juana Anthology*. Alan S. Trueblood, trans. Cambridge, MA: Harvard University Press, 1988.

Kirk, Pamela. *Sor Juana Inés de la Cruz: Religion, Art, and Feminism*. New York: Continuum, 1998.

Labanyi, Jo. *Culture and Society in Modern Spain*, London: University of London, 1993.

Miller, Francesca. "Latin American Women: A Politics of History." In Jack W. Hopkins, ed., *Latin America: Perspectives on a Region*. 2nd ed. New York: Holmes & Meier, 1998, pp. 138–159.

Nash, June C., and Helen Icken Safa. *Women and Change in Latin America*. South Hadley, MA: Bergin & Garvey, 1986.

Paz, Octavio. *Sor Juana, or the Traps of Faith*. Cambridge, MA: Harvard University Press, 1988.

Richardson, Bill. *Spanish Studies: An Introduction*. London: Arnold, 2001.

Stanton, Edward F. *Culture and Customs of Spain*. Westport, CT: Greenwood Press, 2002.

Internet

Asociación Laica para la Opinión en la Iglesia y la Sociedad. <http://www.arrakis.es/alois3/index.html>.

Corriente de Opinión. Chile Unido. <http://www.chileunido.cl>.

The Foundation for International Community Assistance (FINCA). <http://villagebanking.org/home.php3>.

Instituto de la Mujer, Ministerio de Trabajo y Asuntos Laborales (Spain). <http://www.mtas.es/mujer/ principal.htm>.

Las mujeres. <http://www.lasmujeres.com>.

Mujeres en la Red (Peru). <http://www.nodo50.org/mujeresred/peru.htm>.

Social Indicators. The United Nations Statistics Department. <http://unstats.un.org/unsd/demographic/ social/default.htm>.

Sor Juana Inés de la Cruz. Selected poems in Spanish and with translations by Alan Trueblood. <http://www.sappho.com/poetry/historical/j_ines.html>.

Sor Juana Inés de la Cruz Project. Department of Spanish and Portuguese, Dartmouth College. <http://www.dartmouth.edu/~sorjuana/>.

UNIFEM (United Nations Development Fund for Women). <http://www.unifem.undp.org>.

"Women Watch." United Nations. <http://www.un.org/womenwatch/>.

Women's World Banking. <http://www.womensworldbanking.org/Spanish/1000/1000f.htm>.

"The World's Women 2000." The United Nations Statistics Department, May 2000. <http://unstats.un.org/unsd/demographic/ww2000/ww2000pr.htm>.

Video

En el país de no pasa nada (In the country where nothing happens). Videocassette. Costa Mesa, CA: Condor Media. Distributed by Vanguard Cinema, 2001. Color. Spanish with English subtitles. 98 min.

"In Women's Hands." Videocassette. *Americas* series. South Burlington, VT: Annenberg/CPB Collection, 1993. Color. 58 min.

Mujeres al borde de un ataque de nervios (Women on the verge of a nervous breakdown). Videocassette. Pedro Almodóvar, director. Santa Monica, CA: Metro Goldwyn Mayer Home Entertainment, 1988. Color. Spanish with English subtitles. 89 min.

Yo, la peor de todas (I, the worst of all). Videocassette. Maria Luisa Bemberg, director. New York: First Run Features, First Run Features Home Video, 1990. Color. Spanish with English subtitles. 107 min.

Subcomandante Marcos, the leader of an indigenist movement known as the *Ejército Zapatista de Liberación Nacional* (EZLN or Zapatista movement), speaks during a rally in Puebla, Mexico in February 2001. Behind Marcos stand the heads of the Zapatista army. (AP Photo/Victor R. Caivano)

Chapter 9

Indigenous Rights

The indigenous peoples of many countries are making themselves heard now more than ever. In some cases they are asking for reparations for past wrongs that they have suffered at the hands of conquerors or stronger and more numerous national groups; in other cases they demand a greater share in contemporary government, and to get it they have sometimes resorted to lawsuits as well as strikes, blockades and other means of disrupting national life. Do indigenous groups have a legitimate claim to special treatment or restitution for what might have occurred hundreds of years ago? Do they need special protection today?

BACKGROUND

There is no way to know who were the first people—the truly indigenous people—of Spain. Atapuerca, a site near the Castilian city of Burgos, has human remains that date from 800,000 years before the Common Era. These are the oldest human remains yet discovered in Europe. Judging from rock art in several sites in southern Spain, some other early inhabitants seem to have close cultural affinities with Africa. However, there's not much point debating indigenous rights in Spain today.

The Basques certainly have ancient roots and have withstood more than 2,000 years of pressure from Romans, Spanish and French to give up their language, independent government and other cultural traits such as traditional music, dance and festivals. And although they hope for more autonomy (or possibly independence) from Spain and much more respect for their cultural life and language, the Basques are fully integrated into national and international life. For this reason they are unlike indigenous groups in Latin America, many of whom still are not able to participate fully in the life of their nation due to racial and social discrimination.

The other identifiable indigenous community in Spanish territory would be the now-extinct Guanches or Canarios, who inhabited the Canary Islands before the arrival of the Spaniards. Archaeologists believe that these blue or gray-eyed, brown-skinned people with blonde hair arrived in the islands from North Africa during the second or third century B.C. Guanche civilization did not long survive the Spanish invasion and occupation of the islands, but 65% of today's islanders carry some Guanche blood. The Guanche language may have existed into the eighteenth century in a few pockets in the islands. Today, however, only a few surnames, place names and common words remain in use. Today (or at least until very recently) a "whistle language" called *el silbo* endures as a relic of the Guanche past.[1]

The number of indigenous languages in existence in all of Latin America at the time of the conquest is hard to estimate accurately, but was probably several thousand. Since the first years of contact with Europeans many Native American languages have died out, along with the people who spoke them, and this process still continues. Nevertheless, there are several large families of languages in today's Latin American countries, some of which include the Uto-Aztecan, Mayan, Chibcha, Tupi-Guaraní, Quechuan, Carib and Arahuacan language groups. All of these are as different from one another as the Indo-European languages (for example, Spanish) are from the Semitic languages (for example, Hebrew). The existence of so many language families spread across wide areas suggests that the indigenous peoples arrived in a number of waves. Although recent scientific investigations are revealing more intriguing possibilities for early contacts with Europe or Africa, the physiological similarities between indigenous peoples in the Western Hemisphere suggest that by far the largest numbers of early immigrants to the virgin continents must have come from Asia, along the coastline as well as via an inland route through Canada. Artifacts have been dated to a minimum of 10,000 years ago, but new archaeological evidence keeps pushing back the dates of earliest settlements. It seems possible that small communities were living in far South America 25,000 or 30,000 years ago.

As in North America, Native Americans south of our borders don't always agree on what terms should be used to name them. The word *indio* carries negative connotations of conquest and imperialism for many, who prefer the term *indígena* in Latin America or Native American in the United States and Canada. However, all of these "cover terms" blur the distinctions between the very great variety of peoples, cultures and languages that developed over thousands of years and that have endured more than five centuries of conquest, disease, repression and exploitation. In Colombia alone, the 1993 census revealed that 80 distinct ethnic groups speaking 64 different languages comprise the approximately 532,000 indigenous peoples living within the national borders (about 1.6% of the total population).[2] The four largest groups account for about 56% of the total; a handful of small groups have been reduced to 50 or fewer.

On the other hand, after thousands of years of awareness of their linguistic and cultural differences from one another, the Native Americans of both North and South have lately discovered the benefits of uniting behind what they have in common in order to preserve their way of life. This is not the first time that there has been a call for fair treatment of the indigenous communities. Fray Bartolomé de las Casas, the Spanish conquistador turned Dominican monk, was the first person to bring the plight of the Indians to the rest of the world. During the centuries of colonial rule Indians in many parts of Latin America rebelled against the Spanish.[3] Since independence, Indian communities have continued to defend their lands and communal rights against great odds. Population pressure from non-Indian settlers and increased emphasis on export or market-driven agricultural enterprises have driven Indians further into marginal lands. Thousands of indigenous communities have lost their communal lands to outsiders though deceit, political trickery and their low status on the list of national priorities. One recently documented case involves the Wichi of northern Argentina, who have seen their lands dwindle as *criollo* (in this case, non-Indian) newcomers invaded and enclosed their lands. Like many indigenous peoples, the Wichi had little concept of private property and were unprepared to defend their territorial rights. With the help of non-governmental organizations, they made a successful claim to their lands in 1991 but they never received formal title to the 162,000 acres they were promised in the agreement. Since then, development plans have pushed the Wichi further aside to make room for highways and cattle ranches.[4]

Throughout Latin America, indigenous peoples have the highest poverty and infant mortality rates, the poorest health services and the lowest rates of literacy. These statistics are indicative of the low priority that has been placed on the material and educational needs of indigenous peoples in virtually every country. In most Latin American countries, indigenous peoples are more likely than non-Indians to be mistreated at the hands of police or military authorities. In some nations, such as Peru, Mexico and Guatemala, numerous extremely serious human rights violations, including murders and torture, have been common.[5] Over-zealous health authorities have been accused of performing unauthorized sterilizations on Indian women who had entered clinics for cesarean deliveries. International and non-profit organizations have been instrumental in helping indigenous communities and governments to achieve some improvements in the areas of human rights abuses as well as economic development programs at the local level, but much remains to be done. Progress is made more difficult by economic problems, especially the high levels of debt and insufficient economic growth, that all Latin American countries have faced since at least the 1980s.

Bringing the world's attention to the issues that confront indigenous peoples around the world has not been easy. In a world of fast-moving economic and political events, the concerns of indigenous peoples often seem irrelevant. Recently, however, the United Nations created a permanent forum that will examine indigenous issues related to economic and social development, culture, environment, education, health and human rights and advise the UN's Economic and Social Council. The Permanent Forum will have representatives from both indigenous and government bodies.

Latin American writers also have been active in focusing the attention of their own countrymen and the rest of the world on the continuing struggle to obtain dignity, fairness and a way out of the poverty that most indigenous peoples endure. Best known in the United States are Miguel Angel Asturias (Guatemala), Rosario Castellanos (Mexico) and José María Arguedas (Peru).[6] Today, many indigenous organizations get their message out to the world over the Internet.

Here are some of the statements you might hear in a discussion of indigenous rights today:

1. There must be an end to discrimination in language, religion, education and other opportunities.
2. Indigenous peoples need to safeguard themselves and their lands from extinction.
3. Indigenous peoples should have a greater representation in national governments and a role in national affairs.

DISCUSSION

Are Indigenous Peoples Still Victims of Serious Language, Educational and Religious Discrimination?

Agree

The *indígenas* of Latin America have never enjoyed equality with either the people who consider themselves of European origin or the *mestizos*, people of mixed Indian and European ancestry.

Most whites and mestizos viewed Indians as inherently inferior. Some regarded indígenas as little better than a subspecies. A more benign perspective condescendingly considered the Indian as an intellectual inferior, an emotional child in need of direction. Such views underlay the elaborate public etiquette required in Indian-white/mestizo interactions. Common practice allowed whites and mestizos to use first names and familiar verb and pronoun forms in addressing Indians.[7]

Their languages are seldom taught in schools; bilingual education is unavailable in most communities even in primary grades, when children come to school speaking no Spanish. Furthermore, when bilingual education is offered, national governments generally expect to "mainstream" indigenous children as fast as possible into an all-Spanish school system.[8] The message is loud and clear: indigenous languages are second class. In countries such as Peru, Bolivia and Mexico, where many people from indigenous communities migrate to the cities, language loss is occurring rapidly. Modern media, the use of computers and increased educational opportunities—almost always in Spanish—are likely to reduce the numbers of speakers of indigenous languages even further.

Indigenous religions are often considered merely a hodgepodge of superstitions and pagan beliefs or an odd, unsettling combination of Christian and pre-Christian elements. Christian religion was forced upon Indians everywhere soon after the conquest; their forefathers had little choice but to adapt as best they could. They frequently retained a substantial core of their beliefs and practices behind a veneer of Catholic ritual that was sufficient to satisfy colonial officials. For modern Indians who have been able to maintain their traditions and identity, their religious beliefs and practices are an integral part of their rich and long heritage, which stretches thousands of years into the past and gives meaning to their lives. European religions have stressed man's right to dominate nature; Indian religions stress reverence for the earth and nature. These are values that need support, not continual assault by foreign missionaries or the powerful Catholic Church.

Native Americans have much less access to education and opportunities than other citizens of Latin American countries. The mere fact that a person looks "too Indian," dresses like an Indian or speaks an indigenous language amounts to two strikes against him in many localities. In spite of the fact that in some six countries 40% or more of the population identify themselves as *indígenas*, only two countries are "officially" bilingual: Paraguay and Peru. Latin American nations need to invest much more in training teachers who can teach bilingually so that children can get a good start in primary school and go on to be functionally bilingual. This would raise the level of respect for indigenous languages and at the same time ensure that more children were ready to go on to secondary and higher education.[9]

Disagree

What indigenous groups call language discrimination is mostly about the need for a modern country to use a single language for communication. Some countries have 30 or 40 or more indigenous groups, each speaking different languages. How would you accommodate all of these? Educational resources are already stretched to the limit in most countries. Bilingual education for indigenous students is simply not affordable. There are few trained teachers who are bilingual, few programs for training and virtually no teaching materials available. Furthermore, actively encouraging the survival of languages other than Spanish only makes it more difficult for Latin American countries to develop economically and to modernize.

For opponents of this argument, religious discrimination is largely a dead issue. All Latin American countries now recognize the right of individuals to choose and exercise their own religion. Citizens of every country can be Catholics or Lutherans, Pentecostals, Mormons or whatever they choose. Indigenous religions are not the objects of any special discrimination; they deserve no special protection, either. The Catholic Church, in their view, has protected the Indians for centuries and missionaries of other religions have brought literacy and civilization to remote areas that were largely ignored until after the Second World War.

As far as education and other opportunities are concerned, much of what Indians call discrimination has more to do with the fact that indigenous communities are often small and located in rural areas. It's not surprising that, in countries where funds are in short supply, these communities would be the last served. It's also difficult to find teachers who are willing to live in remote areas and without the conveniences of urban life. It is hard to find qualified indigenous bilingual teachers—and few of them are willing to stay long in isolated villages, either.

Can Indigenous Communities Organize to Safeguard Themselves and Retain or Return Lands to Indigenous Control?

Agree

In several countries, among them Mexico, Chile and Ecuador, indigenous groups have already organized to demand a measure of autonomy from the national governments. In Mexico, the Zapatistas (EZLN or *Ejército Zapatista de Liberación Nacional*), an organization that originated in the southern state of Chiapas, successfully resisted the national government's attempts to disarm them and end their takeover of several cities and towns in the state. Later, the Zapatistas rallied most of Mexico's indigenous population for a march on the capital, resulting in at least some changes in government policy.

In South America, CONAIE, the National Confederation of Indigenous Peoples of Ecuador, developed an organization that has represented the indigenous communities, large and small, in all parts of the country. They have become a powerful group in Ecuadorian politics. Their stated aim is to participate in the life of the nation without losing sight of their cultural heritage. The Mapuche tribe in Chile has demanded restitution of its rights to certain areas of the country that it considers its own, and sacred land. Corporación Nacional de Desarrollo Indígena (CONADI), the government bureau charged with oversight of Indian affairs in Chile, has done little to protect Mapuche lands from encroachment by timber companies; hydroelectric projects and highways that will benefit the nation will destroy Mapuche lands. Indeed, CONADI officials were accused of corruption and misappropriation of funds.[10] Without intelligent organization and effective leadership that can make the political processes of the country work for—rather than against—them, these organizations believe that within a few more generations, their cultures will cease to exist and their peoples will continue to be marginalized by the more numerous and more economically powerful members of the Hispanic culture.

In Nicaragua, the small indigenous group known as the Awas Tingni won an important case for indigenous land rights argued before the Interamerican Court of Human Rights. In spite of having occupied the same lands on Nicaragua's Atlantic (Caribbean) coast for generations, the Awas Tingni were not even notified when the national government prepared to grant rights to timber on two-thirds of their land to a foreign lumber company. With legal help from the Indian Law Resource Center in Montana and backing from international human rights and indigenous support organizations, the Nicaraguan Indian community successfully argued that it should be awarded title to the 200,000 acres it claims, as well as damages and legal fees and a time limit to demarcate and title the lands in question. Within six months of the court's decision, a bill had been introduced in the national legislature that would begin the demarcation of all indigenous lands in Nicaragua. The ruling may have important implications for indigenous communities throughout the

Americas, since the case was brought before a court with hemispheric jurisdiction.[11]

Disagree

Critics in some countries view indigenous organizations as obstructionists. In other countries, opponents say Indian leaders are power-hungry, hypocritical charlatans. Some of the leadership, opponents declare, is really Marxist, and wants to organize the Indians and other poor rural people to grab power or destabilize the government. The Zapatistas, for example, were lead by a non-Indian who called himself Subcomandante Marcos and who used the high-tech medium of the Internet to denounce the progress brought by technology and international trade.

Even before his inauguration in 2000, Mexican President Vicente Fox announced an ambitious development plan called Plan Puebla Panama (PPP). The plan, which has backing from international financial bodies, includes superhighways along the Pacific and Gulf coasts running from Mexico to Panama and an expanded highway across the isthmus of Tehuantepec, the narrow band of land separating the two bodies of water in southern Mexico. The plan would increase transportation in the region and open it up for export industries, accelerate the shift from agriculture to manufacture (especially *maquiladora* plants) and expand private property ownership throughout the region, where a substantial part of the land is still occupied by indigenous communities. According to Institute of Current World Affairs fellow Wendy Call, "the success of the project will depend on the indigenous peoples' willingness to abandon their villages and farms, something they may well refuse to do."[12]

A meeting in the southern state of Oaxaca was cancelled by the government, but representatives of over 100 indigenous organizations from Mexico, El Salvador, Guatemala and Nicaragua met over several days to devise a strategy and to issue a statement: "Given that any development plan must be the result of a democratic process, and not an authoritarian one, we firmly reject the Puebla-Panama Plan.... We condemn all strategies geared toward the destruction of the national, peasant and popular economy, [and] food and labor self-sufficiency."[13]

In Ecuador, the confederation of indigenous groups known as CONAIE called for years for a truly democratic government, but critics point out that CONAIE took the lead in a brief, bloodless coup in 1999, forcing the resignation of the elected president of the Republic. CONAIE's detractors say that democracy suited the Indians of the confederation when they had little power. However, when they had more, they resorted to undemocratic means to take over the government.

Should Indigenous Peoples Be Guaranteed Greater Representation in National Governments and a Role in National Affairs?

Agree

Until fairly recently, in many countries Indians did not even have full citizenship. For example, until 1952 in Bolivia, literacy and property requirements barred Indians from voting. Technically they could still be forced to work for the *haciendas* (ranches, estates). While the Indian *pongos* (hacienda workers) were not slaves in the strictest legal sense (they could not be bought and sold, for example), they clearly did not have the ordinary freedoms of other citizens of the country. In countries where they were entitled to vote, Indians were discouraged from participating in elections or were bribed or coerced into voting for a particular candidate or party.

These historical patterns show that indigenous peoples need genuine representation in their national legislatures and at the local level. Only Indians can truly represent the concerns and protect the human and cultural rights of Indians because only they have lived the discrimination and repression that indigenous people have suffered. The assaults on Indian culture, the theft of Indian lands, the poverty that most Indians endure and the human rights abuses against Indians in countries such as Guatemala would not have occurred if Indians had been adequately represented in government.

Generations of neglect, exploitation and violence inflicted by non-Indians have left indigenous populations suspicious of government and marginalized from national life and economic development. In every country, indigenous peoples are the poorest, the least well educated, have the poorest health care—and on and on. Latin American governments must now work to ensure that Indians can address old injustices and participate in the construction of a better future for their nations.

Disagree

While it is true that Indians were discouraged from freely participating in the political process in the past, the principles of democracy do not *guarantee* that any ethnic group will be represented in
proportion to its numbers in the population. If indigenous peoples
are underrepresented, they should vote in larger numbers; they
should bring forward more candidates of their own. Governments
should not make special rules or institute quotas to make sure that
one group of people is guaranteed representation in elected political
bodies. In elections in 2002, Bolivian Indians elected 50 of their own
to the national congress (nearly one-third of the 157 total congress-
men and senators). For the first time in Bolivian history, simulta-
neous translation of congressional debates was provided for
non-Spanish speakers. In contrast, in Ecuador, only four national
legislators and 30 mayors came from indigenous ranks, even though
indigenous groups represent an estimated 30–45 percent of Ecuador's population.[14] These two cases show that *effective* political organization in a democratic framework can bring Indians a voice in
national affairs.

QUESTIONS AND ACTIVITIES

1. What can you learn about the discovery and conquest of the Canary
   Islands? What parallels did this conquest by the Spanish have with the
   conquest of the New World, especially with respect to the fate of the
   indigenous peoples in both parts of the Spanish Empire?
2. The United Nations has a commission on the rights of indigenous peoples. What rights have indigenous peoples around the world demanded?
   Are they different from those that Native Americans in Latin America
   and in North America want?
3. Human rights activist and winner of the Nobel Peace Prize Rigoberta
   Menchú Tum has written and spoken extensively about human rights
   abuses committed against Indians in her own country of Guatemala. She
   also has addressed the issue of indigenous rights in several countries and
   at major conferences. What can you learn about her personal history?
   Some of the work of Menchú has come under criticism. Why?
4. Although nearly one-half (45%) of Peru's more than 27 million people
   are indigenous, Alejandro Toledo, elected in 2001, is Peru's first president of Indian ancestry. What accounts for the fact that few Indians
   have been elected to high political positions in countries like Peru, Bo-

livia, Guatemala and Ecuador, in spite of the fact that they comprise such a large proportion of the population? What are some ways to increase representation of indigenous peoples?

5. Bilingual education is a controversial topic in many Latin American countries. If you were put in charge of designing the schooling for Indian children, would you favor bilingual education in the primary grades? In middle and high school? Explain your reasons.

6. Both the Zapatista movement in Mexico and the Mapuche peoples in Chile have used the Internet effectively to make their point of view known. Choose one of these groups. Use the Internet to discover what their objectives are and what they have done to try to achieve them. Then summarize their objectives and explain if you think their strategies and tactics are likely to be effective.

7. New archaeological discoveries continue to push back the time of earliest pre-Colombian settlements in the New World. Articles on pre-Columbian sites can be found in magazines such as *National Geographic*, *National Geographic en Español*, *Archaeology*, and *Discover*. Is it important to bring discoveries about ancient civilizations to the attention of the rest of the world? Who benefits most and in what ways? Magazine publishers, archaeologists, museums, the descendents of the civilizations being investigated, the tourist industry? Others? Explain why.

VOCABULARY/VOCABULARIO

Nouns/Sustantivos

ancestors	los antepasados
the Basques	los vascos
beliefs	las creencias
bilingual education	la educación bilingüe
the Church	la Iglesia
citizenship	la ciudadanía
communities	las comunidades
conquest	la conquista
customs	las costumbres
descendents	los descendientes
discrimination	la discriminación

festivals	las fiestas
heritage	la herencia
human rights	los derechos humanos
Indian serfs, peons	los pongos (Andes), peones
Indians	los indios
language	el idioma (m.), la lengua (f.)
large landholdings	las haciendas
literacy	el alfabetismo
Mother Earth	La Madre Tierra
Native Americans	los indígenas (m. and f.)
New World	el Nuevo Mundo
opportunity	la oportunidad
pre-Columbian era	la época precolombina
prehistoric times	la época prehistórica
religion	la religión
rights	los derechos
rites, rituals	los ritos, los rituales
school, elementary	la escuela primaria
school, secondary	la escuela secundaria
tribes	las tribus

Verbs/Verbos

conquer	conquistar
disappear	desaparecer
discover	descubrir
exploit, make use of	explotar
exterminate	exterminar
integrate	integrarse
protect	proteger
run for congress	hacerse candidato al congreso, postularse para congresista
unite	unirse
vote	votar

RESOURCE GUIDE

Books and Articles

Arguedas, José María. *Yawar Fiesta*. Frances Horning Barraclough, trans. Austin: University of Texas Press, 1985.

Blouin, Egla Morales. "Rites of Regeneration." *Americas* (March 1992): 14–19.

Casas, Bartolomé de las. *Indian Freedom: The Cause of Bartolomé de las Casas, 1484–1566: A Reader*. Francis Sullivan, ed. Kansas City, MO: Sheed & Ward, 1995.

Chang-Rodríguez, Eugenio. *Latinoamerérica: Su civilización y su cultura*. 3rd ed. Boston: Heinle & Heinle, 1999.

Costales Samaniego, Alfredo. *Daquilema, el ultimo guaminga*. 3rd ed. Quito, Ecuador: Cedime/Ediciones Abya-Yala, 1984.

Gonzalez, Gaspar Pedro. *A Mayan Life: A Birth in the Village*. Fernando Penalosa and Janet Sawyer, trans. Rancho Palos Verdes, CA: Yax Te' Press, 1995.

Howe, James. *A People Who Would Not Kneel: Panama, the United States, and the San Blas Kuna*. Washington, DC: Smithsonian Institution Press, 1998

Hornberger, Nancy N., and Luis Enrique Lopez. "Policy, Possibility and Paradox: Indigenous Multilingualism and Education in Peru and Bolivia." In Cenoz Jasone and Fred Genesee, eds., *Beyond Bilingualism: Multilingualism and Multilingual Education*. Clevedon: Multilingual Matters Ltd., 1998, pp. 206–242.

Hux, Meinrado. *Caciques puelches pampas y serranos*. Buenos Aires: Ediciones Marymar, 1993.

Menchu, Rigoberta. *I, Rigoberta Menchu: An Indian Woman in Guatemala*. Elisabeth Burgos-Debray, ed.; Ann Wright, trans. London: Verso, 1984.

Menchu, Rigoberta. *Me llamo Rigoberta Menchu y así me nació la conciencia*. Elizabeth Burgos-Debray, ed. Mexico: Siglo Veintiuno Editores, 1985.

Meyerson, Julia. *Tambo: Life in an Andean Village*. Austin: University of Texas Press, 1990.

Morris, Walter F., Jr. "Living Maya." *Americas* (January 1988): 14–19.

Rankin, Aidan." 'Real History' Revives Argentina's Indians." *History Today* (June 1995): 8–10.

———. "Landless Protest." *New Internationalist* (October 2000): 8.

Internet

Cultural Survival. <http://www.culturalsurvival.org/home/index.cfm>.
Cultural Survival Quarterly. <http://www.culturalsurvival.org/quarterly/ index.cfm>.
Descendants of the Incas. <http://www.inca.org>.
Development Gateway. <http://www.developmentgateway.org/node/ 130649/>.
Ejercito Zapatista de Liberación Nacional. <http://www.ezln.org/>.
Indígenas de Colombia. <http://www.indigenascolombia.org>.
Latin American Network Information Center (LANIC). <http://www. lanic.utexas.edu/la/region/indigenous/>.

Video/Film

Columbus Didn't Conquer Us. Videocassette. Wendell, MA: Turning Tide Productions, 1992. Color. 24 min.
El Norte. Gregory Nava, dir. Videocassette. Los Angeles, CA: Frontera Films, 1983. Color. 141 min.
"Mirrors of the Heart." Americas series. Videocassette. South Burlington, VT: Annenberg/CPB Collection, 1993. Color. 60 min.

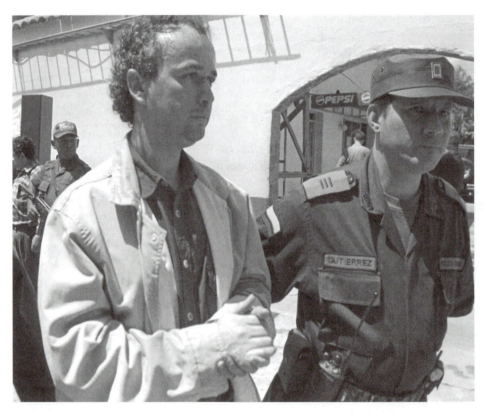

A police officer guards alleged Colombian drug trafficker Jairo Alberto Builes, arrested in Medellín, Colombia, in July 2002. Medellín was the "capital" of the Columbian drug trade during the 1980s. (AP Photo/Luis Benavides)

Chapter 10

Colombia and the War on Drugs

Although other illegal drugs—including marijuana and heroin—are produced in Colombia, its major drug export is cocaine. Every year, hundreds of metric tons of processed cocaine are shipped out of Colombia, most of it headed for the United States. Law enforcement officials of both the United States and Colombia seize a portion of this amount (the United States seized more than 100 metric tons in both 1999 and 2000), but a much larger share—probably two-thirds of the total—slips across our borders undetected.

The production and trafficking of cocaine is a lucrative business. A kilo (2.2 pounds) sold for anywhere from $12,000 to $35,000 in 2001.[1] According to the National Household Survey on Drug Abuse (NHSDA), in 1998 about 1.7 million Americans were current cocaine users (about 0.8% of the total population above 12 years of age). The rate of use was highest among young adults (2.0% of 18- to 25-year-olds). Overall, cocaine leads heroin (and all other drugs) in emergency medical department cases and deaths due to drug use in the United States. The money spent trying to control illegal drugs (all drugs, not just cocaine) and drug-related crime is staggering: in 1999 President Clinton requested $17.3 billion for federal government efforts, while President George W. Bush requested more than $20 billion for 2001. States are thought to spend about the same each year in total costs for police, interdiction of narcotics, prisons and treatment.[2]

What should be done to end—or at least significantly reduce—

the human and economic cost of drugs? Some people favor a more effective or a harsher standard of law enforcement here and in Colombia. Others advocate much more emphasis on education and treatment in the United States and political, social and economic reforms in Colombia, with each country attending to its own end of the problem. Before rushing to make a judgment, we need to look at the history of this issue and its many complicating factors.

BACKGROUND

Colombia is a nation somewhat larger than California, Arizona and Nevada combined. It is located in the northwestern corner of the South American continent, with coastlines on both the Pacific Ocean and Caribbean Sea, and it lies entirely within the tropical zone. In Colombia, the Andean mountain range splits into three long fingers running north and south, giving the country a variety of climates that range from a rain-drenched Pacific coast, to cool valleys in the interior, to a mountain rainforest in the south, along the border with Ecuador. In the east, the *llanos*, a flat plain, stretches toward Venezuela and Peru, along tributaries of the great Orinoco and Amazon rivers.

Bogotá, the capital of Colombia, once proudly called itself the Athens of the Americas, reflecting its reputation as a center of learning and culture. The nation's second largest city, Medellín, was renowned as a garden spot, one of those cities of "eternal spring" seen in tourist brochures. However, today Medellín is best known as the home of the *narcotraficantes* (drug traffickers) of the world's most notorious drug cartel. Colombia has the highest murder rate in the Western Hemisphere, with much of it tied, at least indirectly, to the cocaine trade. How did this transformation take place?

Indigenous (Native American) peoples in parts of Colombia, as well as Peru, Bolivia and Ecuador, have chewed the leaves of the coca plant for centuries for ritual purposes and as a mild stimulant to ward off fatigue, hunger and the effects of high altitude. The leaves contain a very small amount of the cocaine alkaloid. In contrast, street-ready cocaine is a powerful drug produced in several stages (leaf, coca paste, cocaine base and, finally, cocaine). Its processing requires a variety of chemicals during the later stages. Most of the people involved in the process of producing cocaine are simple farmers and pickers who earn little money from growing and picking coca leaves. It is the upper echelon of the drug rings that reaps the enormous profits we associate with the illegal drug industry.

The growing and selling of coca leaves first became big business in colonial Peru, where it was sold to Indians who were forced to work in high-altitude mines. It was known in Europe mainly as a botanical curiosity until a chemist discovered the process to precipitate the cocaine alkaloid from a liquid used to soak the coca leaf mixture. Initially used as a local anesthetic, in the nineteenth century doctors began to experiment with cocaine as a treatment for a wide variety of ailments, often with deadly results, and were at first unaware that cocaine was powerfully addictive. For a time, coca products were used in patent medicines and even soft drinks for their stimulant qualities. Several important European and American pharmaceutical companies manufactured cocaine legally in the nineteenth and early twentieth centuries, but large amounts of their production made its way into illegal markets. Between the First and Second World Wars Japan became the leader in illegal cocaine sales to finance its military expansion, but at the end of the Second World War the Japanese cocaine industry and its coca fields in Java were put out of business.[3]

Cocaine was neither used nor produced in large quantities in Colombia until the 1970s; Peru and Bolivia were the most important Andean producers. The modern Colombian drug trade was born during the 1960s, as local criminal networks became suppliers of marijuana to meet a boom in demand from buyers in the United States. During the next decade, cocaine began to appear more frequently in the United States. Initially, cocaine was thought to be an ideal "recreational drug," a stimulant with no serious side effects and no risk of physical addiction. Only later did the evidence against the use of cocaine begin to mount: death by overdose, severe psychological effects and extreme addictive qualities. "Snorting" cocaine powder can lead to destruction of the palate (roof of the mouth) and perforation of the nasal septum (the cartilage that divides and supports the nose). Cocaine is now implicated in sudden death by stroke in youthful users and damage to internal organs. However, it became chic to use cocaine at parties in the big cities; gradually, its use spread to smaller cities and towns. "Crack" cocaine—cheap and even more highly addictive—swept through the inner cities in the 1980s and eventually wound up in small towns too. The lifestyles of Hollywood and east coast celebrities glamorized the use of cocaine throughout the 1980s, although the media have also made the public aware of the difficulties of quitting cocaine by publicizing the personal ordeals of TV, film and sports stars.

By the time the destructive effects of cocaine were well known, the Colombian criminal networks had been exporting it in massive quantities for years and the cartels were not about to give up their lucrative business. Although the coca plant can grow (and has been grown) in some other areas in the tropics (such as Java), today the cocaine on the world market comes from South America. In recent years, nearly all of the cocaine sold in the United States has been processed and/or exported by Colombian drug traffickers. The remainder comes from Bolivia and Peru, and a small amount is produced in Panama or other Central American countries. Cocaine shipments take many routes, but the majority of the Colombian production eventually enters the United States through Mexico, by ship to the Pacific coast states and Gulf coast states and overland across the U.S.-Mexican border. Colombian smuggling rings still control most of the shipments to the east coast, although the U.S. Drug Enforcement Agency reports that increasingly Mexican traffickers are supplying New York City.[4]

The total amount of cocaine produced is extremely difficult to estimate because of the illegal nature of the business and because the amount of cocaine alkaloid varies in plants produced in different regions and under different growing conditions. Estimates of the total production near the end of the twentieth century ranged from 500 tons to double that—1,000 tons of white powder ready for sale.[5] Intercepting shipments of illegal drugs is made more difficult due to the complicity of members of the police, military and civilian officials in numerous producing and transit countries. To complicate things further, the U.S. Central Intelligence Agency (CIA) has been implicated in protecting drug operators in Central America and Bolivia in the 1980s in exchange for information and influence or to support political groups in favor with U.S. administrations.[6] More recently, press reports allege that the CIA has funded Vladimir Montesinos, former head of Peru's intelligence and internal security, who had ties to Colombian and Peruvian drug rings. At the very least, these activities blur U.S. efforts to combat international drug trafficking. Writing about the agency's involvement in Central America, the authors of *Cocaine Politics* state that "[t]his pattern is deeply embedded in the CIA's history and structure. For the CIA to target international drug networks, it would have to dismantle prime sources of intelligence, political leverage, and indirect financing for its Third World operations."[7]

The so-called Medellín cartel is the best known of the drug rings operating in Colombia. Initially, many of the drug lords were looked upon as local Robin Hoods, men of humble origins who grew rich while thumbing their noses at the authorities. In addition to buying houses and ranches for themselves, they also invested in legitimate businesses and built housing projects and public facilities for poor residents of the city. Some of them even aspired to public office. Pablo Escobar, the head of the Medellín cartel, became an alternate delegate to the Colombian congress.

Not surprisingly, the cartels had another, very sinister side. To maintain their supremacy they employed gunmen to intimidate and often to murder their enemies. These included not only competing drug dealers but also politicians, newspaper reporters and editors or others who objected to the growing influence of criminals in the Medellín area. Killings began to multiply, to the point that murder became a way to settle scores of all kinds.

The Medellín cartel lost its dominant position in the 1980s when its leaders, including Escobar, were jailed. An even more violent drug ring took their place. Assassins, called *sicarios*, could be hired for as little as a few hundred dollars since guns were easy to get and many people were pouring into the cities to escape rural poverty. Drug money was used to buy political influence and police protection. Because the police were unable or unwilling to control the violence, vigilante gangs sprang up to punish the guilty, using beatings and guns. The violence also spread to Bogotá, where kidnappings, murders and bombings became a frequent occurrence.

Impatient with the lack of effective law enforcement in Colombia, the United States arranged to extradite individuals accused of drug-related crimes so that they could be tried and imprisoned in the United States. The drug traffickers responded with a burst of violence designed to terrorize Colombians and turn public opinion against extradition. Eventually the Colombian congress decided that extraditing the criminals was simply too costly in lives and property.

Extradition was abandoned in 1991 and not resumed until 1997. By the mid-1990s, the leaders of the major cartels were in prison and the drug trade was handled by a number of independent criminal rings using high-tech equipment to keep ahead of the police.

Political and economic conditions in Colombia have seriously complicated the process of coming to grips with the drug problem. The upper classes of Bogotá, Medellín and other Colombian cities have always lived well. Known for their industriousness and shrewdness, these Colombians prospered. After the Second World War, an educated, white-collar middle class was growing in the cities. Nevertheless, a much larger number of poor Colombians lived in rural areas, without access to education, social services or decent housing and working conditions.

The upper-class elites ruled the country through two political parties: the Liberals and the Conservatives. Other social classes had no real voice in the political system. The rivalry between the two dominant parties erupted in warfare that lasted almost two decades. This episode, known in Colombia as *La Violencia* (The Violence), may have claimed as many as 200,000 lives between 1946 and 1958. During this time, little was done to improve the lives of Colombians living in rural areas. Political violence and poverty forced many people to abandon their small farms and move to the cities.

By the 1960s the gap in income, opportunities and rights between the privileged middle and upper classes and the poor had grown wider than ever. These conditions were ideal breeding grounds for Marxist-Leninist (Communist) groups. Their recruiters stressed the unfairness of the existing social and economic system, the ideal of a socialist government that would put workers—not wealthy landowners—first, and the need to resort to armed revolution to achieve their ends.

Forced into the mountains and rainforests to hide from the Colombian army, these early revolutionary groups became skilled at guerrilla warfare. Although some of these groups gave up their arms in 1991 to seek change through ordinary political processes (forming political parties and running for office), others continued the armed struggle. At the turn of the twenty-first century, the two most important organizations, the ELN (*Ejército de Liberación Nacional*, or Army of National Liberation) and the larger FARC (*Fuerzas Armadas Revolucionarias de Colombia*, the Revolutionary Armed

Forces of Colombia) controlled roughly the southern third of the nation. Coca is grown in large portions of these areas and guerrilla bands provided protection from the government to coca growers and processors who paid them a "tax" for this service. With financial support from Cuba and the Soviet Union no longer available, the guerrilla organizations have come to rely on coca taxes.

Large landowners, who were opposed ideologically to the guerrillas, organized armed paramilitary groups—private armies—to oppose the leftist guerrillas. Drug money also helps to pay for much of the paramilitary's arms and maintenance. Both the guerrillas and the paramilitaries threatened and killed peasants to keep them from cooperating with the other side.[8]

Recent administrations in Colombia have tried several approaches in dealing with the guerrillas, from anti-insurgency warfare to negotiating for peace. Andrés Pastrana (president, 1998–2002) made seeking peace with the rebels a part of his campaign platform. Recognizing that the guerrillas already had effective control over such a large part of the country, Pastrana promised to end military attacks in that region in exchange for peace negotiations. Later he proposed a $7 billion peace plan called Paz Colombia, which would combine funds from Colombia, the United States and the European community. (A scaled-down proposal called Plan Colombia was finally adopted during the Clinton administration with funds from the United States that provided for more military and less economic aid.) However, Pastrana's attempts to bring the guerrillas into meaningful peace talks failed. In 2002, a series of high-profile kidnappings and attacks by the FARC caused him to call off all peace talks. In May of the same year, Pastrana handed the reins of government to the next elected president, Álvaro Uribe, whose campaign promises to bring guerrilla violence to an end had appealed to a citizenry that was tired of bloodshed and broken promises. Whether or not Uribe will be able to end the civil war, the increased military pressure on the southern coca-growing region that has enjoyed several years of peace will probably mean that more of the coca growing and processing will move back to Peru and Bolivia, and even move into Ecuador.

It is obvious that the causes and effects of the drug war in Colombia are complicated and many-sided. In the following section we will examine several assertions that are commonly made concerning how to put an end to drug trafficking in Colombia:

1. Colombia must take full responsibility for curtailing drug trafficking.
2. The growing of coca must be stopped in order to dismantle the drug industry.
3. The guerrilla organizations must be subdued in order for Colombia to have the strong central government it needs to combat the drug problem.
4. Decriminalizing the use of cocaine (and other illegal drugs) in the United States would be a useful strategy in the fight against drugs.

DISCUSSION

Should Colombia Take Full Responsibility for Curtailing Drug Trafficking?

Agree

Although the U.S. government has spent billions of dollars over the last several decades to stop the flow of cocaine and heroin from Colombia and other South American countries, the amount of illegal drugs headed for the United States has only increased. Critics of the so-called war on drugs in the United States state that the initiative has been a costly failure. Surveys show that the use of crack cocaine has not changed much in 10 years, nor has the general level of illegal drug use. This demonstrates that effective measures in the drug problem will have to come from the producing country.

Colombia must do much more to eliminate coca fields and production facilities. They will also have to do much better at catching, prosecuting and putting drug traffickers in prison for long sentences. Colombia must rid itself of corrupt politicians and police officials who accept bribes to allow the drug trade to continue. Critics of Colombia's record say that the police know who most of the *narcotraficantes* are, but fail to arrest them because of their high-level "connections." Even when the criminals are tried and convicted, they manage to run their drug operations from prison. The Colombian system is too soft on these criminals; the Colombian people must put an end to crime and corruption before they consume the nation.

Disagree

Drug trafficking is a worldwide problem; it is hardly limited to Colombia. A report compiled by the United Nations International Drug Control Program estimated the amount of money exchanged in the drug trade (all illegal drugs, not just cocaine) at $400 billion annually, or about 8% of all international trade. That was more than the trade in textiles, clothing, iron and steel combined.[9]

Of course, cocaine trafficking would not be such big business if the demand for these drugs did not exist. The United States has the largest appetite for illegal drugs in the world. Many Colombians think the United States should clean up its own house first before it meddles any further in Colombia. If the demand for cocaine decreased significantly in consuming countries like the United States, if drug addiction treatment and prevention programs were more effective, if all of the judges and police in our country were free of corruption, no doubt the drug trade in Colombia would decline significantly as well.

Finally, compared to the United States, Colombia is a small and poor country. It already spends a large share of its budget on eradicating coca, on investigating, catching and prosecuting and imprisoning drug dealers and combatting the guerrillas who protect them. It has made significant progress in recent years in jailing major *narcotraficantes* and corrupt officials, even some at high levels in state and national government. Every year it has seized more shipments of cocaine. Numerous Colombian politicians, judges, journalists and policemen have died in the fight against the drug lords. Thousands of Colombians have been jailed and prisons are overcrowded. Most of those in jail are people who turned to working in the drug trade because of poverty. In addition, there are other matters that urgently need attention: education, economic development, housing, water and public health. Colombia is doing all it can; the United States can and must do more.

Is the Eradication of Coca Plants the Most Effective Way to Stem the Flow of Cocaine Coming into the United States?

Agree

The coca fields keep expanding every year. The Office of National Drug Control Policy estimated that total coca acreage in Colombia more than tripled between 1992 and 2000 and reached nearly 420,000 acres in 2001. In the same year, Peru and Bolivia had 133,000 acres of coca under cultivation. United States officials conceded that more potent varieties of coca have been introduced in both Colombia and Peru, increasing the amount of cocaine produced per acre. Eradicating the coca crop is a logical step toward ending the drug trade.

The moneymaking potential of coca makes it hard to simply convince people not to grow it. A small farmer can usually make more from coca leaf production than from growing other crops. Thus, eradication is the most effective way to cripple cocaine production. If the coca is destroyed, farmers will have to turn to other crops and the cycle will be broken. Coca plants can be pulled up or burned or herbicides can be used to kill them. Recently, the Colombian government accepted plans to spray a type of fungus that attacks and kills coca as another means to control the plant. The United States pressed hard for its adoption.

The *cocaleros* (coca growers) look for areas that are hard to reach and far from centers of government control. The mountainous rainforest in southern Colombia, near the Ecuadorian border, is remote and the growing conditions are perfect for coca. *Cocaleros* have also appeared in other distant locations, such as the eastern slopes of the Andes, where they set up their labs and start new plots. Burning and aerial spraying are virtually the only practical ways to keep up with the growers and processors. These methods have been used in Peru and Bolivia; production of coca leaf in those areas declined as a result.

Disagree

At the turn of the twenty-first century, Colombia was growing approximately 80% of the South American coca leaf that was converted into cocaine, up from only about 25% a decade before. Nevertheless, killing all of the coca plantations in Colombia wouldn't stop the flow of drugs to the United States. Because of the huge profits that illegal drugs generate, other sources would be found. Coca growers are both resourceful and mobile. They can simply move on to another area and begin planting there.

Many of the opponents of eradication programs don't oppose getting rid of coca and the cocaine industry, but they object to the methods that are used in an attempt to do it quickly. They have two primary objections. First, rapid extermination of coca plants causes damage to the environment. Burned fields erode easily. In rainy, mountainous terrain, this causes heavy loss of topsoil, which in turn ruins streams. Herbicides are just as bad for erosion. They can also poison the land for years, and pose a very serious hazard to the health of animals and humans in the area. The fungus that may be sprayed to kill the coca plants has the potential to infect other plants as well. Some scientists believe it could threaten food crops and cause environmental damage in unexpected ways. They also believe that it may be dangerous to people with weakened immune systems.

A second argument against rapid extermination is that the people who grow and pick coca are mostly poor rural people who have no other way to make a living at present. For example, two-thirds of the 300,000 inhabitants of the district of Putumayo in southern Colombia are small coca farmers and migrant leaf pickers, and many are refugees already displaced by the civil war between the guerrillas and the army. It is hard to discourage people from growing coca because no other crop will bring the same income. Even so, it is a meager living.

When the coca fields are burned, most often people must replant coca or move away—either to become jobless refugees in the towns or to new fields, in more remote areas. In the absence of economic development, there are no buyers for other crops that can be grown, no innovative ideas to create jobs, and no loans for equipment or education. Without an incentive to find another way to make a living, the rural Colombians that grow the coca leaf have few other choices. And as *cocaleros* retreat into more and more remote areas, they are destroying irreplaceable rainforest, which must be cleared before the coca is planted.

According to the opponents of rapid eradication programs, Colombia needs a long-term development plan, especially in the rural areas. The plan would have to provide seed, tools, loans and expertise to farmers, as well as better education and health care for their families, in order to build a base for a stable economy and a just society. In this setting, few people would be forced to raise coca to feed their families or to risk their lives and liberty to serve as *correos* or *mulas* (low-paid drug runners). This approach would take much more time, but would be more beneficial to everyone, not just a temporary fix to please the U.S. government.

Do the Guerrilla Organizations Have to Be Subdued before Colombia Can Effectively Combat the Drug Problem?

Agree

Guerrilla organizations have become involved in the protection of coca growers and cocaine labs as a way to generate money for their operations against the government. Their critics inside and outside of Colombia also say that guerrilla groups are directly involved in growing, manufacturing and selling illicit drugs. Because the guerrillas are well armed, only the national government has the manpower and equipment to combat them effectively.

The existence of guerrilla groups seriously threatens the sovereignty of the nation. In a third of the country the guerrillas—not the national government—are in control. They even collect "taxes" in these areas, especially from residents who are better off. The country is, in effect, in the middle of a civil war. As long as it lasts, the ability of the Colombian government to combat illegal drugs will be weakened. Some people believe that the United States should help the Colombian government combat the guerrillas by providing the Colombian military with more arms, aircraft and training. Although the U.S. Congress did not back this proposal initially, the designation of the FARC and ELN as terrorist organizations gave greater impetus to using U.S. funds, arms and troops to help the Colombian military.

Furthermore, only a strong national government can put an end to the violence caused by clashes between the guerrillas and the paramilitary "private armies" that oppose them. Civilians, including women and children, are the most frequent casualties in this conflict. Killings of local public officials and attacks on voters during elections have paralyzed parts of the country; thousands of people have fled the violence and have lost their homes and property. Possibly 200,000 Colombians a year become refugees in their own country. The guerrilla groups have also kidnapped numerous Colombians and foreigners to obtain money for their activities. Human rights organizations such as Amnesty International have criticized the guerrillas for their part in killings, kidnappings and bombings and for the recruitment of children as young as 11 or 12 into their ranks.

The outcome of Colombia's war on drugs and the stability of the country depend on subduing the guerrillas.

Disagree

The supporters of the guerrilla movements counter by saying that the government continues to be dominated by the elite, which cares little about the struggles of the poor people that make up the largest share of Colombia's population. *Campesinos* (rural people, farmers) usually agree with this assessment. They point out that, in spite of its promises, the government often fails to help them after coca fields are cleared in eradication programs. The spraying of herbicides has frequently damaged crops and forests outside of coca fields but the government has seldom responded to the peasants' complaints.

The guerrillas deny that they are directly involved in drug trafficking. To show that it was sincere, the FARC offered to guarantee eradication of coca in a substantial area it controlled. As part of the agreement, the government would have to withdraw its troops from the locale, and the international community would need to provide verification and financial assistance for a crop substitution and market development program.

In both Colombia and the United States, some people fear that increasing military aid will increase the influence of the military in the country, undermining the fragile democratic institutions of the country. Focusing on military aid could also create more opposition to the Colombian government, not less. Especially in the United States, critics of military aid also fear being drawn into another civil war between a leftist movement and government with questionable popular support, as happened in Vietnam, El Salvador and Nicaragua. They believe that U.S. aid should have a much larger component for assistance to economic development, education, health and other programs that would strengthen the social fabric of the nation.

Finally, critics point out that the Colombian military has turned a blind eye toward the activities of the paramilitary groups, allowing them a free hand to terrorize civilians and to combat the guerrillas. Independent human rights groups confirm that much of the paramilitary violence in the countryside in and around guerrilla-controlled areas is condoned (sometimes even directed) by the military, which should be protecting civilians. Trying to strengthen the central government by strengthening the military can only lead to more violence.[10]

Would Legalizing Cocaine (and Other Drugs) End the Problem of Drug Trafficking in the United States and Colombia?

Agree

The war on drugs, both in the United States and in Colombia, has been a failure. Legalizing cocaine would put the drug dealers out of business. Although legalization would not mean the end of drug use, it would have many advantages.[11] These include the fact that the current approach is excessively costly to taxpayers: according to some estimates in 2001 the Bush administration requested more than $19 billion for a variety of programs and agencies for drug control efforts.[12] If cocaine and other drugs were legalized, the price to consumers would be lower, robberies and other forms of street crime committed by addicts to pay for drugs would fall, and the number of people jailed would drop dramatically. Currently somewhat more than 20% of prisoners in state jails and 60% in federal prisons are in jail for drug offenses.[13] The loss of income, suffering and disruption to families of drug abusers routinely jailed, even for minor offenses, would be reduced. Other reasons include the fact that as long as cocaine and other drugs are illegal, no one can oversee their purity or potency. Adulterated drugs or a shipment of cocaine that is more potent than normal can lead to injury or even death.

Others who advocate legalization point out that drug abuse prevention, and drug treatment in particular, are much more effective ways to reduce overall drug consumption than trying to intercept drug shipments and/or catch and jail drug users and dealers, especially when costs are taken into account. The demand for drugs is what keeps the drug market flourishing. If demand could be reduced by treating, rather than jailing and punishing, drug users, all of society would benefit. When treatment is available (and drug abusers don't have to wait as they do now), treatment is effective and much lower in cost than law enforcement.

Many proponents of legalization also believe that drug abuse is a symptom, not necessarily the cause, of social malaise. This has been a common view of liberals in the United States: to combat drug abuse we must get at the underlying causes, which are primarily unemployment, poverty, racial discrimination and urban decay. This will mean working toward improving education and job training, especially for disadvantaged youth, a higher minimum wage, better public health programs and adequate housing.[14]

Disagree

Many Americans are uncomfortable[15] with outright legalization of currently illegal drugs, including marijuana. Some of them disagree with legalization of cocaine or any illegal substance on moral grounds, believing that they weaken the character of the person who uses them and that consuming one or more illegal drugs would encourage users to become involved in even more immoral or criminal behavior. To legalize cocaine, they argue, would be to put a stamp of approval on using drugs and would result in an increase in drug use. Even if legalization eliminated much of the criminal element (since, presumably, drug production would be regulated like other "legal" drugs, such as alcohol and tobacco), encouraging anyone to try drugs would be immoral. Others view the drugs as well as the people who deal in them as a threat to national security, a way to weaken the United States through corruption and demoralization, so that it would be less able to defend itself and give criminals even more power than they already have.

A third group believes that while complete legalization is not a good idea (and probably impossible to achieve, given the attitude of the public), harsh penalties are worse. At present we operate under mandatory minimum sentences for drug offenses, sending many people to jail for possessing small quantities. These get-tough policies are too costly and discriminatory, falling mostly on young African American and Hispanic men from inner cities. A segment of this group advocates a "harm reduction" approach, to reduce the harm that drugs do rather than to try to eliminate them altogether (which virtually everyone agrees is impossible). They advocate increased methadone treatment, needle exchanges and heroin maintenance programs for hard-core addicts in addition to drug abuse education and much greater access to treatment for those not so seriously addicted. It is important that the U.S. public begins to understand that dependence on drugs is a public health problem, not a criminal problem.

Still, not everyone can agree that this approach will answer one of our most vexing social issues. Acknowledging that tolerance for drug addicts "provides a welcome alternative to the narrow moralism of the drug war," we also need to recognize that drug addiction is genuinely harmful to the user and his or her family. Harm reduction programs should also be more active in getting addicts into programs where they can address their problems.[16]

QUESTIONS AND ACTIVITIES

1. Do you believe that teenagers in the United States pay attention to information about drugs shown on TV? Why?/Why not? Give several reasons.

2. Write a TV "commercial" in Spanish aimed at discouraging the use of drugs for a Spanish-speaking TV audience in the United States.

3. Does your school system have drug abuse prevention programs? Do you think they are/were effective? What kind of drug abuse prevention program would work best in your school?

4. What information do people in your community know about the war on drugs in Colombia? What are their sources of information? Conduct a survey of family, friends and/or neighbors. Pool your information with other students from your class. Are there differences in their knowledge that appear to have to do with their age or the source?

5. All Latin American countries now face the problem of young addicts. What can you find out about programs to help them? Use the references below to find information on the Internet. Do a search in Spanish, using *drogadictos jóvenes* as your search term. Pick one program and prepare a short report on it.

6. Who should be responsible for solving the problem of growing and processing cocaine in South America? The United States and other consumer nations or Colombia and other producing nations? State at least three actions that you believe should be taken and why they would be effective. Be prepared to take part in a class discussion on this question.

7. Prepare a TV news story on some aspect of the drug problem in Colombia with three or four other students. You should find a news story about a recent event related in a Spanish-language newspaper online, using news sources you can find in LANIC or CNNenespañol. Then present the story to the class as though it were on the TV news (one of you will be the anchor person, another a reporter; others will be the people being interviewed).

8. Imagine that you will be interviewed for a news special that will be shown in Latin America on U.S. opinions on important issues. Choose one of the following questions and prepare your answer for the Spanish-speaking audience.

   a. Do you believe that the United States should continue to provide military support in the forms of aircraft, arms and training to the Colombian military to combat drug growers and cocaine manufacturers? What are the two most important reasons why you support this course of action?

   b. Do you favor sending U.S. troops to Colombia to assist the Colombian military? You should be able to provide several reasons to support your position.

9. Do the potential benefits of introducing new kinds of fungus that attack coca plants outweigh the potential dangers they present to humans and the environment? You and other students will prepare your answers to this question and present them orally to a group of fellow students, in a simulated meeting of the Colombian Anti-Drug Commission. Address them as "Distinguidos Miembros de la Comisión." Be sure to use *usted* forms.

10. As the mayor of a small town in a coca-growing area, you are aware of the number of small farmers who depend on growing coca to make ends meet. An international delegation has come to your area. Are you in favor of the government's eradication program or would you rather have your area left alone? Explain your position to the visiting dignitaries. What are your concerns? Be sure to address these strangers as *usted(es)*.

VOCABULARY/VOCABULARIO

Nouns/Sustantivos

addiction	la adicción
the authorities	las autoridades
coca growers	los cocaleros
coca leaf	la hoja de coca
coca plant	las plantas, las matas
cocaine	la cocaina
consumers	los consumidores

corruption	la corrupción
criminals	los criminales
drug abuse	el abuso de drogas
drug addicts	los drogadictos
drug dealing, selling	el narcotráfico
the drug problem	el problema/el dilema de las drogas
drug traffickers	los narcotraficantes
drugs	las drogas
effects	los efectos, los resultados
the government	el gobierno
the police	la policía, los polícias
politicians	los políticos
rehabilitation	la rehabilitación
rural people, farmers	los campesinos
street children	los niños desamparados/ abandondados; niños de la calle
treatment	el tratamiento
war on drugs	la lucha contra el narcotráfico

Verbs/Verbos

cause	causar
cure	curar
damage, hurt	dañar
eradicate	eradicar, matar, eliminar
fail (to)	fracasar (en)
get hooked	engancharse
jail, encarcerate	encarcelar
legalize	legalizar
reduce	reducir, disminuir
rehabilitate	rehabilitar
spend (money) per year	gastar X dólares al año; cada año se gasta(n)
spend (time)	pasar (tiempo, días, años . . .)

Expressions/Expresiones

[he has] a drug problem [i.e., he is   él es adicto a las drogas
  a drug addict]

in jail   (estar) en la carcel; (estar)
                                                encarcelado/a

RESOURCE GUIDE

Books and Articles

Becker, Gary S. "It's Time to Give up the War on Drugs." *Business Week*,
    September 17, 2001, p. 32.
Clawson, Patrick, and Rensselaer Lee III. *The Andean Cocaine Industry*.
    New York: St. Martin's Press, 1996.
"Drugs in the Andes: Spectres Stir in Peru." *The Economist*, February 14,
    2002, pp. 33–34.
Karch, Steven B. *A Brief History of Cocaine*. Boca Raton, FL: CRC Press,
    1998.
Massing, Michael. "It's Time for Realism." *The Nation*, September 20,
    1999, pp. 11–14.
Scott, Peter Dale, and Jonathan Marshall. *Cocaine Politics: Drugs, Armies,
    and the CIA in Central America*. Updated Edition. Berkeley: Uni-
    versity of California Press, 1998.
"Survey: Colombia." *The Economist* (special section), April 19, 2001, pp.
    1–16.
"Why the Illegal Psychoactive Drugs Industry Grew in Colombia." *Journal
    of Interamerican Studies & World Affairs* (Fall 1992): 37–63.

Internet

Cocaine Anonymous World Services. <http://www.ca.org/index.html>.
"The Contras, Cocaine, and Covert Operations." The National Secur-
    ity Archive. <http://www.gwu.edu/nsarchiv/NSAEBB/NSAEBB2/
    nsaebb2.htm>.
Drug Enforcement Agency (DEA). <http://www.usdoj.gov/dea/pubs/
    factsheet/fact0600.htm>.
Substance Abuse and Mental Health Services Administration (SAMHSA).
    <http://www.samhsa.gov>.
"Truth: The Antidrug." <http://www.theantidrug.com/> and Spanish ver-
    sion <http://www.laantidroga.com/>.

Basque separatist protesters raise their fists during a march by the political party Batasuna in April 2002 in Bilbao, the largest city in the Basque Autonomous Community. Batasuna was banned later the same year because of its links to the terrorist organization ETA. (AP Photo/Aranberri)

Chapter 11

The Basque Question

"*Vascos Sí, ETA No.*" "*¡Basta ya!*" ["Basques yes, ETA no." "Enough!"] These two slogans are seen frequently on banners and posters in the streets of Spanish cities. The people who carry the banners protest the slayings of politicians, journalists, policemen—and sometimes bystanders or the victims' friends, relatives or employees—by members of Euskadi Ta Askatasuna (Basque Land and Freedom) or ETA, a clandestine militant separatist organization. Since its founding in the 1950s, ETA has been responsible for more than 800 deaths and numerous kidnappings throughout Spain. It has also made several unsuccessful attempts on the life of the king.

ETA's goal has been to force the Spanish state to grant complete independence to the Basque provinces (Euskadi and Navarra). Few Basques approve of ETA's violent tactics, but the majority of them favor the right of self-determination for their region.[1] The roots of the conflict go back several centuries. It will be difficult to resolve this question in a way that is satisfactory for the majority of Spaniards on the one hand and the majority of Basques on the other.

BACKGROUND

The Basques are an ancient people. The Romans encountered a group they called the Vascones already established in the northeastern part of the Iberian Peninsula and southwestern France. The

Basque language, known as *euskera*, is unlike any other in Europe, making it quite likely that the Vascones occupied this region earlier than the Indo-European immigrants or invaders.[2]

Waves of speakers of Indo-European languages arrived in the Iberian Peninsula over a period of several thousand years before the birth of Christ. Each time, the Basques maintained their ethnic and linguistic identity. Today the territory occupied by Basque speakers has shrunk to about one-seventh of its size in the Roman era.[3] Nevertheless, today many Basques consider themselves to be not only a unique people but a *nation*, whose right to self-determination has been thwarted time and time again by their larger and militarily more powerful neighbors, the Spanish and the French.

In the Spanish constitution of 1978, the three Basque provinces of Guipuzcoa, Avala and Viscaya (what used to be called el País Vasco, or the Basque Country) was renamed the Basque Autonomous Community (*Comunidad Autónoma Vasca* or CAV). Its name in Basque is *Euskadi*. To the east, bordering the Pyrenees, lies Navarra, another autonomous community[4] with a smaller but significant Basque population. Across the border in France are three more Basque provinces: Labourd, Basse-Navarre and Soule. Modern Basque nationalists argue that *all* of these provinces should be united under a single, independent Basque government.

For a time in the Middle Ages, the Basque Kingdom of Navarre, with its capital in Pamplona (the capital of modern Navarra), was a major power in European politics. Its influence dwindled as it was cut off from the forward advance of the Reconquest,[5] and by the mid-sixteenth century it had ceased to exist as an independent kingdom. Since then, the number of Basque speakers has declined—especially in the twentieth century—and the number of non-Basques living in this region has increased, also most dramatically in the last century. Because Basque is so different from other European languages, outsiders have been daunted by the prospect of attempting to learn it. Its shrinking geographical boundaries have provided more incentive for Basques to learn Spanish or French than for newcomers to learn *euskera*. For these reasons Basque was also late to develop a written literature and to standardize its spelling. Even today several distinct dialects exist in a geographical area approximately the size of the state of Connecticut.[6]

Much of the ability of the Basques to withstand the linguistic and cultural encroachment of their more powerful neighbors comes from their geographic isolation and attachment to rural traditions.[7] Nevertheless, in the past Basques have left their homeland, becoming expert seamen and whalers. A Basque, Juan Sebastian de Elcano, completed the voyage of Magellan and therefore captained the first expedition to complete the circumnavigation of the globe (1519–1522). Economic hardship in their homeland or the lure of the adventure induced many Basques to join the ranks of *conquistadores, colonos* or goverment and church officials: Lope de Aguirre, Catalina de Erauso, the Lieutenant Nun and Ignatius of Loyola (later Saint Ignatius) are the best known. In the New World they have often prospered. Basques have also played an important role in Spain's intellectual life and include such luminaries as Miguel de Unamuno and Pío Baroja of the Generation of '98, contemporary novelist Juan Goytisolo and sculptor Eduardo Chillida. Basque surnames are common in Latin America, and many U.S. Latinos have one or more Basque ancestors in their family tree. In addition, Basques immigrated directly to the United States, especially to Idaho, Nevada, and California, where many originally came to find work as shepherds. Canada also has Basque communities, largely in Quebec.

In the nineteenth and twentieth centuries, the *País Vasco* was one of the first areas in Spain to industrialize, due to its access to iron ore, good seaports and its proximity to the coal of England. The relative prosperity of the Basque Country attracted other Spaniards looking for jobs in the factories of Bilbao and other Basque cities. Today Navarra enjoys one of the highest levels of per capita income in Spain and, although it has slipped some in recent decades, the per capita income for the three provinces that form Euskadi is still above the average for Spain.

Nevertheless, many Basques want to separate from Spain to form a tiny, independent nation-state of their own. Why? And why do a small minority of them approve of violence—including killing—to achieve this end? What are the attitudes of citizens of the Basque provinces and of the rest of Spain's population toward separation from Spain?

In considering these questions and as you read contemporary Spanish sources, you will need to distinguish carefully between the terms *nation, state* and *nation-state* as they are used in the United States and in Spain. In American English sometimes all three terms are used as synonyms, but most often "state" (*estado*) refers to a subdivision of the "nation," in a federal system such as in the United

States of America or *los Estados Unidos de México*. However, in contemporary Spain, Basque and other nationalists (for example, Catalán or Galician nationalists) refer to Spain and its government as *el estado*, or "the state," which they view as an artificial and imposed political entity. On the other hand, *la nación* refers to a culturally and historically congruent people, such as *la nación vasca*, *la nación catalana* or *la nación gallega* (the Basque, Catalan or Galician nation).

Here are questions we will seek to answer in this chapter:

1. Because of their long history, do the Basques constitute a nation and deserve to be recognized as an independent political state?
2. Can only an independent Basque state be trusted to safeguard Basque cultural, civil, economic and human rights?
3. Is independence for the Basques the only way to bring an end to the violence?

DISCUSSION

Because of Their Long History, Do the Basques Constitute a Nation and Deserve to Be Recognized as an Independent Political State?

Agree

Indeed, the Basques are an ancient people. The ancestors of many modern-day Basques settled in the Basque-speaking provinces of both Spain and France long before those of other modern Spaniards. The Kingdom of Navarre, which incorporated a large portion of the seven provinces claimed as the Basque homeland by today's Basque nationalists, predated modern Spain and coexisted with the kingdoms of Castilla and Aragón into the fifteenth and early sixteenth centuries. Culturally the Basques have remained quite distinctive, retaining a unique language and their own traditions. The Basque claim to a unique ethnicity is bolstered by the fact that, compared to other Europeans, a much higher percentage of Basques have Rh negative blood factor, which is relatively uncommon worldwide. They also point to a set of physical traits, such as the shape of the head, which gives Basques a somewhat different appearance than their non-Basque Spanish and French neighbors.

Although Basque nationalists have not reached consensus on political philosophy,[8] they do agree that the Basque desire for self-government has been thwarted for centuries and that the only way to achieve it is through independence from both Spain and France. They call for an independent Basque nation. They point out that in other developed countries, ethnic/national minorities such as the people of Ireland and, more recently, Scotland and Quebec have made similar demands for separation and independence based on cultural, linguistic and historical grounds. Finally, they argue that it is particularly cruel to divide a group like the Basques—who consider themselves one people who share a common culture, language and traditions—between two "alien" powers. The Basque nationalists argue that both the Spanish and French governments have tried to undermine Basque solidarity by dividing Euskadi from the historically Basque region of Navarra and by combining the Basque provinces in France with others of non-Basque language and tradition.

Disagree

Spaniards (including some Basques) who oppose separation of Euskadi (Basque Autonomous Community) and Navarra have several responses to this separatist claim. For them, the argument of the ancient history of the culture is simply irrelevant. What of all the other peoples in the world whose culture was overtaken and surrounded by invaders or neighbors who were more technologically advanced or more aggressive at some time in the past? Granted that we should not condone aggression in our own time, it is totally unrealistic to attempt to undo every twist of fate that occurred centuries ago. Even though a solid majority of Basques favor holding a referendum on the issue of autonomy, in 2001, only 21% of the same individuals surveyed indicated unconditional support of independence.[9]

Opponents of separation also question Euskadi's viability as a small country in the twenty-first century. How will Euskadi be able to compete in the European context? If the Basques are determined to make their own language primary in their new state, with whom will they communicate outside their own borders? They will need to fall back on French and Spanish to trade with their neighbors. If they achieve independence from Spain (and France), the new Basque state will surely need to join the European Union in order to survive.

How sure can they be that they will be accepted? European Union members may decide that accepting the Basques would only encourage violent separatist movements elsewhere.

Those who oppose the Basque nationalist movement also point out that in Navarra, which the nationalists insist should be considered a part of the Basque homeland, a much lower percentage of the population identifies with the nationalist sentiment. What if Navarra refuses to take part in a referendum on the question of independence? What would happen if Euskadi votes to secede and Navarra votes to remain with Spain? A Basque state without the economic power of Navarra would be even weaker.

Finally, the Spanish "statists" oppose the cultural identity argument because they fear a domino effect. Spain is formed of many competing nationalities, several of whom also have some reason to consider themselves "different" from the rest of Spain: the Catalans, the Galicians and the Canary Islanders, to name the most vocal ones. Even Andalucía has experienced stirrings of separatist feeling. If one of the regions is allowed to separate on the basis of cultural distinctiveness, others might follow suit. Will the Spanish state disintegrate? Fear of fragmentation of the Spanish state vía autonomy for the Basque provinces and Cataluña was an important contributing factor in the Spanish Civil War. Although the military (which opposed Basque and Catalan autonomy) is much less of a threat to representative government today than in the 1930s, the loss of any part of peninsular Spain could cause serious tensions inside the remainder of the country.

Can Only an Independent Basque State Be Trusted to Safeguard Basque Cultural, Civil, Economic and Human Rights?

Agree

In the Basque nationalist view, the imposition of Spanish and French and downgrading of Basque in all three parts of the historic Basque region shows not simply a disrespect for the Basques but a deliberate attempt to extinguish their language and culture. During the Franco regime, the Basque language was banned from public media such as newspapers and radio. Basque was forbidden in the schools. As a consequence, many Basques who were born between the late 1930s through the early 1970s became monolingual in Spanish. The number of Basque speakers dropped precipitously and survived mainly in rural communities where police surveillance was more difficult and older people were monolingual in Basque. The experience since the transition to democracy in Spain has been less harsh—there are no legal penalties for the use of Basque and, in Euskadi, *euskera* is co-equal with Spanish. Still, nationalists blame the Spanish and French states for the lack of unanimity among Basques (concerning the desire for separation as well as other questions): "[A]s a result of the influence of the Spanish and the French states, . . . in the Basque homeland there are people who understand the Basque character in very different ways."[10]

Basque nationalists complain that the Spanish state continues to undermine Basque culture and to throw roadblocks in the way of legitimate efforts to discuss self-determination for the Basques.

Basque citizens must begin by overcoming the major obstacles that have been imposed on us [by Spain and France] in order to be able to construct our own democratic architecture. We are convinced that if we simply accept the rules of the game [*el marco*] and what is considered legitimate by the 2 states, the Basque Nation will cease to exist as a distinct people. . . . Those who have divided our people and who have used a variety of subterfuges during the last 200 years have intended to assimilate the Basque nation. [They] have tried to make our collective identity disappear by eliminating the cultural, symbolic and material elements that distinguish us as a people. And now they want to oblige us to accept the current minority status and political forces as a beginning point for [a discussion of future] democratic change.[11]

Spain's growing frustration with the separatist violence has led the government to take measures that have caused alarm, not only among Basques, but also in the wider human rights community. The Batasuna party was outlawed in 2002 for its alleged close ties with ETA; in February 2003, *Egunkaria*, the only daily newspaper published entirely in Basque, was shut down by the government of Spanish Prime Minister Aznar in spite of scant evidence linking it to ETA. The editor of *Egunkaria* accused the police of torture and humiliation during his arrest—one of numerous allegations against police treatment of suspected ETA agents and sympathizers.[12]

Disagree

Those who oppose the separatist position point out that the decline in the geographical extent and the number of users of the Basque language is, in large part, a natural historical evolution that took place as the Basque provinces became more industrialized and came into closer contact with the outside world.[13] While most of the opponents agree that Franco's repression of the Basque language and culture was barbaric, they point out that other minority cultures—especially the Catalans—also suffered under the Franco regime. The Catalans, however, not only preserved their language and cultural heritage, but also have found it possible to live within the 1978 constitution with little violent conflict. In their opinion, the Spanish constitution provides ample protection for the language and culture of all minority language areas.

These same opponents think that the Basque separatists have become paranoid: they find enemies of Basque cultural identity under every bush. In reality, says this group, all that the vast majority of Spaniards want is for the Basques to live in peace with the rest of Spain. According to this group, it is the ETA terrorists who are responsible for any hardening of attitudes that has occurred in Spanish government circles since the constitution was approved. Opponents of separatism, including the past and present governing parties of Spain—the *Partido Popular* (People's Party, or PP) and the *Partido Socialista Obrero Español* (the Socialist Labor Party, or PSOE)—point out that the autonomous Basque government has failed to discourage ETA's terrorism and intimidation, denying the freedom of speech, thought and action that the separatists claim they alone can guarantee to Basques.[14] The position of the Spanish government, under both the PP and the PSOE, of most Spaniards and of a substantial number of people living in the Basque region is that the Spanish constitution provides sufficient protection for minority cultures and for additional changes within a democratic framework.

Is Independence the Only Way to Bring an End to the Violence?

Agree

During the days of the Franco regime, the Spanish National Police and the Civil Guard (*Guardia Civil*) were responsible for law enforcement in the Basque region. Although all critics of the dictator-ship were subject to harsh treatment, police and military rule in the Basque provinces was especially severe. After ETA attempted to de-rail a train carrying Spanish Nationalist veterans to a reunion in 1961, the regime's response was brutal. Many Basques were im-prisoned and tortured; some were executed. Throughout the re-mainder of the Franco period, ETA responded in kind, targeting Civil Guards, Spanish military commanders, prison officials and even Franco's most important and trusted lieutenant, Admiral Luis Carrero Blanco. A vicious circle of repression and retaliation had begun. One of the major concessions to the Basques (and the Cat-alans) in the constitution of 1978 was to give each of these regions a police force under the control of its own elected autonomous com-munity government. Negotiations between the Basques and the cen-tral governments eventually resulted in the release of certain ETA prisoners and the movement of some others closer to home so that family members could visit them more easily.

Nevertheless, the number of terrorist attacks carried out by ETA groups did not subside as most Spaniards had hoped; in fact, be-tween 1978 and 1980 the number of attacks increased dramatically. The Basque provinces had been the only region in Spain where a majority of voters had not accepted the 1978 constitution. As na-tional elections in 1996 approached, violent attacks by ETA began to increase in number again. José María Aznar, the new prime min-ister (*Presidente del Gobierno*), had narrowly escaped an ETA attack several years before. After the PP won the 1996 election, an increas-ing number of the ETA's victims were PP officials—mayors, city council members and regional parliamentary deputies, both inside and outside of the Basque region. Occasionally the gunmen or bombers were tracked down and arrested, but many times they evaded the police since they operated in small "cells" and often were able to slip across the border to France. In 1998 ETA declared a moratorium while it carried out talks with the government. How-ever, in December 1999 ETA resumed its attacks, saying that the talks were going nowhere.

Even if they do not condone the killings, Basque nationalists point out that trying to defeat a small group of very dedicated individuals will be extremely difficult. Police and military solutions, they say, are doomed to failure. Until the Basques are allowed to freely decide their own fate, there will always be a few who will take up arms to continue the battle. As time drags on, the average age of ETA's *militantes*, or active members, is decreasing. These young men and women, now mostly in their twenties, recruited by ETA's youth organizations and schooled in hit-and-run street attacks, seem to lack a clear ideology. Time may be running out for a solution that will satisfy the disaffected young Basques.

Disagree

Many Spaniards are ready to let the Basque Autonomous Community (CAV) vote to determine whether it should remain in Spain or separate formally. However, they are also troubled by the fact that allowing a vote on separation could be interpreted to mean that the Spanish government had capitulated to terrorism. ETA was born in an era of a police state, when Basques were not allowed any form of self-government. Under those conditions, violence was a more understandable—even forgivable—response. Today, however, the majority of Spaniards believe that Spain's political structure provides regional minorities with more than enough liberty; they say that no rational motive now exists to use violence—especially murder—to achieve a political aim.

Complicating the prospect of a political solution is the question of exactly who should be counted as Basque. Which voters will be allowed to decide the fate of the Basques and the Navarese? The militant Basque separatists reiterate the central position of the Basque language in the definition of Basqueness, but at present none of the three Spanish provinces that comprise the CAV have a majority of speakers of *euskera* and only one, Guipuzcoa, even comes close to 50%.[15] Many people who live in the CAV today are of non-Basque ancestry. Will they qualify as Basques in a referendum on independence? (Most people interviewed said these people are also Basques, but about one-fourth believe that a person should have been born in the Basque provinces, and smaller numbers would require true Basques to have Basque parents or speak Basque to qualify.[16]) The reluctance of Navarra to join with the CAV also worries those Spaniards who are inclined to allow self-determination for the Basques. The Basque separatists look upon Navarra as historically a part of the Basque nation, but only about 10% of the Navarese speak Basque and this autonomous community has repeatedly sided with the Spanish national parties, the PP or the PSOE, since the restoration of democracy.

Critics of the separatist point of view state that the CAV government would not qualify for European Union membership because it would not meet the standards of the EU due to of the lack of protection of dissidents inside the boundaries the Basque Autonomous Community.[17] Individuals and groups who oppose ETA or who speak out for an end to violence are threatened; owners of businesses are intimidated into supplying the organization with money that funds its campaign of bombing and assassination throughout Spain. Bands of young men are free to terrorize citizens in many Basque towns and cities with little response from the Basque police forces. Opponents believe that the *Partido Nacionalista Vasca* (PNV or Basque Nationalist Party)—not ETA alone—is responsible for the atmosphere of fear that exists in the CAV today.[18] More and more people in the Basque provinces, ethnic Basques and non-ethnic alike, are leaving to escape the threat of violence. According to various surveys, as many as 15% of the population is considering relocating to other parts of Spain, and close to three-fourths of Basques think terrorist violence is a serious problem (approximately the same as in the rest of the country).[19] In the absence of progress in negotiations, the government and the majority of the Spanish public believe that Spain must continue to pursue ETA terrorists, hoping to find a "police or military solution" if a political one cannot be achieved.

QUESTIONS AND ACTIVITIES

1. Basque nationalists often refer to the situation of the Basques as being "a nation without a state." Explain in Spanish what this means. Be sure you understand what *nación* and *estado* mean in the context of contemporary Spanish politics.

2. In a group of four students, role-play a scene around a Spanish family dinner table: parents and their teenage children discuss the question of Basque nationalism. Represent the two opposing points of view and explain your reasons. After each of you speaks, outline a compromise that would satisfy most of the demands of those who have the strongest difference of opinion.

3. Draft a letter to the editor of an online newspaper in Spain outlining your position on the issue of separation of the Basque provinces from Spain and the formation of a Basque nation. Provide several reasons to support your position.

4. How do you think Americans would react if your state decided to leave

the union? What would be the reasons the rest of the country would accept or reject the succession? Explain this in writing to a Spaniard of your own age.

5. Organize a debate with one team defending and another team opposing the following proposition: There are circumstances that justify the use of violence to obtain the right of self-determination of a people.

6. Do you think that the right of self-determination (*el derecho de auto-determinación*) of a people could ever justify using *terrorism*? Explain your point of view.

7. In your opinion, should the ability to speak *euskera* be required to obtain a job in the Euskadi government? To teach in a school? To vote in elections in Euskadi? According to a survey taken in 2001, about 55% of the population of Euskadi does not speak *euskera* while about 45% does (bilingual, dominant in *euskera* or monolingual). The number of bilingual *euskera* speakers will grow as children now in primary school reach adulthood.[20]

8. If you were a student in one of the Basque provinces, would you want to go to a bilingual school (where your instruction would be delivered partly in Basque and partly in Castilian) or one where all instruction was in Castilian? Explain the reasons behind your answer.

9. Make a list of advantages and disadvantages (for you as an individual, for your community) of being educated and literate in both languages. Try to think of more than one advantage and disadvantage for each. Compare your lists with your classmates.

individual advantage(s)/ ventajas para el individuo	individual disadvantage(s)/ desventajas para el individuo
community advantage(s)/ ventajas para la comunidad	community disadvantage(s)/ desventajas para la comunidad

10. Even if you don't agree with their separatist cause, you can probably appreciate how deeply Basque nationalists feel about their language. Do you believe that a decline in the use of the mother tongue from one generation to the next necessarily brings with it a loss of cultural identity? Support your answer.

11. How do Spanish newspapers differ in the way they report Basque issues? Look for a recent major story related to the topic of Basque nationalism in at least two newspapers online; for example *ABC*, *El País* (both national papers, published in Madrid) and *Diario Vasco*. What differences do you observe in opinions toward the events or the actors in the story ? Does the *Diario Vasco* report the story in a fundamentally different way from the national papers? Where would you

place the three newspapers on a scale of "statism" versus "Basque nationalism"?

12. Choose one of the following regions that have been in the news in recent decades because of separatist movements: Quebec (Canada), Northern Ireland (United Kingdom) or Scotland (United Kingdom). Compare the historical antecedents of modern separatism, the motivation for separation and the tactics of the separatists. What was the outcome? Do you believe the separatists will be satisfied with the outcome? Explain your answer.

VOCABULARY/VOCABULARIO

Nouns/Sustantivos

assimilation	la asimilación
Basque language	el vasco, el euskera
bilingual education	la educación bilingüe
country	el país, la nación, el estado
cultural identity	la identidad cultural
goal	la meta
independence	la independencia
issue	la cuestión
language	el idioma, la lengua
language policy	la política lingüística
liberties, freedoms	las libertades
minority	la minoría
nation (a people)	la nación
nationalism	el nacionalismo
nationalist (person)	el/la nacionalista
policy	la política
politics	la política
repression	la represión
rights	los derechos
self-determination	la autodeterminación
separatism	el separatismo
separatist	el/la separatista
state, national government	el estado

terrorism	el terrorismo
terrorist	el/la terrorista
theme, topic	el tema
violence	la violencia

Verbs/Verbos

achieve independence	independizarse
be in favor of	estar a favor (de)
be opposed to	estar en contra (de)
favor	favorecer
fight, struggle	luchar
oppose	oponerse (a)
separate	separarse
state (an opinion)	opinar
support (a cause, a belief)	apoyar

Adjectives/Adjetivos

| independent | independiente |
| unique, different | único/a |

RESOURCE GUIDE

Books and Articles

Carr, Raymond. *De la restauración a la democracia* (Spanish edition). Barcelona: Planeta Publishing, 1995.

Cenoz, Jasone. "Multilingual Education in the Basque Country." In Cenoz Jasone and Fred Genesee, eds., *Beyond Bilingualism: Multilingualism and Multilingual Education*. Clevedon: Multilingual Matters Ltd., 1998, pp. 175–192.

Clark, Robert P. *The Basques: The Franco Years and Beyond*. Reno: University of Nevada Press, 1979.

Collins, Roger. *The Basques*. Cambridge, MA: Basil Blackwell, 1990.

Douglass, William A., and Jon Bilbao. *Amerikanuak: Basques in the New World*. Reno: University of Nevada Press, 1975.

Estibaliz Ruiz de Azua y Martinez de Ezquerecocha, María. *Vascongadas y America*. Madrid: Editorial MAPFRE, 1992.

Hooper, John. *The New Spaniards*. New York: Penguin, 1995.

Kurlansky, Mark. *The Basque History of the World*. New York: Penguin, 2001.

Laxtalt, Robert. "The Enduring Pyrenees." *National Geographic* (December 1974): 794–819.

———. "Land of the Ancient Basques." *National Geographic* (August 1968): 240–276.

Laxalt, Robert, and Joyce Laxalt. *The Land of My Fathers: A Son's Return to the Basque Country*. Reno: University of Nevada Press, 1999.

Nolan, John E. H. "Life in the Land of the Basques." *National Geographic* (February 1954): 147–187.

Núñez Astrain, Luis. *The Basques: Their Struggle for Independence*. [Cardiff], Wales: Welsh Academic Press, 1997.

Pena Santiago, Luis Pedro. *Leyendas y tradiciones populares del Pais Vasco*. Donostia, San Sebastian: Editorial Txertoa, 1989.

Richardson, Bill. *Spanish studies: An Introduction*. London: Oxford University Press, 2001.

Internet

ABC (national newspaper). <http://www.abc.es>.

Bakio Berbarik Berba (Online database with speech samples). <http://bips.bi.ehu.es/bakio/web/bakio.htm>.

Basque surnames. <http://buber.net/Basque/Surname/surlist.html>.

Basque/Castillian Castillian/Basque online dictionary. <http://www.elhuyar.com/hiztegia/>.

Brief sample of Basque language (audio). <http://www.teleport.com/napoleon/basque/audiosample.html>.

Buber's Basque Page (history, culture, politics). <http://buber.net/Basque/>.

Diario Vasco (news in Spanish from Donostia/San Sebastian). <http://www.diariovasco.com/>.

El Pais (national newspaper). <http://www.elpais.es>.

Larry Trask's Basque Page. <http://www.cogs.susx.ac.uk/users/larryt/basque.html>.

Meet Euskal Herria, the Basque Country. <http://www.geocities.com/Athens/9479/basque.html>.

Noticias de Navarra. <http://www.noticiasdenavarra.com>.

U.S. Border Patrol Agents watch a group of people behind the fence along the U.S.–Mexico border, a traditional staging area for illegal immigration near San Ysidro, California. (AP Photo/Fred Greaves)

Chapter 12

Immigration

> Following the [deaths of] twelve people from Ecuador killed
> when their mini bus was hit by a train on a level crossing . . .
> more details are emerging about the conditions in which
> the paperless immigrants were working. A statement by a union
> spokesman in the area said they worked from dawn to dusk and
> were paid [approximately 3½ cents for every pound] of broccoli
> collected. The union claims that many official complaints had
> been made about the exploitation of immigrants in the area,
> including one made against the employer concerned in this
> case.[1]

Similar news stories are all too common in border and agricultural
areas throughout the United States. But it may surprise you to know
that this tragedy occurred not in the United States, but in Spain,
where Ecuadorians comprise the second-largest group of undocumented immigrants.[2]

The terrorist attacks on the World Trade Center and the Pen-
tagon on September 11, 2001 intensified concerns that many Americans and Europeans already had about immigration. Nevertheless,
people from other parts of the world will continue to seek to live
in North America and Western Europe, with—and often without—
official permission. What compels people to leave their homeland,
often at great sacrifice, and to travel to an unfamiliar country, perhaps never to return? What should the countries that are magnets

for immigrants do about the influx of "undocumented" individuals? The spread of terrorism makes it impossible to ignore. Even in the face of concerns about safety inside the United States, is immigration in general beneficial to the receiving country or is it detrimental?

BACKGROUND

First, we need to be clear about several different motivations for immigration and different types of legal status for immigrants. Some people emigrate[3] to another country to escape turmoil and persecution, most often for political or religious reasons. Certain European countries, such as Germany, France, Sweden and now Spain, have had liberal immigration policies that benefited persons who claimed that they were seeking political or religious freedom. Traditionally, the United States has been another country that opened its doors to people seeking these freedoms. However, standards for proof of persecution have been tightened in recent years for those applying for immigration for reasons of conscience. Another group of persons who seek asylum are women, who want to escape unbearable gender discrimination or brutal customs forced on them in their home countries.

The second category of motivation is for economic and other kinds of opportunity. Countries with robust economies attract immigrants from countries where opportunities for economic and social advancement are poor and where unemployment is high and wages are low.

In the United States, legal immigrants receive approval from the Immigration and Naturalization Service after a formal application, investigation of their case and a relatively lengthy waiting period. Legal (or "documented") immigrants receive a "green card" which shows their legal status. Although the laws change from time to time, in general legal immigrants have the same rights and obligations as native-born or naturalized citizens, although they cannot vote or take part in other activities for which citizenship is required (serve on juries, run for public office, etc.). After another waiting period the immigrant may seek naturalization, that is, a change to American citizenship.

Illegal (also called "undocumented") immigrants have not gone through the formal process or have been denied legal status. Most of them slip into the host country by crossing borders illegally, coming in by boat, hiding in a truck or a container or by using the services of a paid smuggler, called a *coyote* in Spanish. Often undocumented aliens run grave risks to avoid detection by immigration authorities or trust their lives to *coyotes* who may abandon them with no food or water or lock them in trucks or railroad cars to keep them hidden. Another significant number (perhaps as high as 40%) enters the country legally with tourist or other kinds of visas but do not return to their homelands when the visa expires. They disappear into the local population.

The United States is not the only country where immigration laws and the benefits or drawbacks of liberal immigration policies are being debated. All of the countries of the European Union are now receiving growing numbers of people from Eastern Europe, Africa and the Far East. Spain[4] also has experienced a major increase in the number of immigrants from Latin America and North Africa in recent years. Furthermore, unwanted immigration—motivated by economic need or the desire to flee from violence—is a serious issue in areas of several Latin American countries. Let's take a look at the questions about immigration—legal as well as illegal—on both sides of the Atlantic.

1. Should immigration be much more tightly controlled to protect jobs and salaries of home country workers?
2. Do immigrants create burdens on the communities they live in?
3. Do immigrants have an effect of the unity of American (or Spanish) society?
4. Does the presence of illegal immigrants affect the incidence of crime?

DISCUSSION

Should Immigration Be Much More Tightly Controlled to Protect Jobs and Salaries of Home Country Workers?

Agree

Those who answer affirmatively say that our own workers should not have to compete for jobs with people from other countries. We need to take care of the people who are already here. During the decade of the 1990s approximately 10 million people were admitted *legally*—more than twice as many as in the decade of the 1970s. How long can the United States continue to absorb growing numbers of immigrants?

Proponents of this argument are concerned about both legal and illegal immigration, but they are most alarmed by the numbers of illegal immigrants. The U.S. government estimates that in the late 1990s, 300,000 people a year entered the country illegally and five times that number attempted to come into the country each year without proper documents.[5]

Illegal immigration has become a growing problem in Spain as well. Only a few miles separate Spain from Morocco and many individuals, mostly men, attempt the crossing in overcrowded small boats. Others try to enter through the Canary Islands, the Spanish autonomous community in the Atlantic Ocean off the coast of Africa. Their motivation is almost always economic: the unemployment rate is higher in Morocco and the per capita income is about one-fifth of the income of Spaniards. Ecuadorians and other Latin Americans must travel from thousands of miles away and usually enter the country with tourist visas. A common language and cultural similarities, such as religion, facilitate their transition into the Spanish workforce.[6] After a few years in Spain, only about one-third of immigrants express an intention to return to their home countries. In the case of immigrants from North Africa the percentage is even lower, around 15%.

Disagree

Those who oppose tightening immigration laws say that we should not be so concerned about the numbers of immigrants. Many experts believe that immigrants—far from being a detriment to the U.S. economy or hurting our native-born workforce—help our economy to continue to grow. It has been shown that immigrants do many jobs that Americans are increasingly unwilling to do. Many immigrants with very limited English or low-level job skills find work in construction, on farms, in hotels and restaurants, and cleaning homes and offices. American companies have had difficulty in recent years finding enough workers to fill these positions. Motivated to succeed, most immigrants are extremely hard working and often successful; the rate of creation of small businesses is higher among immigrants than among native-born Americans.

Immigrants with skills and high levels of education bring many benefits to our economy, and again, in recent years, the demand has outstripped the supply of workers in certain areas—especially science and technology. The question of depressed salaries is somewhat harder to prove or disprove. However, in areas such as agriculture, construction, hotels and restaurants, consumers benefit from low wages paid by the companies they patronize.

The same arguments are heard in Spain, where immigrants perform many jobs that few Spaniards are now willing to take, particularly as seasonal laborers in the fields and as domestic workers in homes. The largest numbers come from North Africa, especially Morocco, and some Latin American countries, such as Ecuador and the Dominican Republic. In Spain, much of the debate about immigration revolved around extending to immigrants the rights to representation by unions, due process and revising immigration laws. In 2001, under the leadership of the conservative *Partido Popular* (People's Party), the Spanish parliament enacted a law that denied immigrants the right to demonstrate, belong to a trade union or strike and allowed authorities to expel those without the proper documents within 48 to 72 hours of their detention, a policy that was more strict than other EU countries and that was sharply criticized by the opposition. With its extremely low birthrate, Spain will have to accept immigrants to replace many of its retiring workers, since there will not be enough young Spaniards to fill the jobs. Spaniards are finding it hard to face the truth about the need for immigrant workers, as do citizens of other EU nations, which will need something on the order of 44 million new immigrants by the year 2050.[7]

Do Immigrants Create Burdens on the Communities They Live in?

Agree

Many Americans believe that immigrants—especially undocumented immigrants in low-paying jobs—put a heavy burden on public facilities, such as emergency rooms and schools. Since most are unable to buy homes, they contribute little in property taxes. To avoid detection, illegal immigrants often prefer to be paid in cash, and so they are able to avoid state and federal income taxes. This means that the rest of the population ends up paying for the services used by immigrants. Furthermore, a substantial percentage of immigrants send much of their earnings to their families back home instead of spending it in the host country, where it would produce taxes and generate more jobs. In effect, the host country ends up subsidizing families in the country of origin of the immigrants as well.

Approximately 20% of legal immigrants in the United States come from Latin America: Mexico, the Dominican Republic, Cuba, El Salvador and Colombia supply the largest numbers. School systems in California, Arizona, Texas, Florida and certain other states are especially affected by large numbers of children from Spanish-speaking families. In 1982, the U.S. Supreme Court ruled that schools could not deny admission to children of illegal immigrants. Immigrants typically have larger families than non-immigrants in both the United States and Spain. Their children need special classes so that they can learn English (or in Spain, Spanish); therefore, areas with large immigrant populations will be especially hard hit.

Proposition 187, a hotly debated referendum approved by 52% of voters in California in 1994, attempted to deny public benefits and services (for example, public schooling and non-emergency medical care) to illegal aliens and required personnel in state facilities such as schools, clinics and hospitals to report all suspected illegal aliens to the appropriate state authorities. (Many of the provisions of the proposition were later ruled unconstitutional.)

Some people on this side of the issue would like to bring back a version of the *bracero* program, which from 1942 to 1964 allowed Mexican agricultural workers to work legally in the United States. This kind of controlled admission of foreign workers would lessen the impact on services and still provide the labor force that American farmers and businesses say they need.[8]

Disagree

Those who disagree contend that immigrants actually contribute more to the host country than they get out of it in services.[9] Because schools receive much of their support from state and federal funds based on enrollment, these sources of income help to offset increases in student enrollment at the local level that are caused by an influx of immigrant children. Furthermore, undocumented workers pay taxes, particularly sales taxes, to state and local governments. If taxes are withheld from their paychecks, they seldom file for tax refunds because they fear that their illegal status will be discovered. For the same reason, undocumented aliens often do not ask for services from local and state governments.

Many illegal immigrants would become citizens or permanent residents if they had the chance. For many people on this side of the issue, it makes sense for the federal government to declare an "amnesty," which would allow undocumented aliens who have resided in the United States for a specific period of time to "regularize" their status. This was done in 1986 and a more restrictive program was signed into law in December 2000.[10] However, the cost for application for regularization of immigrant status was high ($1,000) and the conditions for approval of the application were both complicated and impractical. Mexican president Vicente Fox has made reforming immigration a key to a new relationship with the United States.

Spain experienced a period not too long ago when its own citizens needed to emigrate for economic reasons. In the 1960s tens of thousands of Spanish workers, mostly men from rural areas, left to work in the factories of Germany, France and in service industries in England and other European countries. Their *giros* (money orders) sent back to families in Spanish towns and villages helped to fuel Spain's spectacular economic recovery and paved the way for the development of democracy. Several decades of prosperity have dimmed the memories of immigrant life, however, and the Spanish public is no longer necessarily sympathetic to immigrants on its own soil. Nevertheless, stories in the Spanish press of abuses of immigrant workers have awakened many people in Spain to the need to regularize undocumented workers who have a long period of residence. Under pressure from Spanish human rights groups, new regulations were issued in the year 2000, and in that year alone 140,000 of the estimated 300,000 undocumented immigrants living in Spain were granted legal status.[11]

Do Immigrants Have an Effect on the Unity of American (or Spanish) Society?

Agree

According to many Americans, the United States has always been a "melting pot" where people of different ethnic and national origins came together and quickly embraced the American way of life. This included accepting English as the mother tongue and accepting American values. More recent immigrants have been less willing to do this. Little Havana (Miami), East L.A. and Calle 8 (Los Angeles) and Little Mexico (Chicago) attest to the concentration of Latinos in certain *barrios* of major U.S. cities. They demand bilingual education that only perpetuates their isolation from mainstream American culture. Bilingual ballots and official notices, mandated by federal law, are costly and should be unnecessary. While local and ethnic customs are colorful and even economically beneficial in some cases, in general we should encourage everyone to become a part of the mainstream.

The English language is an especially important component of American culture. The "English Only" movement has attempted to have English named as the *official* language of the United States and to eliminate programs of bilingual education that aim to do anything other than move children from first language to English in the shortest possible time. For this reason, the advocates of English Only support English immersion programs rather than bilingual education.

In Spain, although there is some concern over concentrations of immigrant populations, to date there has been less public anxiety over issues of the cost of public services, such as schooling and health care. In part this may be due to Spain's more centralized system of collection of taxes and distribution of government funds. In addition, many immigrants, both legal and illegal, come from Spanish-speaking countries, and fewer arrive with or arrange for the arrival of their families due to the distance and expense involved. Nevertheless, as the numbers of immigrants have grown rapidly, Spaniards have grown more concerned. Between 1996 and 2001, the attitudes of Spanish citizens showed considerable change. In 1995, only 29% believed there were too many inmigrants; by 2001 42% held this view.[12] Tensions have risen, too. Fights between immigrants and Spaniards and hate crimes committed against immigrants attest to the lack of acceptance of newcomers, especially those whose linguistic and cultural differences make them more visible. In recent years, Spain has seen a disturbing rise in the number of "skinhead" and neo-fascist groups.

Disagree

Studies show that in most immigrant communities in the United States, English quickly becomes the dominant language in the younger generation. In fact, by the third generation, most immigrant families have lost the "home" language for all practical purposes. Latino families also undergo a significant reduction in the use of Spanish that accelerates with each generation in the United States.

Spanish maintains a higher percentage of speakers than most other languages for several reasons. These include proximity to Spanish-speaking homelands, particularly Mexico and Puerto Rico; the over-all larger number of Spanish-speaking immigrants; and, finally, their concentration in several states and metropolitan areas.[13] There are upwards of 35 million people in the United States who call themselves Hispanic.[14]

Most Latinos say that learning English is very important. Far from discouraging their children to learn English, most Hispanic families impress upon their children the need to learn English as important to success in school and future jobs. Ironically, we discourage immigrant families from maintaining their home country languages, often claiming that bilingualism holds children back in school, and then spend money to teach some of the same tongues as foreign languages to other children in our schools and colleges.

Many researchers point out that fear of immigrants is nothing new in the United States. Italians, Irish, Germans, Chinese, Jews, Poles, Japanese and other immigrant groups who immigrated to the United States in large numbers in the 1800s and the early twentieth century were often accused of clannishness, slowness to learn English, ignorance and immorality. Today it would be hard to say that these groups did not go on to integrate themselves successfully into the fabric of American life. People on this side of the issue ask: Is American culture not richer for whatever part of their cultural heritage these groups were able to sustain—music, food, celebrations, contributions to our language, values and traditions?

Does the Presence of Illegal Immigrants Affect the Incidence of Crime?

Agree

Some published articles conclude that crime goes up in localities where immigration is high, whether from crime that victimizes immigrants or from immigrants that commit offenses. Many immigrants come from countries where banks are unreliable or they may not be familiar with setting up and using a bank account, so they prefer to carry or hide their savings in cash. Knowing this, criminals target them for robbery. "Con artists" also prey on immigrants' poor knowledge of American laws and English, charging them for services that are unnecessary or free. Because illegal aliens fear exposure and deportation they are much less likely to report crimes, and even legal immigrants are often hesitant to get involved with the police. Communities that experience an influx of immigrants may also report increases in illegal drugs, gang activities, robberies and violent crimes. In response, critics say, the economy worsens in these communities, too. People on this side of the issue often point out that employers of illegal immigrants are rarely punished, although the Immigration Reform and Control Act (IRCA) of 1986 made knowingly hiring an undocumented person an offense punishable by fines from $250 to $10,000 for each unauthorized worker and a maximum six-month prison sentence if a pattern of illicit hiring behavior was discovered.

The United States is not alone in treating immigrants with suspicion. A student of immigration policy in Spain notes "the marked contrast between the integrationist rhetoric accompanying these laws . . . and their actual content, which systematically marginalizes immigrants and circumscribes their rights."[15] Furthermore, although nearly 95% of Spaniards consider themselves tolerant of immigrants and believe they are entitled to live and work abroad, around 45% say that they notice that other Spaniards appear to be suspicious of immigrants.[16]

Disagree

Both sides agree that immigrants are often targets of crime and exploitation. However, advocates of more liberal immigration laws point out that it is the illegality of undocumented aliens that makes them especially vulnerable. If immigrants didn't fear deportation, they would be much more likely to step forward to report crimes and unfair treatment. As it is, the cycle of crime within immigrant communities goes largely unchecked by authorities, and unscrupulous employers can pay wages far below the minimum legal wage. For the same reasons illegal aliens are also reluctant to join unions or other groups that would fight for their rights and better treatment. Progressive communities with substantial immigrant communities provide information in Spanish or other appropriate languages to help their residents understand the services that are available and the rules that are supposed to protect privacy of personal information. The private sector, such as banks, can also help to reduce robberies by providing low-cost, easy-to-understand basic banking service to community members who are unfamiliar with using financial institutions.

People on this side of the issue point out that the vast majority of immigrants, both legal and undocumented, are hardworking, honest people (as honest as the rest of the population). Amnesty (granting legal status) to immigrants who can show a long period of residence and no record of serious offenses would go a long way in reducing crime against immigrants. Asking employers to be responsible for policing immigrant status is inappropriate because it leads to discrimination against all "foreigners" as well as U.S. citizens who may look or sound "different" from the local majority. This approach is also ineffective because immigration or citizenship documents can be forged.

The federal government has increased the number of Border Patrol officers dramatically in recent years, but illegal immigration has not declined; meanwhile, hundreds of men and women have died—most of them from dehydration and exposure—in Southwestern deserts or at the hands of *coyotes*. The solution lies not in law enforcement and legal barriers, but in better economic conditions in Mexico,[17] Central America and other poor countries.

Spain faces a similar situation. In the year 2000 the bodies of about 100 immigrants were washed up on Spanish beaches; others who drowned were surely never found. Every week, Spanish newspapers report the apprehension of more illegal aliens or, tragically, the discovery of more would-be immigrants who did not survive the nighttime boat ride across the Strait of Gibraltar. Differences in income and opportunities between Spain and the countries of origin of its illegal immigrants push people to take enormous risks.

Ironically, in both the United States and Spain, evidence is mounting that professional criminal rings are replacing small-time operators in the business of smuggling people across international borders. Often these criminal gangs have extensive experience in other illegal operations, such as drug trafficking. Tight immigration policies only make it more profitable for large-scale criminal organizations to become involved. The charge for smuggling an illegal immigrant across the Strait of Gibraltar in an inflated rubber raft was estimated at around $550 in the year 2000; for the same crossing by ferry, with forged documents and a bus or train ticket waiting on the other side, an illegal alien would have to pay around $2,000.[18]

QUESTIONS AND ACTIVITIES

1. Developments in immigration law are followed closely by the Spanish language news media in the United States. Monitor the issue in a regional Spanish-language newspaper from your area or Spanish-language television news. What is the latest development in immigration policy? Write a short paper explaining any new changes.

2. Not all Hispanics favor lenient immigration laws. Make a list of questions to elicit opinions about immigration and recent changes (or proposed changes) to immigration policy. Interview several people from the Hispanic community in your town or city. Be sure to determine age, place of birth and, for people born outside the United States, how long they have lived in the United States and if they are resident aliens or U.S. citizens. Their level of education and occupation might also be data you should collect. Report what you learn in writing or in an oral report. Compare what you learn with other students and present your findings to the class in Spanish. You could also use the same information for a special report in a class in Civics or American Government.

3. Immigrants, whether they arrived legally or illegally, often have interesting or dramatic life stories. Interview a Latino immigrant to discover why he/she decided to come to the United States. Describe his/her difficulties (if any) in obtaining permission from the home country to leave or from the United States to enter and settle here. What has been this person's experience in the United States? Make a list of questions to guide the conversation to obtain the information you are most interested in. If your subject agrees, make a tape recording of the interview. Then write a report and present an oral summary of the report to the class.

4. Imagine that you and your classmates have been called to testify before a fact-finding group that will report on the experience of Latino immigrants at an international meeting to be held in Costa Rica. Divide into two groups. One will explain the viewpoint of *opponents* of liberalizing U.S. immigration laws; the other will speak about reasons why the laws should be liberalized.

5. Other countries in the Western Hemisphere have substantial immigrant populations as well. Mexico, for example, has had a large group of refugees from Guatemala, mostly indigenous people living near the

Guatemalan border. Use Spanish-language newspapers (published in the United States or on the Internet) to investigate the reasons refugees (*refugiados, exiliados*) left Guatemala and conditions in refugee communities.

6. Investigate the reasons for the large numbers of Ecuadorians and/or Dominicans who have recently emigrated to Spain. Online editions of Spanish newspapers and newspapers from Ecuador and the Dominican Republic will be your best sources of information. Search for relevant articles with terms such as *emigrante* or *emigrar* and *España/Ecuador/ Republica Dominicana*. The term *inmigrante(s)* will also yield results.

7. Ecuador and other countries sharing a border with Colombia have experienced a rising number of immigrants from that nation. (The United States also has a substantial number of Colombian immigrants.) Use online newspapers and other Internet services to discover the reasons behind the increase in Colombian emigration. Prepare a news story on the Colombian emigrés and the effect of this emigration on Colombia's neighboring countries.

8. The film *Cartas de Alou* (*Letters from Alou*) portrays the obstacles facing illegal immigrants in Spain; *El Norte* relates the odyssey of two young Guatemalans who flee to the United States. View one of these films. Explain the reasons for emigrating, hazards and conditions facing illegal immigrants portrayed in the film. Do you think the film was realistic? Explain why or why not.

9. The largest group of foreign nationals living in Spain is from Morocco. Do research to discover discrepancies between the professed attitudes toward North Africans and the treatment and conditions of North African immigrants. Contrast the attitudes expressed in surveys with the first-person account of Francisco Goldman in "Moro Like Me."[19]

10. What effect does the growing Hispanic population (estimated at more 35 million) have on North American business culture? Investigate the response of businesses and media to the news of the surprising growth of this population and the roughly $400 billion it spends annually inside the United States. Prepare a report using news sources. If possible, use a searchable database, such as Lexis-Nexis, at your school or public library. Look for sources in Spanish as well as English. Useful Spanish terms will include *censo, población,* and *crecimiento*.

11. If your city has a sizable Latino population, do the public service sector (hospitals, utilities, city services, schools) and major businesses (banks, large employers, large retail outlets, major grocery store chains) offer information and/or advertise in Spanish? If your school has Spanish-speaking students or parents with limited English skills, is there infor-

mation available in Spanish to explain the most important school and school district policies?

VOCABULARY/VOCABULARIO

Nouns/Sustantivos

abuse	el abuso
age	la edad
agriculture	la agricultura
amnesty	la anmistía
attitude	la actitud
boss	el jefe
business	las empresas, los negocios
citizenship	la ciudadanía
conditions, living	el nivel de vida
conditions, working	las condiciones de trabajo
discrimination	la discriminación
dream	el sueño
effect	el efecto
fear	el miedo
growth (in size)	el crecimiento
housing	la vivienda
immigrant	el/la inmigrante
immigrant, illegal	el inmigrante ilegal, el indocumentado
immigration	la imigracion
information	la información
job	un trabajo, un empleo
laws	las leyes
media	los medios de comunicación
migrant	el migrante
Moors	los moros
Morroco	Marruecos
Moslems	los musulmanes
nationality	la nacionalidad
necessity, need	la necesidad

news	las noticias
opponent	el opositor
owner	el dueño
permission	el permiso
place of birth	el lugar de nacimiento
police	la policía, las autoridades
population	la población
poverty	la pobreza
protection	la protección
reason, motive	el motivo, el impulso
refugees	los refugiados
residence	la residencia
residence (home)	el domicilio
restriction	la restricción
rights	los derechos
services	los servicios
speaker, native	el/la hablante nativo/a
speaker of Spanish	el/la hablante de español, el hispanohablante
unemployment	el desempleo
violence	la violencia
wages, salary	el pago, el salario
wealth	la riqueza
work	el trabajo, el empleo

Verbs/Verbos

abuse, mistreat	abusar
admire	admirar
be unemployed	estar sin trabajo
die	morir
earn (money)	ganar
favor, be in favor of	favorecer, estar a favor (de)
fear, be afraid	tener miedo (de)
give amnesty	amnistiar
grow	crecer

immigrate	imigrar
interview	entrevistar
look down upon	despreciar
motivate	motivar
oppose	oponerse (a)
protect	proteger
refuse	negarse (a), rechazar
travel	viajar

Adjectives/Adjetivos

hardworking	trabajador/a
lenient, permissive	permisivo/a, liberal
poor	pobre
realistic	realista (m. and f.)
strict	estricto/a

RESOURCE GUIDE

Books and Articles

Baron, Dennis. *The English-Only Question: An Official Language for Americans?* New Haven, CT: Yale University Press, 1992.

Becerra, Hector, and Fred Alvarez. "Census Reflects Large Gains for Latinos." *Los Angeles Times*, May 10, 2001, Section 2, p. 1.

Calavita, Kitty. "Immigration, Law, and Marginalization in a Global Economy: Notes from Spain." *Law & Society Review* 32(3) (1998): 529–566.

Castaneda, Ruben. "Some Domestics Left Open to Abuse, Study Says." *Washington Post*, June 14, 2001, p. B3.

Chavez, Lydia. *The Color Bind: California's Battle to End Affirmative Action.* Berkeley: University of California Press, 1998.

Goldman, Francisco. "Moro Like Me." In C. Chiawei O'Hearn, ed., *Half and Half: Writers Growing Up Biracial and Bicultural.* New York: Pantheon, 1998, pp. 49–70.

Harwood, Edwin. "Can We Solve the Illegal Immigration Problem?" *Business Forum* (Fall 1985): 20–21.

Hooper, John. *The New Spaniards.* New York: Penguin, 1995.

LeMay, Michael, and Elliott Robert Barkan, eds. *U.S. Immigration and Naturalization Laws and Issues: A Documentary History*. Westport, CT: Greenwood Press, 1999.

Sole, Carlota, "Racial Discrimination against Foreigners in Spain." *New Community* 21(1) (1995): 95.

Internet

Boletín. Centro de Investigaciónes Sociológicas (CIS) (Spain). <http://www.cis.es/boletin/index.html>.

Center for Immigration Studies. <http://www.cis.org>.

Eurostat (European Union). <http://europa.eu.int/comm/eurostat/>.

Immigration and Naturalization Service. <http://www.ins.usdoj.gov/graphics/index.htm>.

Video

El Norte. Gregory Nava, director. Videocassette. [Los Angeles, CA]: Frontera Films, 1983. Color. 141 min.

El Súper. Leon Ichaso and Orlando Jimenez-Leal, directors. Videocassette. New York: New Yorker Video, 1979. Color. 80 min.

Las Cartas de Alou [*Letters from Alou*]. Montxo Armendáriz, director. Videocassette (Spain). Santa Monica, CA: Connoisseur Video Collection, 1994. Color. 100 min.

Nueba Yol. Ángel Muñiz, director. Videocassette. [United States]: Kit Parker Films, 1995. 102 min.

The Ties That Bind: Immigration Stories. José Roberto Gutiérrez, director. Videocassette. Princeton, NJ: Films for the Humanities & Sciences, 1996. Color. 56 min.

Chapter 13

Catholicism

Some 90% of Spaniards and as many as 97% of the population of some Latin American countries say that they are Roman Catholics, yet only about one-fourth or fewer attend church on a regular basis. What is the future of the faith that put its stamp on Hispanic cultures on both sides of the Atlantic?

BACKGROUND

Christianity sank roots very early in Spanish soil. Legends told of visits of St. James the Apostle to Spain in the first century and how his body was inexplicably transported by sea to Galicia, in the far northwestern corner of the Iberian Peninsula, to be found centuries later in a place that would be named Santiago de Campostela.

Spanish prelates played significant roles in early church history. As Roman civilization faltered and then crumbled, the Church in Spain—as elsewhere throughout Western Europe—became the refuge of learned men and culture in the Dark Ages. St. Isidore, bishop of Seville, for example, authored theological and historical works as well as the *Etymologiae*, a compendium of classical learning that became the mainstay of medieval libraries not only in Spain but also throughout Europe for several centuries.[1]

During the Middle Ages and early modern times, the Church and Spanish kingdoms developed side by side. The *Reconquista* (Reconquest), a centuries-long campaign to recover lands lost to the Moors

Women and girls wearing black dresses
and mantillas walk in a daylight Holy
Week procession in Zamora, Spain. (Stephanie Maze/CORBIS)

in the eighth century, pushed the goals of church and state even
closer as the Reconquest gradually took on the quality of a crusade
against the Moslem occupiers. Once a region where Jews, Moslems
and Christians coexisted and even intermarried with some frequency, by January of the year 1492 the Christian monarchs of
Spain accepted the surrender of the last remaining Moorish kingdom. The Jews were forced to either convert or leave Spain in the
same year; Moslems would follow during the next century. It was
clear that Spain would no longer tolerate any religion other than
Christianity.

The sixteenth and seventeenth centuries brought the conquest and
colonization of much of the Western Hemisphere and Spain's *Siglo
de Oro* (Golden Age) as well as a protracted struggle to defend
Roman Catholicism from twin enemies: the heretical Christian Prot-

estants of northern Europe and the powerful Islamic Turks in the eastern Mediterranean.

Spanish monarchs, determined to defend the Catholic faith at any cost, drove Spain deep into debt. Phillip II's dream of forcing England to return to the Catholic fold was thwarted by the defeat of the Great Armada. Nevertheless, the loyalty of most of Spain's populace to the Church (as well as to the monarchy) did not falter. To insure this, the Inquisition or Holy Office (*el Santo Oficio de la Inquisición*) watched over the doctrinal correctness of Spaniards' beliefs and the moral correctness of their behavior from 1478 until 1834. The Inquisition also censored ideas: books had to be approved before they were published inside Spain or imported from abroad.[2]

The *Ilustración* (Enlightenment) of the eighteenth century, however, represented a turning point in Spanish religious history. New ideas were circulating in France, England and the rest of Europe. Some Spanish intellectuals defied the Inquisition's attempts to control their spread by smuggling in and circulating the writings of French philosophers such as Voltaire and Rousseau, as well as scientific tracts. These *ilustrados* (men of the Enlightenment) looked to reason, not faith alone, for an explanation of the natural world and solutions to their practical problems. They also questioned the authority of the Church and the behavior of the clergy.[3]

As the nineteenth century dawned, Spain was no longer a Catholic monolith. The abdication of the young king Ferdinand VII and occupation of Spain by Napoleon's troops in 1808 helped to rupture the unity of the populace. The strongly nationalistic clergy supported the people's revolt against the invaders. Many of the *ilustrados* were torn between their loyalty to their homeland and their impatience with the backwardness of traditional Spain. After the defeat of the French and the restoration of the Spanish monarchy, nineteenth-century Spanish governments seesawed between conservative governments that backed the Church to the hilt and liberal governments that wanted to separate the state from the Church, dismantle its landholdings and loosen its control over education. By mid-century, other political developments began to exacerbate the existing tensions. The Spanish masses had, for the most part, gone along with the Church throughout the seventeenth and eighteenth centuries; now they began to see the Church as parasitic and as a supporter of the rich against the poor. In the cities and in the rural south, working-class Spaniards were attracted to socialism and anarchism, which gave voice to their political grievances and to their growing anticlerical sentiments.

By the end of the nineteenth century, Spanish intellectuals were talking about the two Spains: one yearning to be progressive, democratic and decidedly anticlerical, the other traditional, monarchist and Catholic. This growing dissension came to a head in the 1930s, when a tide of antimonarchist sentiment forced King Alfonso XIII to leave the country. The new government that formed in the power vacuum was republican (i.e., an elected government without a monarch) and anticlerical. Internal divisions on the left allowed a Catholic party, the Spanish Confederation of the Autonomous Right (*Confederación Espanola de Derechas Autonomas*, or CEDA), to rule briefly, but new elections ushered in another leftist administration, which could not control—some said did not want to control— the anticlerical extremists. Priests were harassed; several churches and convents were sacked and burned.

The Republic lasted only a few years; in 1936 the military rose against it. In the ensuing three years of civil war, the Nationalists (a coalition of the military, monarchist, antisocialist/anticommunist and Catholic factions) united together against the anticlerical, mostly left-wing republicans. By the spring of 1939 the Republic was defeated, but *Generalísimo* Francisco Franco, commander in chief of the rebel forces, still needed the backing of the Church. The Church feared the anticlerical left and supported the Nationalist government.[4] Under Franco, the Church received money to rebuild churches damaged or destroyed in the war; the sale of contraceptives and divorce (legalized under the Republic) was abolished and religious instruction was mandated in all schools. The Church was given the power to censor publications, films and broadcast media. This marriage of Church and state received the title of *Catolicismo Nacional* (National Catholicism).

Nevertheless, after several decades the Church began to distance itself from the dictator. Following the lead of the Second Vatican Council and a Church leadership that was more sensitive to the needs of the lower classes and to the changes taking place outside of Spain, by the end of the 1960s the Church began to press for political and social changes. When the *Generalísimo* died in 1975, Cardinal Enrique y Tarancón placed the crown on his successor, Juan Carlos II, knowing that the Catholic Church had helped to move Spain away from dictatorship and toward democracy. He also surely knew that things would never again be the same for the Church in Spain. Once Spain had closed the door on dictatorship, the task for the Church would change from pressing for general freedoms to looking out to assure its own freedom in an increasingly secular environment.

And what about Latin America, today the home of approximately 300 million Hispanic Catholics? Beginning with the conquest of the Americas, Spain's colonies became new ground for the expansion of Christianity. Initially Franciscan and Dominican friars, and then other religious orders and "secular" clergy (i.e., not affiliated with one of the religious orders), came to the New World to indoctrinate indigenous peoples and to serve the spiritual needs of growing numbers of Spanish colonists, *mestizos* and other members of colonial society.

The history of the Church is somewhat different in each Latin American country, but in general the Church enjoyed immense influence and economic power during the three centuries of Spanish colonial rule. After 1810, when independence movements took shape, the Church hierarchy was loyal to Spain, but many local priests were sympathizers and even leaders of independence movements. Examples from Mexico are Miguel Hidalgo and José Morelos, both of whom paid for their political convictions with their lives. After independence, the Church broke with the new nations. In some countries years passed before priests could hold public services. As in Spain, the power and privilege of the Catholic Church came under attack by the liberal parties during the remainder of the nineteenth century. Church property was expropriated (for example, under the Reform Laws in Mexico in the 1850s). After the Mexican Revolution (ca. 1910–1920), even the church buildings became the property of the state and priests were forbidden to wear cassocks.

However, in other countries church and state relations returned to a more comfortable level a few decades after independence. True freedom of choice in religion did not become a reality until the twentieth century in Latin America. Separation of church and state functions is still problematic in some countries (for example, legalization of divorce, public health issues involving abortion and contraception and religious instruction in the schools). In several Latin American nations the clergy has played an important role in denouncing human rights abuses (for example, in El Salvador) or in aiding victims of repressive regimes and their families (as in Chile during the Pinochet dictatorship). However, in a few countries members of the clergy stood by during the torture and murder of civilian prisioners of repressive governments—most notably during the so-called Dirty War (*Guerra Sucia*) in Argentina.

What are some of the questions people have asked about the modern Church and its future in Spain and Latin America?

1. Will Spain and Latin America continue to be bulwarks of Catholicism in the twenty-first century?
2. Do Spanish and Latin American Catholics support the doctrines and policies of the Catholic Church at the turn of the twenty-first century?
3. Are citizens and religious institutions satisfied with the relationship between church and state in Spanish and Latin American governments?

DISCUSSION

Will Spain and Latin America Continue to Be Bulwarks of Catholicism in the Twenty-First Century?

Agree

For hundreds of years Spain produced a surplus of priests. Many of them went to Latin America and even the United States to work in parishes or as missionaries. A Spanish priest, José María Escrivá de Balaguer, founded the influential and controversial Opus Dei (the Work of God) in 1928. Spain and Latin America are strongholds of this organization, which is comprised mostly of laymen and women and who number about 80,000 worldwide today, including members in the United States. The conservative religious and political views of Opus members fit well with Franco's Spain, and lay members were instrumental in saving Spain from financial collapse at the end of the 1950s and setting it on its way toward an "economic miracle" in the 1960s. Today the Opus operates numerous schools and several universities. Many prominent religious, economic and political leaders in Hispanic countries are said to be members.[5] While only a small minority, they exert an important influence in secular and Church affairs.[6]

As birthrates plummet in traditional European Catholic strongholds such as Spain, Italy, France and Germany, the relative importance of Latin American prelates and their brethren from other developing nations is likely to grow. Just under 300 million—about one-third of the world's Catholics—live in Latin America. Sheer numbers alone will guarantee that Latin America will figure prominently in the Church in the future. In 2001 Pope John Paul II appointed 12 new cardinals from Latin America, bringing their total number to 27 of the 135 cardinals and ensuring a greater voice for Latin American Catholicism in the international Church.

The Church has had and continues to have significant moral authority and political influence in Latin America, though much less so in Spain today. In the recent past Catholic clergymen and women played critical roles in bringing attention to the plight of victims of political oppression and poverty, sometimes at the cost of martyrdom. In the United States, the best known of these was Salvadoran Archbishop Oscar Romero. He was eventually slain on orders of powerful ultra right-wing individuals who wanted to silence his denunciations of their political violence. The activism of the Church received encouragement from a movement called liberation theology, which grew out of the work and writings of Latin American theologians in the 1960s and gained momentum in the 1970s. By encouraging the poor to examine and take an active role in seeking solutions to their problems, liberation theology attracted critics who accused religious leaders of promoting Communism. Under John Paul II, the focus of the Church has moved sharply away from social activism toward more traditional moral and pastoral concerns. However, in recent years members of the Church hierarchy have not been silent with respect to other kinds of problems and, in doing so, have often risked their lives. Bishops in Mexico and Colombia who have spoken out against corruption and the influence of drug dealers have been gunned down, and no doubt murders like these will continue as long as criminals derive so much power from the profits of illegal drugs.

On a more positive note, the prominence of Christian Democratic parties in several countries means that the voice of the Church may be able to play an important role in integrating Latin Americans into the international political and economic scene. Christian Democratic parties have a special opportunity to support democracy and the humane growth of capitalism:

Substantial evidence exists that Latin Americans desire free market reform, but also insist upon policies that mitigate [its] initial, painful effects.

... A party with both a genuine respect for, and healthy fear of, capitalism reflects the desires of the majority of Latin American voters. That is why Catholic social thought, which combines this respect and fear and appeals to Latin America's overwhelmingly Catholic majority, stands the best chance of implementing free market reform in Latin America without undermining the region's hard-won democratization.[7]

Disagree

People who believe that the influence of the Catholic Church is waning point out that fewer Spaniards and Latin Americans attend church regularly now than in the past. A very large proportion of Catholics in both Spain and Latin America are "cultural" Catholics, ones who show up for important life events (baptism, marriage, funerals) but seldom attend church. In Latin America, the number of Catholics who regularly attend Sunday mass is estimated at 6 to 10%. Some of the poor attendance is attributed to the shortage of priests, about 1 per 6,000 of the population in Chile, for example.[8] In Spain, recent estimates calculate that about 25% of Catholics attend services regularly. However, the majority of regular attendees are older people. Interest in religion among youth, and the number of young men enrolling for study for the priesthood in particular, has declined dramatically in Spain.

In both Spain and Latin America, the clergy place much of the blame for the lack of interest in religion on the increasing degree of secularization and consumerism in modern life. In the past, attendance at mass followed by a family gathering was the norm for most families. Nowadays, weekends, including Sundays, are the time when Latin Americans and Spaniards flock to soccer games, parks, department stores and *hipermercados* (malls) to be entertained and to consume the merchandise advertised on radio and television. In Spain, legislation allowing increased hours of service on Sundays met with criticism from the clergy, who pointed out that not all of life is production and consumption (*"no todo es producción y consumo"*[9]). They reminded Spaniards that Sundays serve an important social as well as religious purpose: they are a time for the family to be together and a needed antidote for the incessant pressure of work—more important than ever now that more women are employed. Frequent admonitions that non-attendance at mass is a grave sin and that Sunday is for God and not for soccer has had little discernible effect on increasing the numbers in the pews on Sunday.

In addition to the general downturn in attendance, the Catholic Church is faced with growing competition from other religions. In Spain, for example, the fastest-growing faith is Islam, which is said to have more than one-half million adherents.[10] Traditional Spanish Moslems probably account for about 30,000 and are, for the most part, moderate Islamic Spaniards whose families have been Spanish citizens for generations. The largest number of Moslems in Spain are recent immigrants from North Africa and the Middle East, most of whom are fundamentalists.

Although both Jews and Moslems are present in small numbers in Latin America, Protestantism is the fastest-growing faith in Hispanic countries in the Western Hemisphere. Estimates of the numbers of Protestants vary rather widely, from about 50 to 65 million in 1997.[11] While virtually all Protestant sects are represented in Latin America, Evangelical churches have grown spectacularly in recent decades. About three-fourths of these new converts belong to Pentecostal or charismatic groups. Evangelicals are most successful with the poor.[12] Although in most countries it is unlikely that Protestants will outnumber Catholics any time soon, five or six countries may have Protestant majorities by 2010. In a few countries, such as Guatemala, Protestants already claim 30% of the population. Furthermore, because so many of the region's Catholics are Catholic in name only, experts believe that *active* church membership is already about the same for both groups in many countries.[13] After decades of dismissing the growth of Protestant churches, the Catholic Church hierarchy is now showing real concern about the need to evangelize more actively, especially in the rapidly expanding urban areas, and a need to provide for more priests.

The first Protestants to make an impact in Latin America arrived shortly after independence in the early 1800s. Initially Protestants attracted considerable public hostility, and there was strong social pressure to remain within the Catholic fold. However, changes that took place in the second half of the twentieth century, especially urbanization and increasing secularization of society, have loosened social networks. Protestantism began to grow in the 1940s, and the pace of growth has not slowed. One reason for the success of Protestantism is its flexibility. In many Protestant denominations, ministers can easily come up through the ranks of the faithful. They do not need to invest long years of study to qualify for the ministry: anyone can preach. Some of the Protestant denominations, such as

Pentecostals, also stress healing, which is a powerfully attractive element, especially among the poor. In addition, the emphasis that many denominations place on individual control and family responsibility also has strong appeal:

Marginalized people tend to have difficulty holding down jobs, controlling drinking, [and] keeping families intact. Pentecostals have gone to the poorest sections of cities. . . . They've gotten people to stop drinking, and taught them to read and to take family responsibilities seriously. Consequently, Protestantism has created upward mobility. As people become more self-disciplined and responsible, they start to become leaders in their businesses and communities. In addition, such churches become places where people who are nobodies can become somebodies. People whose voice does not matter in society can prophesy in the church.[14]

African American religions (for example, Ifa or Yoruba religion in Cuba and santería in the Caribbean, among others[15]) and indigenous religions also have a significant following in certain areas. Syncretism, or the blending of African or indigenous religious beliefs and customs with Catholic ones, is visible in the popular Catholicism in many areas. During the last decade, indigenous groups in particular have pressed for greater respect for their ancestral religions and less interference from the national religious establishment and from aggressive missionary activity.

Do Spanish and Latin American Lay Catholics Support the Doctrines and Policies of the Catholic Church at the Turn of the Twenty-First Century?

Agree

Pope John Paul II has been a popular figure among the populace in Latin America in particular, and his numerous visits have drawn huge crowds to open-air masses. In Spain, where there is less overt enthusiasm for the pope, a surprising number of the public—including young people—turned out for his visits, the first of which occurred in 1982.[16] The increase in the number of Latin American cardinals, several of them Opus members, should guarantee a continuation of conservative leadership in the Hispanic hierarchy in the near future.

Spanish and Latin American Catholics are among the strongest supporters of the pope and Catholic doctrine. One example of their support is found in the growth of Opus Dei. Opus members are among the staunchest supporters of the Church, and especially of the pope. The founder of the order, José María Escrivá de Balaguer, was raised to sainthood in October 2002, only 27 years after his death in 1975. The Opus is a vigorous supporter of Church doctrine, including all of the most visible issues in the twenty-first century Church debates: celibacy of the clergy, restriction of the priesthood to males, opposition to artificial contraception or abortion for any reason and papal infallibility. Another group that champions orthodoxy is the Legion of Christ (*la Legión de Cristo*), described in *The National Catholic Reporter* as a "highly disciplined, hierarchical and militant" organization that has taken on the task of warding off the enemies of the Catholic Church, "including communists, socialists, Masons, secular humanists and even Catholics considered to be 'dissidents.' "[17] The order, founded by a Mexican priest in 1941, is making advances within the Catholic Church that contrast markedly with the steady decline of longtime orders such as the Jesuits. The Legion, which has more than 500 priests, some 2,500 seminarians (mostly in Latin America) and a lay organization called Regnum Christi, has been an implacable foe of liberation theology (see below) and is said to be influential with conservative Catholic Bishops in the region.[18]

The theological battles of the 1960s, 1970s and early 1980s, inspired by the rise of a movement called liberation theology, are, if not buried, at least substantially muted in Latin America. Liberation theology sought to "reinterpret the Christian faith from the perspective of the poor, struggling to overcome oppression. . . . [P]roponents of liberation theology employed 'Christian-Marxist' analysis and a liberationist reading of the Bible to highlight the ideologies they saw as perpetuating unjust economic and social systems in the developing world."[19] The "preferential option for the poor," espoused by liberation theologists, brought them into conflict not only with politically conservative politicians but also with the Vatican, both groups fearing the possible implications of the clergy's support of a class struggle pitting the poor against the middle and upper classes. The economic downturns of the 1980s and return to market-oriented capitalism in the 1990s combined with the replacement of retiring liberationist bishops. The result was less energy for social and political mobilization of the working classes on the one hand and a Church hierarchy that was much less sympathetic to supporting these activities on the other.

Disagree

Catholics in Spain and Latin America are not monolithic in their agreement with official Church policy or theology. There are considerable numbers of progressive Catholics in both regions who disagree on issues such as right to birth control, all-male clergy, celibacy, the role of laypersons in the Church and, to a lesser extent, abortion. Organizations of Catholics in Spain have been especially critical of the religious hierarchy's stand on celibacy and women's role in the Church. In March 2002 more than 150 Catholic organizations joined to call for an end to obligatory celibacy for priests. In their statement, the dissident priests and lay members also called for opening the priesthood to women, greater internal democracy and renunciation of the Church's "trappings of wealth and ostentation."[20] Many of these complaints have wide support from other groups within the country. The low levels of men entering seminaries alarms lay Catholics and the religious establishment alike. Most Spanish Catholics probably recognize that women (as well as married male priests) will be allowed into the priesthood when the shortage of celibate male priests becomes so acute that the Church has no choice. Mercedes Carrizosa, a female theologian, expressed the opinion that there were many more women interested in the priesthood than generally thought.[21]

Another disagreement with the hierarchy concerns the status of sexual orientation, both in the general community and within the priesthood. As in the United States, Catholics agonized over whether homosexuality reflected part of the wide but normal range of human behavior or was sinful conduct that is learned, and therefore could be unlearned. The official position of the Church has been to "condemn the sin but love the sinner," a stance not unlike that of numerous Protestant denominations but one that has received criticism from progressive circles within the Catholic Church itself. The Spanish public is relatively tolerant of homosexuality and Spanish parishes, when confronted with the revelation that their priest was homosexual, have often asked that their priests be allowed to continue to serve.[22]

Supporters of liberation theology in Latin America are profoundly disappointed by the turn the official Church has taken since the decade after the first, groundbreaking conference of bishops in Medellín, Colombia in 1968, when the leaders of the Catholic Church of Latin America broke with centuries of alignment with the wealthy elites to speak out against poverty and oppression. Encouraged to share the lives of the humble and powerless, the clergymen and women who joined this movement contributed to the empowerment of the poor and to a more democratically organized religious structure with a greater role for the laity in small groups called "base communities." Calling for a reevaluation of the message of Christianity, liberation theology had a significant effect on North American Catholic thinking and theological training and was not limited to the Catholic Church alone. Indeed, many influential liberation theologians are Latin American Protestants. Serious disagreement developed, however, between conservatives and progressives within the Catholic Church. The second conference, held in Puebla, Mexico in 1976, brought differences out into the open, when journalists and some prominent liberationist churchmen were refused entrance to the meeting. The conservatives found a like-minded ally in the new pope, John Paul II, whose tenure began in 1978 and whose experience in Poland under the Communists left him wary of the Marxist analysis of socioeconomic conditions on the one hand and inexperienced with the give and take of democracy on the other. Since that time, according to Penny Lernoux, a journalist specializing in the church in Latin America,

The rightward shift in the church threatens to alter [the emphasis on peace and justice] by reemphasizing piety at the cost of solidarity [with the poor] and by slowing the institutional momentum behind the base communities. . . . In many countries the lessons in democracy learned in the communities proved vital to the creation of other neighborhood groups that gave the poor a public voice. These offshoots will continue to grow, but increasingly they will have to do without the support of the institutional church.[23]

Are Citizens and Religious Institutions Satisfied with the Relationship between Church and State in Spanish and Latin American Governments?

Agree

The degree of separation between the church and state (or secularization of the state) still varies from one country to another, and therefore makes it impossible to answer this question in either the negative or the affirmative. However, progress has been made recently in several Hispanic nations toward resolving disagreements over freedom of religion. For example, the constitution of Paraguay that was in effect between 1967 and 1997 made Roman Catholicism the official religion of the nation and stipulated that the president of the Republic had to profess the Catholic faith. The new document recognizes freedom of religion, worship and ideology. No specific religion now has official status, and the constitution stipulates that no person shall be harassed, questioned about or compelled to profess his beliefs or doctrines. The Catholic and Protestant churches as well as the two leading national political parties agreed upon these important changes. Since the Second Vatican Council (1960–1962), the Catholic Church has steadily moved toward a clear separation of church and state, noting that both will better fulfill their roles if they maintain their independence. This has had a positive effect in most Hispanic countries.

At the other extreme in church-state relations was Cuba, which declared itself a Marxist, atheist state after the Cuban Revolution in 1959. Following the Bay of Pigs invasion in 1961 (which was viewed by many Cuban Catholics as a religious crusade), all of the private schools were nationalized and more than 100 priests were deported. Public ceremonies were forbidden, and many of the remaining Catholic priests, brothers and nuns left the country. Only a few, mostly older, people continued to go into the churches. As in other Communist countries, religious affiliation came at a high cost: practicing Christians were denied university fellowships or promotions at work; Christians were not eligible for membership in the Communist Party. Following an initial period of repression, the leadership of the Catholic Church came to terms with the Cuban regime and President Fidel Castro has, for the most part, tolerated the presence of the few remaining clergy. After almost 40 years, driven by the loss of the Soviet Union's patronage and pressure to show openness to the non-Communist world, Castro invited Pope John Paul II to visit Havana and loosened restrictions on religious freedom. The celebration of Christmas, officially banned in 1969, was reinstated in 1997 as one of the conditions for the pontiff's official visit to the island. Today Cubans have greater religious freedom, though decades of official atheism have taken their toll, particularly since many Cubans who were disturbed by the loss of religious freedom had gone into exile or emigrated years before the reversal in policy toward religion. Estimated at 100,000 to 200,000 in 1992, the numbers of Catholics and church attendance are growing slowly and requests for baptisms continue to rise,[24] but individual Christians still must endure the hostility of neighbors. Modest public processions are allowed on major religious holidays, but only the Catholic Church is able to get much cooperation from the government. The government continues to harass religious organizations to some extent by delaying necessary permits, visas and other bureaucratic maneuvers.[25]

Disagree

Even in countries where the two have coexisted more peacefully, citizens continue to negotiate the relationship between church and state. In Spain, for example, the progressive leadership of Cardinal Enrique y Tarancón had steered the Catholic Church through the delicate task of extricating the Church from its close ties to the Franco regime. With Tarancón's obligatory retirement in 1982, a more conservative leadership emerged. It has focused more on upholding traditional views of sexual morality, the family and Catholic teaching. However, at times it clashed with government, as when it attacked the Socialist ruling party for promoting the use of condoms to prevent the spread of AIDS.[26] More recently, the question of public funding of optional religious education classes in public schools and the content of these classes has come under scrutiny in Spain.[27] State funds pay for the salaries of more than 10,000 religious education teachers in Spanish public schools; the teachers are nominated and can be terminated by Catholic Church officials.[28] In spite of the fact that a small number of other Christian denominations as well as Islamic religious communities exist in the nation, only the Catholic Church receives a subsidy from the Spanish state, a form of assistance that originally was intended to ease the transition to financial independence after democracy was restored. The more conservative *Partido Popular* (People's Party, or PP) has closer ties to the Church. In 2000–2002 religious education in state-funded schools was extended, in spite of the opposition of the PSOE (*Partido Socialista Obrero Español*, the Socialist Labor Party). In a similar situation in Peru, the state pays bishops and some other members of the Church hierarchy an allowance. The Catholic Church is exempt from certain taxes and is free to establish educational institutions of any level, to open cemeteries and to serve as chaplains, and has other privileges that other faiths must obtain the right to on a piecemeal basis.[29]

In both Spain and Latin America, supporters of the Catholic Church often believe that education should include religious instruction, and they frequently criticize governments that want to remove religious teaching from education or secularize public education (*educación laica*). Secular education breeds atheism, some Catholics maintain. They blame rising crime rates and violence on the absence of religion from public schools.[30] In a number of Hispanic countries, state funds help to subsidize schools run by religious organizations.[31]

Critics believe that the Church still exerts influence and interference in civil affairs that are inappropriate in modern democracies. An example is the Church's unyielding opposition to divorce in Spain (and more recently in Chile), where a majority of the population favored legalization. The same critics call attention to the incongruity between the Church's disapproval of divorce on the one hand and its acceptance of annulments (religious decrees that dissolve marriages under certain conditions). Spain legalized divorce after a bitter battle in the *Cortes* (Parliament) and the media. At the turn of the twenty-first century, Chile was one of the few countries in the world that did not recognize divorce. The Chilean Catholic Church opposed a modern divorce law, proposing instead a lengthy process of counseling and mediation that could last three to four years. Annulments, which essentially deny that the marriage was valid in the first place, are speedy affairs but costly and encourage Chileans to lie about the circumstances of their marriages. Finally, critics insist that the high rates of informal unions (couples living together without formal marriage) and illegitimate births in Chile have been in part due to the impossibility of ending bad marriages: the poor simply cannot afford annulments and so many couples live in informal unions with their second partner. In addition to possibly encouraging less stable families, these unofficial unions have legal disadvantages: for example, a lack of clarity when "spouses" must make decisions that affect the fate of children or the right to decide on medical treatment for a family member.

The Church also wields indirect influence that can have a chilling effect on freedom of speech and other civil rights. One case involves an independent television station that in 1997 broadcast a story of nine ex-priests who claimed to have been sexually abused by the founder of the Legion of Christ while they were students in schools run by the order. Companies began canceling advertising contracts with the station immediately and within months it had lost all of its major advertisers and was close to bankruptcy. The story did not appear again in the Mexican press until Mexican Church authorities admitted in April 2002 that some of their clergy had been guilty of sexual abuses. A story published in the *Washington Post* stated that "Media companies fear enraging the church and its powerful friends. 'There's no doubt about it, it's fear and it goes directly to economics,' said Raymundo Riva Palacio, a leading Mexican journalist. He said conservative Catholic business leaders 'supply most of the advertising to the Mexican media.' "[32]

QUESTIONS AND ACTIVITIES

1. The separation of church and state is a thorny and hotly disputed issue everywhere. Explain what you believe are reasons for and against teaching a specific religious doctrine (or set of religious teachings) in a public school.

2. The ministry of education in some Hispanic countries has approved the inclusion of required "ethics" components that would include the history of religions or a comparison of religions. Imagine a debate between two groups of parents, some who believe this is a reasonable approach and others who believe that if almost all families consider themselves Catholic, the "ethics" component should consist of Catholic religious instruction.

3. In Spain, public tax money is used to pay the salaries of religious education teachers in optional religious education classes, all of which teach a Catholic curriculum. Minority religious groups, such as Moslems, have begun to complain. Should Spain cease using public money for optional religious education or should it extend classes to include other religious affiliations?

4. In one Spanish community, a Moslem father refused to send his daughter to school, saying that the education of women violated his religious beliefs. The state planned to force him to send the girl to school. Prepare an argument for the state and for the family. What do you think the young woman would want, if she were free to express herself?

5. In 2002, the Chilean Catholic Church told its parishioners to vote against candidates who supported the bill to legalize divorce in Chile. Another group said that this was inappropriate behavior in a democratic

country. What do you think? How far should a religious organization go in influencing its followers?

6. To what extent should members of the clergy (Protestant, Catholic or other) become involved in helping groups to organize for political or social action? Think of some cause that you support. What are reasons why your (or other) religious leaders should become involved in promoting that cause? Now think of a cause that you oppose. Should religious leaders help to promote or organize others for this cause? How do your answers differ (if at all) and why?

VOCABULARY/VOCABULARIO

Nouns/Sustantivos

abortion	el aborto
anticlerical	el anticlerical
atheist	el ateo
base communities	las comunidades de base
birth control	el anticonceptivo(s)
bishop	el obispo
Catholic(s)	los católicos
Catholic Church	la Iglesia Católica
Catholicism	el catolicismo
Christian	el cristiano
clergy	el clero
contraception	el anticonceptivo(s)
divorce	el divorcio
doctrine	la doctrina
Enlightenment	la Ilustración
Evangelical	el evangélico
Golden Age	el Siglo de Oro
hierarchy	la jerarquía
Inquisition	la Inquisición
Jew	el judío
lay person	el miembro laico
liberation theology	la teología de liberación
majority	la mayoría

malls	los centros comerciales, hipermercados
materialism	el materialismo
materialist	el/la materialista (m. and f.)
men of the Enlightenment	los ilustrados
minority	la minoría
Moslem	el musulmán
parish	la parroquia
the Pope	el Papa
priest	el cura, el sacerdote
Protestant	el protestante
Reconquest	la Reconquista
school, private	el colegio
school, public (or non-religious)	las escuelas laicas
university	la universidad

Verbs/Verbos

annul	anular
attend (an event)	asistir (a)
divorce	divorciarse
go to mass	ir a misa, oir misa
grow (in size)	crecer
organize	organizarse
take communion	comulgar

RESOURCE GUIDE

Books and Articles

Berryman, Phillip. "Church and Revolution." *NACLA Report on the Americas* (March–April 1997): 10–15.

Brassloff, Audrey. *Religion and Politics in Spain: The Spanish Church in Transition, 1962–96.* New York: St. Martin's Press, 1998.

Cleary, Edward L., ed. *Born of the Poor: The Latin American Church since Medellín.* Notre Dame, IN: University of Notre Dame Press, 1990.

Cleary, Edward L., and Hannah Stewart-Gambino, eds. *Conflict and Competition: The Latin American Church in a Changing Environment.* Boulder, CO: Lynne Rienner, 1992.

Hooper, John. *The New Spaniards.* London: Penguin Books, 1995.

Lynch, Edward A. *Religion and Politics in Latin America: Liberation Theology and Christian Democracy.* New York: Praeger, 1991.

Martin, James, S.J. "Opus Dei in the United States." *America*, February 25, 1995, pp. 8–17.

Miranda, Porfirio. "Laicismo es ateísmo." *Proceso*, April 9, 2000, p. 44.

Payne, Stanley G. *Spanish Catholicism: An Historical Overview.* Madison: University of Wisconsin Press, 1984.

Ranzato, Gabriel. *The Spanish Civil War.* New York: Interlink Books, 1999.

Internet

The Catholic Encyclopedia. <http://www.newadvent.org/cathen/08186a.htm>.

Legion of Christ. <http://www.legionofchrist.org/>.

National Catholic Reporter online. <http://www.natcath.com/>.

Opus Dei. <http://www.opusdei.org>.

Opus Dei Awareness Network, Inc. <http://www.odan.org/whatisopus.html>.

Video

Romero. John Duigan, director. Digital Videodisk. [New York]: Trimark Home Video, 2000. Color. English and Spanish. 105 min.

Romero. John Duigan, director. Videocassette. Santa Monica, CA: Vidmark Entertainment, 1990. Color. 105 min.

The Spanish Civil War. Videocassette. Princeton, NJ: Films for the Humanities and Sciences, 1991. Black and white. 27 min.

Chapter 14

Peace and Justice

Almost 150 years ago, Mexican president Benito Juárez put it very succinctly: *"El respeto al ajeno es la paz."* (Peace is respect for the other.) He knew from firsthand experience what he was talking about. Growing up in the turbulent years of the War of Independence, through a combination of good fortune and dedication to study and hard work he went from life in a Zapotec Indian village in Oaxaca to the study of law and service in the local and national legislatures. In 1855 Juarez became minister of justice and public instruction and then presiding judge of the Supreme Court. The new administration abolished special courts for the church and the military, forced the Church to sell its enormous property holdings, and created a new, liberal constitution. His dogged resistance to French invasion and the puppet ruler Maximilian preserved Mexico's independence, and he then served as president until his death in 1872. He worked to eliminate special privileges and to develop strong democratic institutions that are the best guarantee of fair treatment to the greatest number of citizens. Unfortunately, the quest for peace and justice in Mexico and in other Latin American nations remains unfinished. Special privilege, unequal justice, and great differences in material wealth characterize too many countries in the Hispanic world.

Aymara women wait to receive their pension payment in La Paz, Bolivia. According to official reports, almost 80% of Bolivians, mostly indigenous peoples, live in poverty. (AP Photo/Dolores Ochoa)

BACKGROUND

Although it enjoys greater prosperity and democracy today, Spain entered the twentieth century in a different state. A weak constitutional monarchy governed the country, led by a king who liked to meddle in politics and a cynical political system in which the two major parties managed elections so as to alternate in power and political patronage. Spain was economically backward and socially divided into haves and have-nots. The Catholic Church had sided decades before with the upper classes. A pointless war in North Africa cost the lives of thousands of conscripts, while wealthy young men could buy their way out of military service. In the period after the First World War, a dictatorship replaced the ineffectual parliament. By 1931 the Spanish public had had enough of the monarchy. The king went into exile, and a Republic was declared: a new era had begun.

However, the euphoria didn't last long. Beset by especially hard economic times (the Great Depression had just begun), severe class divisions and internal political differences, the Republic was rocked by strikes, dissension and political violence. In 1936 the Spanish military revolted, hoping to quickly topple the republican government. Although unable to achieve immediate victory, the army, supported by opponents of the Republic, gained control of two-thirds of the country within months. The Republic held on for almost three years, but the cost was truly devastating. Probably 200,000 had been killed in battles and bombings; as many as 125,000 more were brutally massacred in villages and cities, the victims of zealots on both sides of the conflict.[1] During the final months of the war thousands of others fled into exile, crossing the border to France in the snow.

The war came to an end in 1939, but human suffering did not. The dictatorship imposed by *Generalísimo* Francisco Franco was unrelentingly vengeful. Supporters of the republican cause were rounded up and imprisoned. Some were sent to work camps and others were executed. Most of the people imprisoned or killed were not guilty of anything more serious than being members of a political party that had supported the Republic or for fighting on the losing side of the civil war. The years following the war were difficult ones for almost all Spaniards: food and medicine were scarce and a black market flourished. Spaniards had little contact with the outside world as the dictatorship kept a tight rein on its citizens.

There was only one avenue for political expression: a single party, modeled on fascist lines that became known as *el Movimiento* (the Movement). Other political parties were outlawed. The government censored all publications and media. The Spanish Catholic hierarchy, which had backed Franco's movement during the war, gave his regime its full support during the early years and returned to its role as supervisor of education, as well as public and private morality, which it had lost under the Republic.

Franco's dictatorship survived until 1975. Although in its later years Spaniards sometimes referred to it as a *dictablanda* (a "soft" dictatorship) rather than a *dictadura* ("hard" dictatorship), the fact remained that, until its last years, freedoms of ordinary Spaniards were limited and secret police spied on everyone. Political correctness *a la* Franco was required for upward mobility, even though the economy had improved at least somewhat for nearly everyone.

As Franco's death approached, Spaniards grew uneasy. The horrors of the civil war lived on in the memory of the public. Franco had named Prince Juan Carlos de Borbón as his "heir," but few Spaniards thought that the young man, educated in Spanish military schools and groomed by the dictator, was capable of leading their country. People worried that another civil war might be unleashed after the *caudillo's* (military leader's) demise.

For once, luck was on Spain's side. The king was considerably more astute than the public believed. The next two years saw a change that few Spaniards could have imagined: with considerable arm-twisting and incentives from the new king and his prime minister, the old guard of the Franco regime legalized other political parties and stepped aside. Leaders representing almost the entire political spectrum drafted a new constitution. It was a constitution of many compromises, but it was one that almost all Spaniards could support. When it was put before the people in December 1978, the constitution was overwhelmingly endorsed by the voters. Another era had definitely begun.

Since that time Spain has endured its share of scandals, two foiled coups by disgruntled military men, political reverses, periods of unemployment and economic downturns and a continuing struggle against the terrorism of ETA[2] as well as triumphs. Importantly, however, it is now a country where people have freedom of expression, political and labor organization, choice of religion and more equality between the genders. It is not a perfect country, but it is one where people can live with relative prosperity, peace and justice.

Peace and justice, respect for the other—these are not as evident in Latin America. In an address reported in the *Journal of Third World Studies*, 1987 Nobel Peace Prize winner and former Costa Rican President Oscar Arias spoke about the need to think of peace in terms of human security. He said, "Human security is not just a concern with weapons—it is a concern with human life and dignity. The martyred Salvadoran Archbishop, Oscar Romero, eloquently expressed this idea. He told his people that 'the only peace that God wants is a peace based in justice.' "[3]

As leader of a small Central American country, Arias is familiar with conflict. His peace plan helped to bring an end to civil wars that were ravaging the neighboring countries of El Salvador and Nicaragua. But he knows that an absence of war is not the same as peace.

[W]e have another option. Instead of permitting the dominant values of selfishness, military buildup and love of money to prevail, we can choose to reclaim our most noble aspirations. . . . There are ethical maxims that guide virtuous communities but that have been too quickly overlooked in recent times: that all people have a right to work for a living wage. That all have a responsibility to live in harmony with the natural environment. And that all people should have equal opportunity to access educational, cultural and financial resources.[4]

At the turn of the twenty-first century all but one of the Hispanic Latin American countries had elected governments; nevertheless, democracy is still fragile. In many countries the military still exerts too much influence. Human rights violations have occurred on a large scale, even under several technically democratic governments; political opponents still face threats. Another dimension to this issue is economic justice. Over the last 20 years the standard of living for the majority of people in many Latin American countries has actually declined due to recession, huge national debts and mismanagement or corruption. The entrance of Latin America into the global economy has produced mixed results and the swing toward free market economies, which has the blessing of the United States, may not be the best solution for Latin America.

Here are some questions to consider as we look at the topic of peace and justice:

1. Are Hispanic countries making progress toward full democracy?
2. Is the incidence of human rights violations declining, and have those responsible for past abuses been identified and punished?
3. Can poverty and the gap between rich and poor be reduced in important ways?

DISCUSSION

Are Hispanic Countries Making Progress toward Full Democracy?

Agree

In the case of Spain, the answer is yes. Spaniards have embraced democracy and have weathered three major changes in governing parties with no ill effects. Naturally, not all Spaniards are happy with the current government, but it falls well within the center-left–center-right spectrum of European democracies and is a member of the European Union. The military in Spain is no longer a threat.

Costa Rica is often named as the best example of democratic government in the Latin America region. Relatively peaceful since independence, Costa Rica has seen a gradual development of democracy, interrupted by some periods of military rule. Since 1948 it has been governed under a constitution that eliminated the army, gave the vote to women and African Americans as well as all other adults over 18, and prohibited consecutive presidential terms. The disavowal of a standing army has meant that the country could invest more in education, health care and other social benefits, all of which have given the country's populace a longer life expectancy and higher level of education than most other Latin American countries, political stability and a relative freedom from domestic strife unmatched in the other republics.

The last decade of the twentieth century brought a swing back to democracy in Latin America that had been unparalleled in its history. All countries but one (Cuba) were considered democracies, although some were less completely democratic than others. Nevertheless, none of these nations were living under military or other dictatorial rule, which had been the case in several countries only 15 years before. Chile, for example, continued to make a successful transition back to democracy after more than a decade and a half of dictatorship (1973–1989) under General Augusto Pinochet. Bolivia, Paraguay, Uruguay and Argentina also ended dictatorships to join the ranks of democratic nations during the 1980s and 1990s. In Central America, two long civil wars came to an end and elections took place. In Nicaragua, the Sandinistas, who had triumphed in their civil war, handed over power when they were voted out after one term in office. In Mexico, cracks began to appear in the creaking structure of the PRI (*Partido Revolucionario Institucional*), the party that had ruled since the 1920s. The candidate of the major opposition party, PAN (*Partido de Acción Nacional*), won the presidential election to begin the new century.

Disagree

Democracy requires more than elections—that was evident from the control that the PRI exerted in Mexico for several generations. Elections can be rigged, ballot boxes can disappear or voters can be frightened away from the polls. Fraudulent elections were commonplace in Mexico up into the 1990s, and many Mexicans believed that the PRI had stolen the presidential election in 1996. Nevertheless, international observers considered the election generally honest, in spite of some irregularities, and the PRI candidate, Ernesto Zedillo, was declared the winner with 49% of the vote.[5]

One other example, taken from South America, shows that democracy is not as firmly planted as one would hope. In 1990 in Peru, a relative unknown, Alberto Fujimori, defeated the early favorite, Mario Vargas Llosa, in a stunning victory for the underdog. Fujimori campaigned against the free market[6] economic reforms espoused by his opponent and "politics as usual" in the Peruvian Congress, and capitalized on his outsider status as a Japanese-Peruvian in campaign tours through the heavily indigenous rural areas. However, shortly after taking office, Fujimori reversed himself and began a very rigorous program designed to put Peru back into the good graces of the international financial community. To bring down Peru's extremely high inflation, he cut the national budget and opened Peru's markets to competition from imports. Soon many people found themselves unemployed as publicly owned companies

Portrait of Augusto Pinochet with President Jimmy Carter. While this official photograph suggests warm relations between the two leaders, President Carter encouraged the democratic opposition in Chile that eventually brought Pinochet's military dictatorship to an end. (National Archives, Jimmy Carter Library, Atlanta, GA)

were sold to private international buyers and Peruvian goods faced greater competition from imports. The jolt was so severe that Peruvians called it "Fujishock." In spite of the hard times his policies were causing, Fujimori maintained his popularity with voters. A major reason for this was the success of the police in capturing the head of the terrorist group Shining Path. Since the Shining Path (*Sendero Luminoso*) had first appeared in 1980, it had sown terror in rural villages and increasingly in the cities. Between the Shining Path guerrillas and the army troops sent to combat them, thousands of Peruvians, mostly Indian villagers, were killed and many more driven from their homes.

But Fujimori could not push through the legislation that he wanted. As an outsider he had no real political base in the Congress. He forged close ties to the military and the head of his intelligence service, Vladimir Montesinos. Unable to get what he wanted from the legislative branch, Fujimori arranged a *golpe de estado* (a *coup d'état*). With the blessing of the military, the president closed the Congress and the courts, arrested opponents and ruled by decree for about six months. The event was promptly labeled an *autogolpe*, or self-coup. Other governments, including the United States, denounced the *autogolpe* but Fujimori was reelected in 1995 under a new constitution. His opponents cried foul, accusing his supporters of voting irregularities and campaign tricks. His authoritarian habits continued and the public's enthusiasm cooled, especially when he ran for a third term. The constitution stipulated a limit of two terms, but Fujimori argued that since the first term had been carried out under the old constitution, he was entitled to two full terms under the new one. Again he was accused of unfair tactics, of planting false stories in newspapers and using the secret police for political undercover work.

After the election, which he "narrowly" won against opponent Alejandro Toledo, the truth about Fujimori's regime began to come out—on videotapes broadcast nightly on the Peruvian news. His right hand man, Montesinos, had been selling favors and buying votes in the Congress. Hundreds of Peruvian businessmen and politicians appeared on tapes that had secretly been made by Montesinos but had fallen into the hands of the press. Within a few months Fujimori took advantage of an official trip to Japan to go into exile there. The next year new elections were held and the new president, Alejandro Toledo, took office in 2001.

The Fujimori years show how a government that lacks strong judicial and legislative institutions can be manipulated and overshadowed by the executive branch, especially when it has the support of the army, giving room for many abuses.

Is the Incidence of Human Rights Violations Declining, and Have Those Responsible for Past Abuses Been Identified and Punished?

Agree

Some important progress for human rights was made in the 1990s, along with many setbacks. The best-known positive development was the detention of former Chilean dictator Augusto Pinochet in 1998 while he was in the United Kingdom for medical attention. Although the British government agreed to extradite him to Spain, where the warrant was issued, Pinochet was returned to Chile when the British determined that he was too ill to stand trial. Because of lengthy appeals based on his physical and mental disabilities, the general never stood trial for the murders and torture he was accused of ordering. However, in an important decision, the Chilean court stripped Pinochet of the immunity granted to him as Senator for Life. Pinochet's indictment opened the door to finally bringing criminal charges against other Chilean officials accused of torture and murder of political prisoners during the dictatorship.

The Pinochet case was not the only example of attempts to extradite persons accused of grave crimes. In Argentina, the scene of a brutal "dirty war" against dissidents during the period of military dictatorship from 1976 to 1983, thousands—perhaps as many as 15,000 or even 30,000—"disappeared" while in the custody of the police or the military. After the fall of the military government in 1983, five members of the ruling *junta* (group, governing council) were found guilty of ordering these crimes. But as the courts attempted to prosecute hundreds of lower-level officers, the still-powerful armed forces were able to intimidate the democratically elected government into suspending the trials and to granting amnesty to the remaining defendants in 1986 and 1987. Eventually all 10 men convicted for human rights crimes were pardoned. However, due to continued work of relatives, human rights organizations, prosecutors and judges, in 2001 the amnesty of those accused of torture and extrajudicial execution was finally declared unconstitutional and in violation of Argentina's international human rights agreements. Not only Spain but also Italy, France, Germany and Sweden requested the extradition of Argentineans they accused of torture and murder of their citizens. Although the Argentinean government refused to extradite these men, investigation and prosecution of human rights cases did at least resume within Argentina. Furthermore, several former top members of the military government were accused and awaiting trial for organizing the illegal transfer and adoption of babies of women political prisoners to members of the military and others connected to the government.[7] These were important steps in bringing human rights criminals to justice.

The 1990s also saw a sharp decline in political terror carried out by the Shining Path (*Sendero Luminoso*, or SL), an ultraradical Communist group that recruited among students and peasants in the most poverty-stricken regions of Peru. After a decade of attacks designed to annihilate anyone who disagreed with it in any way, the SL was finally crippled in 1992 when its leader, Abimael Guzmán, was captured along with several other high-level *senderistas*. Before this, however, thousands of people, mostly peasants, were killed by both the SL and the armed forces in an attempt to pacify areas where the terrorists were supposed to be hiding among the populace. After the departure of Alberto Fujimori, a "truth commission" was set up and began to investigate the stories of massacres and disappearances and attempt to identify those who were responsible, including high-ranking military or police officers.

Disagree

While the incidence of human rights violations has declined sharply in Spain since the Franco years, both terrorist and police violence mar the country's record. Continued terrorism at the hands of ETA, the Basque separatist organization, has caused more than 800 deaths since its inception in 1959. Unfortunately, in spite of strenuous efforts by the police, the *Guardia Civil* (Civil Guard), the intelligence forces and the opposition of the vast majority of Spaniards, small cells of ETA terrorists continue to strike at journalists, police, politicians and members of the judiciary. Amnesty International reported that in 2001, 15 people died from ETA attacks (and more were injured).[8] On the other hand, in the same document, Amnesty International also reported allegations of mistreatment of migrants and suspects in police custody, including beatings and torture of ETA prisoners at the hands of police. In addition, 14 members of the police or the *Guardia Civil* imprisoned for torture were released as part of a mass amnesty to celebrate the new millennium.

The Spanish judiciary system has been reluctant to dig into abuses that took place under Franco. While Spaniards were coming out of their long period of dictatorship, leadership was uncertain and the possibility of civil violence or a military takeover was in the back of the minds of politicians and the public alike. It became clear that the majority of Spaniards wanted a government that could steer a middle course. According to John Hooper, author of *The New Spaniards*, "The mood of the moment was reconciliation and it was clear that whichever party could embrace supporters as well as opponents of Francoism would stand a good chance of winning the [first general] election."[9] But this has also lead to a kind of historical amnesia. By the 1990s Spanish children didn't know much about Franco and his regime. The same writer says, "The spirit of the transition is sometimes described as being that of 'forgive and forget.' That is not entirely correct. Since no one in Spain was ever judged [for the crimes they were alleged to have committed], forgiveness never entered into it. It was just a matter of forgetting."[10] The Amnesty International report cited earlier echoes this reluctance to dig into the ugly past and, at the very least, reveal embarrassing information about people who have been prominent in the post-Franco era. The Amnesty International report declares that granting of pardons to torturers, lax enforcement of sentences and allowing prisoners to be held incommunicado contributed to an atmosphere of impunity among the police (and is disturbingly similar to police practices under Franco).

Human rights organizations stress the issue of impunity (lack of punishment or legal consequences) because it undermines all other efforts to bring about true democracy. In *Peace without Justice*, legal and human rights expert Margaret Popkin explains the difficulties in reforming the judicial system, a critical part of the settlement of the 10-year civil war in El Salvador. Before the war, the activities of the police and military were not subject to public scrutiny in El Salvador. Persons accused of crimes could be held for periods of up to 15 months without charges, bail was generally impossible to obtain and the accused did not have the right to see a lawyer until the final phase of his case before a magistrate who had been the investigator, prosecutor and judge. Honest judges were threatened; timid and dishonest judges did as they were told or were paid to do. In effect, the only hope of release was to obtain the help of someone with influence. Experienced lawyers bypassed the courts and went to the military to buy their clients' freedom. As in far too many countries around the world, the police routinely tortured prisoners to get confessions, and extrajudicial executions (i.e., taking the prisoner out and shooting him or her) were a common occurrence, especially in the case of political prisoners.

This civil war eventually received attention in the American media, as Salvadorans fled to Mexico and the United States in increasing numbers to escape the violence and as the Reagan administration poured money and advisors in to support the Salvadoran government. The negotiated settlement to end the war included instituting meaningful reforms in the system of justice. In spite of millions of dollars in grants and loans and the assistance of teams of experts in designing reforms, Popkin concludes that the effort has produced few really positive results. Although El Salvador now has a political system that meets some of the criteria of a democracy, the system of justice has not changed much, largely due to a lack of involvement of the Salvadoran civil (i.e., ordinary, non-military) society in designing the reform process. As a result, reforms in the police and court system that were planned have not been carried out. The institutions that were supposed to safeguard human and civil rights are weak and there is still little effective oversight of police and judicial officials. To make things worse, a crime wave, led by gangs of ex-soldiers or guerrillas, came on the heels of the war. Afraid to report gangs to the police, ordinary Salvadorans despair and have even taken matters into their own hands.[11]

Learning from the mistakes made in El Salvador, judicial reforms in Guatemala made at the end of its 36-year war had a more promising beginning. Nevertheless, the climate of fear and the distrust of authorities—too often well placed—continue, along with abductions, threats and murders of people who cooperate in uncovering the truth about the horrendous human rights abuses of the past. According to José Pilar Alvarez, a Lutheran pastor in Zacapa, Guatemala,

The peace process has stalled because there is no political will for it to prosper, because there are sectors of the powerful who are addicted to unjust economic and political structures, and they don't want to see things change. They don't want to see peasants and the indigenous have more space for a dignified life.[12]

Can Poverty and the Gap between Rich and Poor Be Reduced in Important Ways?

Agree

One of the biggest obstacles to peace and justice is poverty. Of all the world's regions, Latin America has the greatest disparity between the rich and the poor. It is not uncommon for the wealthiest 10% of a Latin American nation's population to control 40% or more of the wealth, while the poorest 20% control 10% or less. This very disproportionate distribution of wealth makes the average, or per capita, income quite misleading. For example, the per capita income for Bolivia was reported at $2,600 for the year 2000 (or slightly more than $200 per month), but most Bolivians did not earn that much. Seventy percent of the population lived below the poverty line (most often defined as daily expenditure of $2 per person for food, clothing, shelter and other expenses), and the poorest 10% of the population earned only 2.3% of the country's income. That meant that the poorest of the Bolivian poor—mostly indigenous peoples—had an income of less than $60 per person per year.

Microcredit, or small loans (usually $50 to $500), is one approach to helping people out of poverty that gained momentum during the 1990s. Loans are usually taken out to start or improve a small business—for example, to buy supplies, a farm animal or other small but significant economic step for the family or a group. The typical microcredit client is a married woman with children. The microcredit organizations use local staff and keep costs down, but charge a reasonable rate of interest and are serious about collections. Since 80% of all businesses in Latin America can be described as microbusinesses, and one-third of the labor force is employed in them, providing credit for these enterprises has the potential to improve the standard of living of much of the region's poor. The Interamerican Development Bank reports that its microcredit institutions reached 600,000 microentrepreneurs in Latin America and helped to create or strengthen 1.8 million jobs during the decade of the 1990s. USAID, the foreign aid branch of the U.S. government, and several non-governmental agencies also sponsor microcredit programs.

Education, particularly greater emphasis on improving access to primary and secondary education, is also seen as essential for Latin American nations to improve their quality of life. While Latin America has made important strides in the area of education, other world regions have done better and the gains in Latin American nations are uneven. For example, illiteracy in some rural areas in Mexico is 21%, double the national average, and while the upper 10% of the population receive 12 years of schooling, the poorest 10% average just two years. In most countries too much of the budget has gone to university-level education, heavily attended by the upper classes, who could afford private university tuition. Teacher salaries are low and teacher training needs much improvement. The education of women, the rural poor and indigenous peoples, all long-neglected by national educational systems, should be given special priority.[13]

Finally, a highly influential group of countries and organizations, spearheaded by the United States, the World Trade Organization (WTO), the International Monetary Fund (IMF) and the World Bank, advocates global trade as the solution to development and reducing poverty. Lowering trade barriers through participation in multinational trade agreements, such as the North American Free Trade Agreement (NAFTA) or the proposed Free Trade Area of the Americas (FTAA), will stimulate trade between all participants and result, eventually, in higher incomes for Latin Americans. Free trade advocates say that trade is good for economic growth of both developed and undeveloped countries and that the income of the poor rises in step with growth in the national economy. They point to China as a recent example of a poor country that has experienced unprecedented growth as a result of embracing global trade.

There are other benefits to the free market as well, say supporters of free trade. Putting obstacles in the way of trade, such as tariffs and complicated regulations, protects local producers but at a cost of inefficiency and corruption. Competition doesn't eliminate corruption, but it makes it harder to hide. When foreign companies move some of their operations to a developing country, the country receives new technology and new jobs. And although U.S. companies often set up plants abroad to reduce their labor costs, the wages they pay are generally higher than those paid by local employers.

The evidence suggests that multinationals pay a wage premium—a reflection, presumably, of efforts to recruit relatively skilled workers. . . . [T]he wages paid by foreign affiliates to poor-country workers are about double the local manufacturing wage; wages paid by affiliates to workers in middle-income countries are about 1.8 times the local manufacturing wage.[14]

Disagree

Critics of neoliberal (free trade) policies say that trade alone is not the answer. Free trade policies include not only the lowering of tariffs but also the privatizing of nationally owned companies, relaxing of labor laws and eliminating subsidies on many products (including food, fuel and other essentials). While these protectionist measures make national companies and goods less competitive with foreign ones and create more expense for the government, if they are dismantled across the board or too quickly their elimination causes great hardship, especially on the poor, who are least equipped to absorb more losses.

Organizations that work in Third World development accuse the developed nations of hypocrisy in promoting world trade. While the United States, members of the European Union and other developed nations demand that poor nations open themselves to trade, the developed countries continue to subsidize some of their own products (corn, rice and soybeans in the United States are examples). Frequently, these subsidized products are then sold in developing world markets for less than foreign farmers or manufacturers can produce them. In other instances, the United States still protects local industries from imports from Latin America. The Andean Trade Preferences Act, passed in 1991, lowered tariffs on certain items from Colombia, Bolivia, Peru and Ecuador, but when the time came to renew the agreement in 2001, the U.S. Congress was in no hurry to approve it. A proposal to add textiles and tuna to the list met with opposition from U.S. business interests. Oxfam, a prominent non-governmental anti-poverty agency, estimates that a 1% increase in world-export share for each developing region could reduce world poverty by 12%. However, *equitable* growth—giving the poor their fair share of improvement in the economy—will require the development of effective strategies and a determination to protect the interests of the poor, neither of which figure in the orthodox neoliberal framework.

Other organizations question the very nature of world trade: by encouraging poor nations to focus on exports, it discourages food production for local needs and intensifies pressure on the environment. Exports to First World markets concentrate on luxury products, such as shrimp, flowers and specialty foods, supplied by corporations for rich First World consumers while destroying the resource base and livelihood of small farmers and fishermen.[15] And unlike the European Union, which works to equalize development among its members, NAFTA and FTAA only serve to make Latin American countries more subject to domination by the United States, providing us with new markets, protecting our own and doing nothing to bring backward economies up to our standard of living.[16]

The inequities of neoliberal economic policies are already evident in several Latin American countries. The ones that have been studied best are Chile and Mexico. Chile began its conversion to neoliberal economic policies shortly after the military-led coup that overthrew the government of Salvador Allende. The military leaders were anxious to dismantle the socialist economic framework of the Allende administration and brought in a team of American-educated economists who put Chile on a capitalist fast track. By cutting government expenditures, selling nationalized industries and services to private, mostly international companies and focusing on exports to raise revenues, the Chilean government was able to reduce its large foreign debt, although at the cost of widespread unemployment and hardship for the working class. Since then, the Gross Domestic Product (the sum of the all the goods and services produced within the country) has grown at a better rate than other Latin American nations and, along with it, per capita income. However, many of the jobs created are seasonal agricultural jobs in agribusiness, which has forced out small farmers who were unable to afford the improvements needed to compete in international markets. Multinational timber companies have been given concessions that will allow them to cut old-growth rainforests to produce wood pulp. The gap between the wealthy and the poor did not improve much during the last half of the 1990s.[17]

Mexico, a partner with the United States and Canada in NAFTA, has also experienced mixed blessings from free trade. During the 1990s, a period that encompasses pre- and post-NAFTA, the Gross Domestic Product for the nation increased, but so did poverty. In other words, the distribution of wealth became more unequal during the decade. These findings ran contrary to the promises of NAFTA supporters in the United States and Mexico. The number of jobs did increase in *maquiladoras* (assembly plants for U.S. companies) but in few other areas, except for financial services that are linked to the *maquila* industry. Assembly-line jobs (mostly clothing and manufacture) have increased wages in the areas where plants are located, but additional economic benefit to the community is limited. *Maquiladoras* are also concentrated near the U.S.-Mexican border, contributing to a widening gap between the more prosperous North and the South, which is getting poorer. Many of the plants prefer to hire female workers, giving them greater economic opportunity, but plants have been accused of unfair labor practices regarding women, too.[18]

One very big step toward reducing poverty would occur if the wealthy nations forgave the debts now owed by the poorest nations, that is, to substantially reduce or wipe out the debt entirely. The World Bank and the International Monetary Fund (IMF), which make loans to developing countries, instituted a debt reduction program in 1996 to assist the most heavily indebted, poorest countries. The World Bank estimated that the program would reduce by approximately one-half the $90 billion owed by countries that qualified. The goal was to bring down debt to "sustainable" levels. Most of the countries in this category are located in Africa, but three of them were Latin American nations: Nicaragua, Honduras and Bolivia.

Some non-profit organizations have advocated eliminating the debt altogether—in conjunction with requirements that the poor nations develop plans to alleviate poverty, improve education, tackle corruption and other reforms—to give struggling nations a chance to get on their feet. Debt reduction programs in place today have not gone nearly far enough. Ecuador, for example, had a public debt of $15 billion in 1998, equal to 82% of the Gross National Product. That year interest payments on the debt were twice the amount spent on education and health care combined, and 50% of Ecuador's population was living below the poverty line. In spite of these alarming figures, Ecuador was not classified as one of the most heavily indebted countries and therefore not eligible for the World Bank's debt reduction program:[19] its per capita income was too high.

Countries must also change their spending priorities, whether or not they engage extensively in global trade. More than half of the world's governments currently spend more on their military than on health care for the entire nation. Military spending costs the world about $800 billion per year. According to Oscar Arias, if $40 billion of that total were dedicated not to arms and armies but to anti-poverty programs each year, within 10 years *all* of the world's population could have access to basic services that should be the right of all people: education, basic health care, safe water and waste facilities. If $80 billion—only 10% of the current military expenditures—per year were available, all people could live above the poverty line for their countries.[20]

The social and political benefits of not having to support an expensive military apparatus can be seen in Costa Rica, where the 1948 constitution eliminated the armed forces. Costa Rica was one of the few countries to maintain an unbroken record of democratic governments in the second half of the twentieth century. Other Latin American countries are beginning to see the wisdom of reducing military budgets. In 2001 President Toledo of Peru proposed an arms expenditure agreement, as well as a freeze on the purchase of expensive offensive weapons such as missiles, to free up funds for much-needed social services that would help the poor. As a result of the debate sparked by Toledo, for the first time 19 Latin American nations voted in favor of the principle of limiting arms spending. In 2002, Peru and Ecuador (who had invaded each other's territory three times in the past 50 years due to a simmering border dispute) began negotiations to increase mutual trust and reduce their military budgets. Since the two countries spent roughly $1 billion and $720 million, respectively, per year on arms and military personnel, this proposal offered good hope for channeling savings into improvements in health, education or other social development services.[21]

QUESTIONS AND ACTIVITIES

1. The Spanish police have been cited for mistreatment of immigrants and for the deportation of child immigrants without papers (*inmigrantes sin papeles*). Has the situation improved? See Amnesty International's annual report on the Internet. Look for articles in the Spanish press. How does the United States compare?

2. The civil war in Colombia has lasted for more than four decades. President Alvaro Uribe, elected in 2002, promised an all-out military cam-

paign to subdue the rebel guerrillas, known as the FARC and the ELN. Human rights advocates feared another increase in killings of civilians. Use the Internet to find out about the human rights record of the current Colombian administration. Use Amnesty International or Human Rights Watch. Prepare a short report.

3. A number of non-governmental organizations work in Latin America to improve living conditions, community health or education. Look into the Latin America projects of one of these organizations by reading its pages on the Web: Amigos de las Americas or American Friends Service Committee. What kinds of activities does the organization sponsor? Is there a minimum age? What skills do volunteers need? Would you rather spend two or three weeks on an ordinary vacation in one of the same countries or participate in one of these projects? Explain your reasons.

4. Use the Internet to look for organizations that subscribe to fair trade. One of them is Global Exchange <http://www.globalexchange.org> but there are others. Develop a definition of "fair trade." Do you think fair trade can be effective in reducing poverty in a community? Would it have other benefits? Explain your opinion.

5. Many stores now sell "fair trade" coffee, which usually costs more than ordinary coffee. Would you pay more week in and week out for fair trade coffee? Explain your answer.

6. If you had to live on $2.00 a day in the United States, what would you be able to eat? Put together a menu for breakfast, lunch and supper and estimate the cost of each meal. Will you have to skip one or more meals? Can you find some low-cost foods that will satisfy your nutritional needs? Compare your menus with those of other students and come up with the best one.

7. What are the common foods of the poor in different regions of Latin America? If you know (or can e-mail) someone from another country, find out what foods you would find on the table of the poor in Mexico, Central America, the Caribbean or the Andes.

8. *Missing* and *Romero* are two films that show people who confront a violent regime that acts with impunity. View one of these films. How does the major character react initially? What causes him to change his views and his response?

9. In 2002, in spite of the opposition of local authorities and a referendum by the townspeople, a U.S. mining firm planned to open a pit mine in a part of the town of Tambogrande, located in a productive agricultural area of Peru. Imagine that the dispute has been brought before a court to decide. What arguments would the townspeople present? What

counterarguments would the mining company have? As judge, what is your ruling?

10. The EZLN (Ejercito Zapatista de Liberación Nacional) has vigorously opposed NAFTA. Use their website to determine why they are so opposed to this agreement and report your findings.

11. Is NAFTA a success or a failure? Explain your conclusions.

12. Agencies of the United States have participated in covert—or secret—operations in a number of Latin American countries since the end of World War II. These activities have ranged from funding the campaigns of candidates favorable to the United States to training Latin American military who have later become dictators and human rights abusers to participation in the planning and execution of military coups. Use books and documents published on the Internet to research the United States' role in Latin American affairs of one of the following countries: Chile, Cuba and Guatemala.

VOCABULARY/VOCABULARIO

Nouns/Sustantivos

agreement	el acuerdo
civil war	la guerra civil
company	una compañía, una empresa
corruption	la corrupción
debt	la deuda
farmer	el campesino
free market	el mercado libre, el libre comercio
immigrants, illegal	los inmigrantes sin papeles, los indocumentados
impunity	la impunidad
justice	la justicia
killer	el asesino
military	los militares
neoliberalism	el neoliberalismo
peace	la paz
people	la gente, la población
plant, assembly	la maquiladora
politicians	los políticos
poverty	la pobreza

power	el poder
rebels	los insurgentes
regime	el régimen
rights, civil	los derechos civiles
rights, human	los derechos humanos
Shining Path	el Sendero Luminoso
standard of living	el nivel de vida
terrorism	el terrorismo
terrorist	el terrorista
trade, fair	el comercio con justicia
trade, global	la comercio global, la globalización

Verbs/Verbos

develop	desarrollar
imprison	encarcelar
kill	matar
live in peace	vivir en paz
mistreat	maltratar, abusar
murder	asesinar
trust (in)	confiar en

RESOURCE GUIDE

Books and Articles

Arias, Oscar. "Confronting Debt, Poverty, and Militarism: A Humane Program of Support for the Developing World." *Journal of Third World Studies* 17(2) (2000): 113–127.

"Cramming Them in." *The Economist*, May 11, 2002, pp. 34–35.

Garreton, Manuel Antonio. "Human Rights in Processes of Democratisation." *Journal of Latin American Studies* 26 (1994): 221–234.

"Grinding the Poor." *The Economist*, September 27, 2001, pp. 10–13.

Griswold, Daniel T. "The Blessings and Challenges of Globalization." *International Journal on World Peace* 17(3) (2000): 3–22.

Guillermoprieto, Alma. *The Heart that Bleeds.* New York: Vintage Books, 1995.

————. *Looking for History: Dispatches from Latin America*. New York: Pantheon Books, 2001.

Handy, Jim. *Gift of the Devil: A History of Guatemala*. Toronto: Between the Lines, 1984.

Harvey, Neil. *The Chiapas Rebellion: The Struggle for Land and Democracy*. Durham, NC: Duke University Press, 1998.

Menchu, Rigoberta. *I, Rigoberta Menchu: An Indian Woman in Guatemala*, edited and introduced by Elisabeth Burgos-Debray; translated by Ann Wright. London: Verso, 1984.

Merrill, Tim L., and Ramón Miró, eds. *Mexico: A Country Study*. Washington, DC: Federal Research Division, Library of Congress, 1996.

Nelson-Pallmeyer, Jack. *School of Assassins: The Case for Closing the School of the Americas and for Fundamentally Changing U.S. Policy*. Maryknoll, NY: Orbis Books, 1997.

Sunstein, Cass R. *Free Markets and Social Justice*. New York: Oxford University Press, 1999.

Internet

Amigos de las Americas. <http://www.amigoslink.org/>.

Amnesty International. <http://www.amnesty.org/>.

Annual Human Rights Reports (country index), U.S. Department of State. <http://www.state.gov/g/drl/rls/hrrpt/2001/wha/>.

Center for Trade Policy Studies. <http://www.freetrade.org/>.

Derechos Chile. Chile Information Project (CHIP). <http://www.chip.cl/derechos/index_eng.html>.

Fair Trade Federation. <http://www.fairtradefederation.com/index.html>.

Global Exchange. <http://www.globalexchange.org>.

Human Rights Watch (index for the Americas). <http://www.humanrightswatch.org/americas/index.php>.

Maquiladora Health and Safety Support Network. <http://mhssn.igc.org>.

National Security Archive. <http://www.gwu.edu/nsarchiv/latin_america/>.

Oxfam. <http://www.oxfam.org/>.

School of the Americas Watch. <http://www.soaw.org>.

Washington Office on Latin America. <http://www.wola.org>.

Video

El Norte. Gregory Nava, director. Videocassette. Los Angeles: Frontera Films, 1983. Color. 141 min.

The Evolution of Chile: Prosperity for Some. Marc DeBeaufort, director. Videocassette. Princeton, NJ: Films for the Humanities, 1998. Color. 29 min.

Get up, Stand up. Marc DeBeaufort, director. Videocassette. *Americas* series No. 8. South Burlington, VT: Annenberg/CPB Collection, 1993. Color. 60 min.

La boca del lobo [*The Lion's Den*]. Francisco J. Lombardi, director. Videocassette. New York: Cinevista Video, 1990. Color. Spanish with English subtitles. 111 min.

La historia oficial [*The Official Story*]. Luis Puenzo, director. Videocassette. New York: Fox Lorber Home Video, 1985. Color. Spanish with English subtitles. 111 min.

Missing. Costa-Gravas, director. Videocassette. Willowdale, ON: MCA Universal Home Video, 1982. Color. 123 min.

Notes

INTRODUCTION

1. Lars Gyllensten, "Presentation Speech," The Nobel Prize in Literature, 1982, *Nobel e-Museum*, April 18, 2002, accessed June 9, 2002, <http://www.nobel.se/literature/laureates/1982/presentation-speech.html>. "For a long time Latin American literature has shown a vigor as in few other literary spheres. It has won acclaim in the cultural life of today. Many impulses and traditions cross each other. Folk culture, including oral storytelling, reminiscences from old Indian culture, currents from Spanish baroque in different epochs, influences from European surrealism and other modernism are blended into a spiced and life-giving brew. From it García Márquez and other Spanish-American writers derive material and inspiration. The violent conflicts of political nature—social and economic—raise the temperature of the intellectual climate. Like most of the other important writers in the Latin American world, García Márquez is strongly committed politically on the side of the poor and the weak against oppression and economic exploitation."

2. Gabriel García Márquez, "Nobel Lecture 8 December 1982," *Nobel e-Museum*, November 19, 2001, accessed June 9, 2002, <http://www.nobel.se/literature/laureates/1982/marquez-lecture.html>.

CHAPTER 1

1. The co-equal status of *catalán, euskara* or *vasco* and *gallego* is relatively new, as of 1978, when the new constitution was approved.

2. Languages are less likely to borrow sounds or aspects of morphology and grammar. Apart from lexical (vocabulary) borrowing, the effect that speakers of one language have on another, either as speakers of the dominant group (superstratum) language or the dominated (substratum) group language, is often unclear.

3. A feature of pronunciation, grammar or vocabulary can *stigmatize* or negatively mark a dialect as lower class, rustic, and so on. Examples from English are the use of "ain't" and the double negative "I never saw nothing."

4. That is, in sound and in the form of the word. An example is the verb "*puchar*," meaning "to push." It has been adapted in its sound (the "sh" sound has been changed to "ch") and, with the appropriate verb ending -ar, it is ready to be used like any other Spanish verb: *Púchalo*. (Push it.)

5. Code-switching has been studied extensively by linguists. See Kristin R. Becker, "Spanish/English Bilingual Codeswitching: A Syncretic Model," *Bilingual Review* (January–April 1997): 3–30.

CHAPTER 2

1. Carrie B. Douglass, *Bulls, Bullfighting and Spanish Identities* (Tucson: University of Arizona Press, 1997), p. 101. This brief history of the attempts to prohibit the *fiesta de toros* and much of the other information in this chapter is taken from Douglass' book.

2. For other countries see Toros y Toreros, Señal Colombia, <http://www.torosytoreros.com/>.

3. "Madrid Slammed over Decision to Remove Anti-bullfighting Poster," World Society for the Protection of Animals (WSPA), *WSPA News Archive*, May 2000, accessed July 27, 2001, <http://www.wspa.org.uk/news/archive/oldnews45.html>.

4. Quoted in "Citas sobre la tauromaquia y la tortura de toros," *Arco de Noé*, Angel de la Web, July 27, 2001, <http://usuarios.tripod.es/arcadenoe/toros.htm>.

5. Douglass, *Bulls, Bullfighting and Spanish Identities*, pp. 37–45.

6. This point of view is articulated well by Carlos Fuentes in "La virgen y el *toro*," in *El espejo enterrado* (part 1), videocassette ([s.l.]: Public Media Video, 1991), color, 59 min.

7. "Cruel Sports," World Society for the Protection of Animals, *WSPA News Archive*, October 1995, accessed July 27, 2000, <http://www.wspa.org.uk/news/pres-rel/cruel02.html>.

8. This quotation and other data in this section come from news releases published by WSPA. See their index of news archives at <http://www.wspa.org.uk/news/archive/index.html>. The WSPA also reported that 86% of Spaniards had "no interest" in bullfighting and that fewer

than 13% considered themselves *aficionados*. However, the survey was reported in *La Vanguardia*, the largest newspaper in Catalonia, which is an area of little support for the *corrida*. See <http://www.wspa.org.uk/news/archive/oldnews32.html>.

9. "Empresa española pretende organizar una corrida en La Habana," Efe News Services, April 28, 2000, online, LexisNexis™ Academic, accessed July 31, 2001.

10. John Hooper, *The New Spaniards* (New York: Penguin, 1995), pp. 357–358. The author cites a poll published in *El Tiempo* in 1985, one of only a handful that he considered reliable that had been published in the 20 years prior.

11. Douglass, *Bulls, Bullfighting and Spanish Identities*, pp. 37–45.

12. "Rabbi Says Bullring Off Limits to Orthodox Jews," The Associated Press, August 31, 1986, LexisNexis™ Academic, accessed July 30, 2001.

CHAPTER 3

1. See "Valoración de la Monarquía," *25 años sin Franco*, *El Mundo*, special supplement, November 2000, accessed December 20, 2000, <http://www.elmundo.es/noticias/2000/graficos/noviembre/semana3/monarquia.html>. See also Centro de Investigaciónes Sociológicas, *Datos de Opinion: Boletín* #20, <http://www.cis.es/boletin/20/index.html>, for similar statistics.

2. After several decades of civil war and political turmoil, the short-lived First Republic was declared in 1873; the Borbón monarchy was restored in 1874. For this reason the republic that was declared in 1931 is known as the *Second* Republic.

3. The Spanish Civil War began in 1936 and ended with the fall of the Republic in 1939.

4. "Intensa actividad de don Felipe durante su viaje a Nicaragua," *¡Hola!* January 1, 2002, accessed May 25, 2002, <http://www.hola.com/2002/01/11/felipenicaragua/>.

5. Sanjuana Martinez, "Voces en España en favor de la República: Que la figura del rey deje de ser tabú." *Proceso*, May 10, 1998, pp. 46–50.

6. Ibid.

7. "Valoración de la Monarquía."

8. "King Juan Carlos of Spain and Former U.S. President Jimmy Carter Awarded Unesco's Peace Prize," UNESCO Press Archives (1995), <gopher://gopher.undp.org:70/00/ungophers/unesco/press/95_12/951205150105>.

9. These arguments, made by Julio Anguita, former head of Izquierda Unida (United Left) Party, are summarized in "Anguita insta a partidos posicionarse a favor [de la] 3ª república," Efe News Services, January 26, 2001, online, LexisNexis™ Academic, accessed May 20, 2001.

10. "An Assault on Spain's Monarchy," *The Economist*, September 21, 1996, p. 54.

11. Robert, Latona, "Juan Carlos," *Europe* (October 1993): 19.

12. See John Hooper, *The New Spaniards* (New York: Penguin, 1995) for information on the Transition and attitudes toward the Monarchy.

13. "Valoración de la Monarquía."

14. "El Rey don Carlos y el Principe Felipe luchan por el título en la Regata Freixenet," *¡Hola!* May 19, 2002, accessed May 25, 2002, <http://www.hola.com/2002/05/19/regatafreixenet/>. *¡Hola!* is the best known of the society magazines that cover the comings and goings of royal and other celebrities.

15. "Debate por una princesa," *El País*, May 6, 2001, accessed May 20, 2001, <http://www.elpais.es>.

CHAPTER 4

1. The Spanish government was rather surprised to find out that many Americans, particularly the Native Americans, would not accept the idea that the Americas had been discovered by any European and that, in any event, they viewed the arrival of Colombus as the beginning of a brutal repression. Eventually, the "discovery" was referred to as "El encuentro de dos mundos" (the Encounter of Two Worlds).

2. Gianni Granzotto, *Cristopher Columbus*, trans. Stephen Sartarelli (Garden City, NY: Doubleday, 1985).

3. Ibid.

4. Once known as Watling Island, this unimposing island has been re-christened "San Salvador," the name given to it by Columbus.

5. This observation is echoed in the meaning of the word *taino*, "good" or "noble," which the Tainos apparently used to distinguish themselves from the bellicose Caribs to the south. See Irving Rouse, *The Tainos: Rise and Decline of the People Who Greeted Columbus* (New Haven, CT: Yale University Press, 1992), p. 5.

6. The Caribs, rather than the more numerous Tainos, gave their name to the Caribbean Sea.

7. The countries of Haiti and the Dominican Republic share the island today.

8. Granzotto, *Christopher Columbus*, pp. 207–208.

9. Ibid., pp. 220–225.

10. See Alfred W. Crosby, *The Columbian Exchange: Biological and Cultural Consequences of 1492* (Westport, CT: Greenwood Press, 1972).

11. Granzotto, *Christopher Columbus*, pp. 56–58.

12. Columbus' possible voyage to Greenland is mentioned only once, in the memoires of the explorer's son, Fernando Colombus. Bruce Auster, "A Leaf from Leif," *U.S. News & World Report*, July 24, 2000, pp. 69–70.

Fray Bartolomé de las Casas notes that Colombus wrote that he had sailed 100 miles west of Thule. Granzotto, *Christopher Columbus*, p. 36.

13. Gonzalo Fernández de Oviedo y Valdés, *Los viajes de Colón*; nota preliminar por Jaime Delgado (Madrid: Ediciones Atlas, 1944). See also Miles H. Davidson, *Columbus Then and Now* (Norman: University of Oklahoma Press, 1997).

14. Rouse, *The Tainos*, p. 154.

15. See Jan Rogozinski, *A Brief History of the Caribbean: From the Arawak and the Carib to the Present* (New York: Facts on File, 1992) for a discussion of the fate of the Taino (Arawak) Indians and the introduction of slaves.

16. See Charles Gibson, *The Black Legend: Anti-Spanish Attitudes in the Old World and the New* (New York: Knopf, 1971) for a brief selection from Las Casas' work. Under the lens of the Leyenda Negra there was nothing in the Spanish character worthy of admiration. Another contributor to the Black Legend, an English scientist named Francis Willughby, wrote after a short visit to Spain: "Spain is in many places, not to say most, very thin of people, and almost desolate. The causes are (1) a bad Religion, (2) the tyranncial Inquisition, (3) the multitude of Whores, (4) the barrenness of the Soil, (5) the wretched laziness of the people, very like the Welsh and Irish, walking along slowly and always cumbred with a great Cloke and long Sword." From *Relation of a Voyage Made Through a Great Part of Spain, 1664*, quoted in Gibson, *The Black Legend*, p. 63.

17. Rouse, *The Tainos*, p. 158.

18. Michael S. Berliner, "The Christopher Columbus Controversy: Western Civilization vs. Primitivism," Ayn Rand Institute, March 13, 2002, <http://multiculturalism.aynrand.org/columbus.html>.

19. John Charles Chastain, *Born in Blood and Fire: A Concise History of Latin America* (New York: W.W. Norton, 2001), p. 29.

20. Ibid., p. 15.

21. Daniel Alder, "Columbus Day Stirs Mixed Emotions in Latin America," United Press International, October 11, 1992, LexisNexis™ Academic, accessed May 17, 2002.

22. "Conflicto indígena: Tension en el sur," La Tercera en Internet, May 20, 2002, <http://www.tercera.cl/casos/indigena/noticias/1999/octubre/noticia06.html> and "Govt Tones Down Columbus Day Celebrations Due to Indigenous Pressure and Anger at Spain over Pinochet Case," CHIP News, October 13, 1999, online, LexisNexis™ Academic, accessed May 20, 2002.

CHAPTER 5

1. John Hooper, *The New Spaniards* (New York: Penguin, 1995), pp. 197–198.

2. Data in this paragraph come from a summary of the report of the Ministry of the Interior's *Plan Nacional de Drogas*. See "El 43.5% de Estudiantes fuma a diario," *El Mundo*, July 11, 2001, accessed August 10, 2001, <http://www.elmundo.es>. For additional articles see the Web site of the Ministry of the Interior, <http://www.mir.es/pnd/noticias/index. htm>.

3. Mayka Sánchez, "El consumo de alcohol provoca en España más de 13.000 muertes anuales," *MedSpain*, June 13, 2000, accessed August 3, 2001, <http://www.medspain.com/ant/n14_jul00/alcohol.htm>.

4. Luiz Izquierdo and Celeste López, "El Gobierno prepara una ley para vetar el consumo a menores de 18 años," *La Vanguardia*, February 15, 2002, accessed March 22, 2002, <http://www.lavanguardia.es>.

5. CIS carries out a monthly survey called the *Barómetro*. Most months, interviewees are asked to name the three most important problems facing Spain. Interviewees' five-year predictions were published in Centro de Investigaciones Sociológicas (CIS), *Boletín: Datos de opinión 10*, December 1996, accessed January 3, 2002, <http://www.cis.es/baros/frame. html>.

6. David Holley, "Tobacco's Reign in Spain May Fall in Court," *Los Angeles Times*, August 19, 2001, p. A3, accessed August 21, 2001, <http://www.latimes.com>.

7. Mariano Rajoy (Minister of the Interior), quoted in "Uno de cada cinco estudiantes entre 14 y 18 años fuma porros habitualmente," *El País*, June 24, 2001, accessed August 3, 2001, <http://www.elpais.es>.

8. Otto Pohl, "La Vida Loca? In a Plaza in Madrid," *New York Times*, August 9, 2001, p. A10, accessed August 13, 2001, <http://www.nytimes. com>.

9. "El ocio de los jóvenes: La batalla del 'botellón,' " *El País*, February 4, 2002, accessed March 22, 2002, <http://www.elpais.es>.

10. Michael Gilbert, "Doc against Drugs," *New Statesman & Society*, May 21, 1993, p. 12.

11. The CIS survey data were reported in *Boletín: Datos de Opinión 3*, February 3, 1996, <http://www.cis.es/boletin\3/est1.html> and *Datos de Opinión 4*, March 4, 1996, <http://www.cis.es/boletin\4/est1.html>. The report of workplace smoking "La prohibición de fumar se incumple en el 46% de los espacios públicos" appeared in *El País*, February 1, 2003, <http://www.elpais.es>.

12. Marta Costa-Pau, "En España el tabaco es demasiado accesible a los menores," *El País*, May 30, 2001, accessed August 3, 2001, <http:// www.elpais.es>.

13. "Zapatero se compromete a crear un Ministerio de la Juventud si llega al poder," *El País*, February 18, 2002, accessed March 22, 2002, <http://www.elpais.es>.

14. "El ocio de los jóvenes: La batalla del 'botellón,' " *El País*, February 4, 2002, accessed March 22, 2002, <http://www.elpais.es>.

CHAPTER 6

1. Data for world population (estimated): beginning of the Christian era, about 300 million; by 1750, 800 million; around 1800, 1 billion; by 1930, 2 billion; 1960, 3 billion; 1974, 4 billion; before 1990, 5 billion. "Population," *Encyclopaedia Britannica Online*, accessed July 8, 2001, <http://search.eb.com/bol/topic?eu=115183&sctn=33>.

2. Susana Guzman, "Mexico Opens National Crusade for Forests and Water," Environment News Service, March 7, 2001, accessed May 25, 2002, <http://www.ens.com>.

3. Harvesting Brazil nuts from the rainforest floor is a sustainable development activity.

4. The six so-called greenhouse gases (GHGs) include carbon dioxide, methane, nitrous oxide, hydrofluorocarbons, perfluorocarbons and sulphur hexaflouride.

5. "Cambio climatico: Ecologistas en accion pide a Matas ratificar el acuerdo de Kioto," Efe News Services, April 2, 2001, online, LexisNexis™ Academic, accessed July 13, 2001.

6. Alexander F. Watson, Assistant Secretary for Inter-American Affairs, address to the Council of the Americas, May 1995.

7. Vinod Thomas and Tamara Belt, "Growth and the Environment: Allies or Foes?" *Journal of Social, Political and Economic Studies* 22(3) (1997): 327–334.

8. A few of the organizations advocating sustainable development include the United Nations, the Inter-American Development Bank (IBD), United States Agency for International Development (USAID), Oxfam, World Watch and Alianza Centroamericana para el Desarrollo Sostenible.

9. Michael Moore, "Environmentalism for the Twenty-First Century," *IPA Review* (September 2000): 3–8.

10. See John O. Browder, ed., *Fragile Lands of Latin America: Strategies for SustainableDevelopment* (Boulder, CO: Westview Press, 1989).

11. Hillary Lane, "Coffees with Conscience," *E Magazine: The Environmental Magazine* (January–February 1994): 40–41 and "Starbucks to Expand Sales of Shade-Grown and Organic Coffee," *American Journal of Alternative Agriculture* 15(3) (2000): 109.

12. See Planeta.com, <http://www.planeta.com>, a comprehensive source of information on ecotourism including publications, events, organizations and companies that offer tours. See Martin Mowforth and Ian Munt, *Tourism and Sustainability: New Tourism in the Third World* (London: Routledge, 1998) for a critique of tourism in developing countries.

13. "Economic Man, Cleaner Planet," *The Economist*, September 27, 2001, pp. 103–106.

14. Both of these views are expressed in Fundación Chile Unido, *Corriente de Opinion* no. 2, May 2000, <http://www.chileunido.cl>. For a

similar opinion in the United States see Joyce Morrison, "Do Your Emissions Offend God?" *Illinois Leader,* December 10, 2002, <http://www.illinoisleader.com/columnists/columnistsview.asp?c=3301>.

15. "UE-Aceite: Defensores naturaleza piden profunda reforma de ayudas al aceite," Efe News Services, June 18, 2001, online, LexisNexis™ Academic, accessed July 13, 2001.

16. "Oil and Cloud-Forests Don't Mix," *The Economist,* June 21, 2001, p. 67.

17. Since all species are candidates for eventual extinction, biologists now use the term *premature extinction* to refer to the loss of species due to man-made causes, such as elimination of habitat, pollution, hunting, and so on.

18. Ethnobotanist Michael Malick, quoted in Angela M.H. Schuster, "On the Healer's Path: A Journey through the Maya Rain Forest," *Archaeology* (July–August 2001): 34–38.

19. A combination of "ecology" and "tourism," ecotourism refers to travel to see and experience flora and fauna, usually of exotic places, such as rainforests, arctic or other unusual environments.

20. The best-known and most comprehensive is the Convention on International Trade of Endangered Species of Wild Fauna and Flora (CITES), an international agreement whose aim is to "ensure that international trade in specimens of wild animals and plants does not threaten their survival." "What Is CITES?" CITES, May 15, 2002, <http://www.cites.org/eng/disc/what_is.shtml>.

21. *CIA Factbook,* July 13, 2001, <http://www.odci.gov/cia/publications/factbook/index.html>.

22. Benjamin Jones, "Saving Doñana Nature Reserve," *Europe* (October 1998): 43–46 and "Vertido Tóxico: Director Parque Doñana Cree Rápida Intervención Evitó Catástrofe," Efe News Services, April 24, 2001, online, LexisNexis™ Academic, accessed May 20, 2002. At the average exchange rate in 2000, the cost was approximately US$135 million.

23. Will Nixon, "Rainforest Shrimp," *Mother Jones* (March–April 1996): 30–35.

24. Peter W. Huber, *Hard Green: Saving the Environment from the Environmentalists: A Conservative Manifesto* (New York: Basic Books, 1999).

25. Daniel C. Esty, "GATTing the Greens," *Foreign Affairs* 72 (November/December 1993): 36. See also Marian R. Chertow and Daniel C. Esty, eds., *Thinking Ecologically: The Next Generation of Environmental Policy* (New Haven, CT: Yale University Press, 1997). Many of Esty's articles have been published on the Internet in *World Link: The Magazine of the World Economic Forum,* <http://www.worldlink.co.uk>.

CHAPTER 7

1. Mexico D.F, São Paulo and Rio de Janeiro (Brazil), Buenos Aires (Argentina), Bogota (Colombia) and Santiago (Chile) come in ahead of Madrid, Spain's largest city, which had a population of 5.1 million in 2000.

2. International Conference on Population and Development, Programme of Action, Chapter 6, Part 1, February 29, 1999, accessed February 13, 2001, <http://www.agora21.org/cipd/frame05.html>.

3. See Antonio Barrero, "Espacios Naturales Protegidos . . . Parcialmente," *Ecosistemas*, 1996, accessed June 10, 2001, <http://www.ucm.es/info/ecosistemas/espacios.htm>.

4. See John O. Browder, *Fragile Lands of Latin America: Strategies for Sustainable Development* (Boulder, CO: Westview Press, 1989), pp. 1–7 for a summary of approaches.

5. See Ronald Bailey, "Billions Served: An Interview with Norman Borlaug," *Reason*, April 1, 2000, pp. 30–37 for a discussion of the results of the "Green Revolution" as well as a harsh critique of environmentalist approaches.

6. Conclusions and data in this section on birth control programs, contraceptive use and abortion from Mexico, Peru and Latin America as a whole come from Imogen Evans, "What Do You Do, Partner?" *The Lancet*, July 27, 1996, pp. 211–212 and "Cada año hacen en Latinoamérica 6 millones abortos clandestinos," Efe News Services, November 3, 1999, online, LexisNexis™ Academic, accessed July 15, 2001. Statistics on abortion, unwanted pregnancies and contraceptive use are subject to wide variation.

7. On average, infant mortality falls by 25% when pregnancies are separated by at least two years. Thomas McDevitt et al., *Trends in Adolescent Fertility and Contraceptive Use in the Developing World* (Washington, DC: U.S. Bureau of the Census, 1996), p. 8.

8. See "Legislación sobre el aborto en países de América Latina y el Caribe," Campaña del 28 de septiembre: Día de despenalización del aborto en la América Latina y el Caribe, May 16, 2002, <http://www.campanha28set.org> and especially <http://www.campanha28set.org/E2001/html/fmapa_legislacao.html>.

9. "Afirman que se registran hasta 350.000 abortos al año [Lima, Peru]," Efe News Services, September 30, 1999, online, LexisNexis™ Academic, accessed July 15, 2001.

10. Robert F. Drinan, "Church Grapples with Crowded Planet," *National Catholic Reporter*, December 3, 1999, p. 18.

11. Statistics from Population Reference Bureau. The figures mentioned in the text for South America do not include Brazil, which (at 70% contraceptive use) would inflate the percentages compared to the Spanish-language countries. Figures were not available for Argentina, Chile or

Uruguay. Spain, the United States and Puerto Rico have rates that are very close.

12. More than 40% of married women have chosen tubal ligation in these two countries. See Michael Klitsch, "The Global Status of Sterilization," *Engender Health Update, a Quarterly Newsletter*, 2000, <http://www.engenderhealth.org/pubs/ehnews/fl02/fl_02_1.html>.

13. An example of typical materials in Spanish is *Creando Vida* (Chile), <http://www.creandovida.cl/vientos/capitulo1/9b.htm>, which stresses responsible sexuality and recommends "natural family planning" as the only safe and ethical kind of birth control.

14. For a comparison of views see "Restoration of the Mexico City Policy Concerning Family Planning," July 23, 2001, <http://www.usaid.gov/bush_pro_new.html> and Liz Creel and Lori Ashford, "Bush Reinstates Policy Restricting Support for International Family Planning Programs," Population Reference Bureau, 2001, July 5, 2001, <http://wwwprb.org/press/bushreinstates.html>.

15. Creel and Ashford, "Bush Reinstates Policy Restricting Support for International Family Planning Programs."

16. Xavier Bosch, "Investigating the Reasons for Spain's Falling Birth Rate," *Lancet*, September 12, 1998, p. 887.

17. Xavier Bosch, "Spain's Birth Rate Drops to an All-Time Low," *Lancet*, January 8, 2000, p. 26.

18. See Mariela Sala, "Entre Dos Fuegos: Descubren campaña de esterilización forzada," *Mujer/Fempress* (April 1998), July 20, 2001, <http://www.fempress.cl/198/revista/pe.html> and Federico R. León et al., "Counseling Sterilization Clients in Peru: Before, during, and after Method Choice," American Public Health Association, November 13, 2000, accessed July 10, 2001, <http://apha.confex.com/apha/128am/techprogram/paper_11372.htm>.

19. *Report of the International Conference on Population and Development* (Cairo, 1994), Chapter 6, Part 21 (6.21), <gopher://gopher.undp.org:70/00/ungophers/popin/icpd/conference/offeng/poa>.

20. "Indigenas [de] México Denuncian Campaña Masiva [de] Esterilización [en] Chiapas," Efe News Services, December 9, 1999, online, LexisNexis™ Academic, accessed July 23, 2001.

CHAPTER 8

1. Sor Juana Inés de la Cruz, "Hombres necios que acusáis," in *A Sor Juana Anthology*, Alan S. Trueblood, trans. (Cambridge, MA: Harvard University Press, 1988), pp. 110–113.

2. Jan Brogger and David D. Gilmore, "The Matrifocal Family in Iberia: Spain and Portugal Compared," *Ethnology* 36(1) (1997): 13–30.

3. "La violencia doméstica," Centro de Investigacion Sociológica, *Boletín* #27 (January–December 2001), March 13, 2002, <http://www.cis.es/boletin/27/violencia.htm>.

4. "The World's Women 2000." The United Nations Statistics Department, May 2000, accessed November 13, 2001, <http://unstats.un.org/unsd/demographic/ww2000/ww2000pr.htm>.

5. For information on these projects and issues see UNIFEM, <http://www.unifem.undp.org/index.htm>.

6. Rolando Andrade, "Jose Alfredo Jimenez: A Cultural Dilemma," *Studies in Latin American Popular Culture* 16 (1997): 147–161.

7. This is the view of the Catholic Church. See issues of *Corriente de Opinión*, July 15, 2001, <http://www.chileunido.cl>.

8. Magaly Llaguno, "El movimiento anti vida en Latinoamérica: Un resumen," *Vida Humana*, November 17, 2001, <http://www.vidahumana.org>.

9. Statistics from the United Nations Statistics Division, November 17, 2001, <http://www.un.org/Depts/unsd/social/index.html>.

10. "Igualdad hombre mujer: Un mito que no hace bien," *Corriente de Opinión*, November 15, 2001, <http://www.chileunido.cl>.

11. "The World's Women 2000."

12. Juan G. Bedoya, "El congreso de teólogos exige que la mujer pueda acceder al sacerdocio y al episcopado," *El País*, September 10, 2001, accessed November 18, 2001, <http://www.elpais.es>.

13. Excerpts from "Proponen a los cubanos rescatar el arte del buen piropo," Agence France Presse Spanish, June 17, 2000, online, LexisNexis™ Academic, accessed November 11, 2001.

14. "Novela intriga Lorraine Ladish defiende piropo español tomado acoso sexual [en] eeuu," Efe News Services, Spanish Newswire Services, June 17, 2001, online, LexisNexis™ Academic, accessed November 17, 2001.

15. "Piropos y preguntas en la calle," *El País Internacional S.A.*, June 6, 2001, p. 3.

16. Susana Pérez De Pablos, "El 23% de los chicos de 14 a 18 años cree justificado que las mujeres cobren menos: Un estudio revela que uno de cada cuatro adolescentes tiene opiniones discriminatorias," *El País*, July 31, 2001, <http://www.elpais.es>.

17. Brogger and Gilmore, "The Matrifocal Family in Iberia."

18. See Neil Buckley and Peter Norman, "Court Backs Jobs Affirmative Action: Equally Qualified Women May Be Appointed before Men Where Women Are Under-represented," *Financial Times* (London), November 12, 1997, online, LexisNexis™ Academic, accessed November 17, 2001.

CHAPTER 9

1. "Actuales islenos proceden 65% guanches y resto luso y castellano," Spanish Newswire Services, June 29, 2001, online, LexisNexis™ Academic, accessed May 10, 2002. Little published material is available on the Guanches in the United States. For more information, search the Internet. One site (English and Spanish) is Los Guanches, May 2, 2002, <http://www.geocities.com/jrancel/canguan1-esp.html>.

2. Indigenas de Colombia, November 15, 2001, <http://www.indigenascolombia.org/pueblos.htm>.

3. Some of the best known were Tupac Amaru (1570s) and Tupac Amaru II (1780s) in Peru. In Chile the Arauacos were able to resist total control until well into the nineteenth century.

4. Adain Rankin, "Real History Revives Argentina's Indians," *History Today* (June 1995): 8–10 and "Landless Protest," *New Internationalist* (October 2000): 8.

5. The best-known denunciation of human rights violations, including torture and murder of Indians, is contained in Rigoberta Menchu, *I, Rigoberta Menchu: An Indian Woman in Guatemala*, ed. Elisabeth Burgos-Debray, trans. Ann Wright (London: Verso, 1984).

6. See biographies and excerpts of works of these and other authors at El Poder de la Palabra, April 10, 2002, <http://www.epdlp.com/>.

7. Dennis M. Hanratty, ed., *Ecuador: A Country Study* (Washington, DC: Federal Research Division, Library of Congress, 1989), p. 87.

8. Ana Saroli, "Can Quechua Survive?" *Cultural Survival Quarterly* (July 2001): 40. Peru, Ecuador and Bolivia began to recognize a need for bilingual education in the 1970s, 1980s and 1990s, respectively. Mexico and Guatemala also provide bilingual education in some areas. Guatemala, which began its successful programs in the 1970s, reached only about 15% of Mayan-speaking children in the mid-1990s, according to "Costs and Benefits of Bilingual Education in Guatemala," *HCO Dissemination Notes* 60, October 23, 1995, <http://www.worldbank.org/education/economicsed/finance/demand/related/note60.html>. See the Resource Guide for Chapter 9 for articles on bilingual education.

9. In 2001, Peru's President Toledo proposed making Quechua, the most widely spoken Indian language, an option for students taking a foreign language in the nation's schools.

10. Rosamel Milaman, "Mapuches Press for Autonomy," *NACLA Report on the Americas* (October 2001): 10–12.

11. Catherine Elton, "Indians' Heritage Gets a Legal Stamp," *Christian Science Monitor*, December 4, 2001, p. 6; and Danielle Knight, "Nicaragua

Honors Court Ruling on Indigenous People," Interpress Service, February 25, 2002, online, LexisNexis™ Academic, accessed May 25, 2002.

12. Wendy Call, "Plan Puebla-Panama," *NACLA Report on the Americas* (March–April 2002): 24–25.

13. Wendy Call, "A Man, a Plan, Expansion: The Puebla-Panama Plan," Institute of Current World Affairs, June 1, 2001, reprinted by Global Exchange, May 26, 2000, <http://www.globalexchange.org/campaigns/mexico/ppp/icwa060101.html>.

14. Jan Rocha, "Democracy Dawns for Bolivia's First People," *The Guardian* (London), August 3, 2002, online, LexisNexis™ Academic, accessed March 3, 2003 and "Ecuador Ecuadorian Indians Hail Example Set by Bolivia's Morales," Efe News Services, July 9, 2002, online, LexisNexis™ Academic, accessed March 3, 2003.

CHAPTER 10

1. "Drug Trafficking in the United States," U.S. Drug Enforcement Administration, <http://www.usdoj.gov/dea/concern/drug_trafficking.html>.

2. National Institute on Drug Abuse (NIDA), *NIDA Info Facts*, "Crack and Cocaine," <http://www.nida.nih.gov/Infofax/cocaine.html>; "Major Drugs of Abuse in ED Visits, 2001 Update," U[nited]S[tates] Department of Health and Human Services, Office of Applied Studies, *The DAWN Report*, October 2002, accessed February 22, 2003, <http://www.samhsa.gov/OAS/2k2/DAWN/majordrugs2k1.pdf>; Judy Mann, "Money Spent on Drug War Could Be Put to Better Use," *Washington Post,* October 17, 2001, p. C12.

3. Steven B. Karch, *A Brief History of Cocaine* (Boca Raton, FL: CRC Press, 1998).

4. "Trafficking by Colombian and Mexican Organizations," Drug Enforcement Administration, May 12, 2002, <http://www.usdoj.gov/dea/pubs/intel/01020/index.html#c1>.

5. Office of National Drug Control Policy, "The National Drug Control Strategy: 1996," quoted in Karch, *A Brief History of Cocaine.*

6. Jo Ann Kawell, "Coke and the CIA: The Real Thing?" *Nation*, September 28, 1998, pp. 25–31.

7. Peter Dale Scott and Jonathan Marshall, *Cocaine Politics: Drugs, Armies, and the CIA in Central America* (Berkeley: University of California Press, 1998).

8. *The Economist* is a good source of information on the Colombian political and drug situations.

9. "Drugs Uncovered: The Profit Motive," *The Observer* (United King-

dom), April 21, 2002, online, LexisNexis™ Academic, accessed February 21, 2003.

10. See the Washington Office on Latin America (WOLA) for recent reports on Colombia and other Latin American nations, including "A Better Approach: Finding New Solutions to Old Problems," WOLA, May 16, 2002, <http://www.wola.org>.

11. Carl M. Cannon, "Tempering the War," *National Journal*, August 18, 2001, pp. 2592–2597.

12. Ibid.

13. Figures in this paragraph come from Cannon, "Tempering the War," p. 2592.

14. Michael Massing, "It's Time for Realism," *The Nation*, September 20, 1999, pp. 11–14.

15. Polls conducted in 2000 and 2001 showed that 64% believed that marijuana use should not be legal (Gallup, 2000). Another survey done for the Pew Center for People and the Press in 2001 showed that Americans were divided on the issue of whether possession of small amounts of marijuana should be a criminal offense. The same survey indicated that half of Americans think drug addiction should be treated more like a disease than a crime but are divided on the question of prison sentences for non-violent offenders. See Public Agenda, "Illegal Drugs," <http://www.publicagenda.org/issues/majprop.cfm?issue_type=illegal_drugs>.

16. Massing, "It's Time for Realism."

CHAPTER 11

1. The Basque Nationalist Party (Partido Nacionalista Vasca, or PNV), along with a more radical party, won a slight majority of votes in the 2001 elections.

2. Their languages included Latin (and its successors the Romance languages—French, Spanish, Italian, Catalán, etc.), the Celtic and the Germanic languages.

3. The Basque region once extended north to Bordeau and east to near Toulouse (both in France), to Andorra, south to near Zaragoza and Soria. Now Basque speakers are found in the three Basque provinces, about one-quarter of Navarra, and the three Basque provinces of France.

4. In the context of the Spanish political system, the terms autonomous community or *comunidad autónoma* do not imply complete independence but rather something similar to the limited powers of states in the United States. Since adoption of the 1978 constitution these communities (consisting of one or more provinces) have their own legislative bodies, governors and jurisdiction over certain areas of public life.

5. The Reconquest of Muslim-held territory in the Iberian Peninsula began in the early ninth century and ended with the conquest of Granada in 1492.

6. For example, the name of the Basque language is *euskera*, *euskara* or *uskara*, depending on the dialect spoken in a particular part of the Basque-speaking region.

7. See various articles in *National Geographic Magazine* and books by U.S. novelist of Basque descent Robert Laxalt.

8. There are several Basque nationalist parties, ranging from those that espouse Marxist ideology to the Carlists, who are ultraconservative.

9. "El 57% de los vascos apoyaría un referéndum de autodeterminación," *Diario de Noticias de Navarra*, Decembeer 30, 2001, <http://www.noticiasdenavarra.com/ediciones/20011230/espana/d30esp0103.php>.

10. "Euskal demodrazia proposamena (Bases y formas de desarrollo para conformar la democracia vasca)," Euskal Herria, November 1999, accessed January 6, 2001, <http://www.euskal-herritarrok.org/ed/oindee.htm> (translation by the author).

11. Ibid.

12. "Blaming the Messenger," *Time Europe*, March 13, 2003, accessed March 13, 2003, <http://www.time.com/time/europe/magazine/article/0,13005,901030317-430697,00.html>. Amnesty International expressed concern about ambiguous language in the Law on Parties and reiterated an urgent call for a full investigation of the case involving the closing of Egunkaria and detention of its staff. Amnesty International, "Spain: The Lethal Cost of Freedom of Expression in the Basque Country," February 11, 2003, <http://web.amnesty.org/ai.nsf/Index/EUR410012003?OpenDocument& of=COUNTRIES\SPAIN> and "Spain: Only Adequate Safeguards Will End Torture, and Claims of Torture," March 11, 2003, accessed March 13, 2003, <http://web.amnesty.org/ai.nsf/Index/EUR410032003?Open Document&of=COUNTRIES\SPAIN>.

13. Julio Caro Baroja, *El laberinto vasco* (San Sebastian: Editorial Txertoa, 1984).

14. Ernesto Saavater, "Discurso de Fernando Savater en el Parlamento Europeo," Basta Ya, Documentos, January 5, 2001, <http://www.geocities.com/bastayaonline/>.

15. Luis Núñez Astrain, *The Basques: Their Struggle for Independence* ([Cardiff], Wales: Welsh Academic Press, 1997). The number of Basque-speaking children is growing, however, due to the use of Basque in schools.

16. "El 57% de los vascos apoyaría un referéndum de autodeterminación."

17. "Euzkadi-Europa," *El País*, March 22, 2001, accessed May 15, 2001, <http://www.elpais.es/elecciones/pvasco2001/hemeroteca/editoriales/ed32201a.html>.

18. Saavater, "Discurso de Fernando Savater en el Parlamento Europeo."

19. "El 57% de los vascos apoyaría un referéndum de autodeterminación"; and Centro de Investigaciones Sociológicas, *Barómetro*, November 2001, accessed December 30, 2001, <http://www.cis.es/baros/frame.html>.

20. *El País*, May 7, 2001, accessed August 3, 2001, <http://www.elpais.es>. Just prior to 1998, nearly 40% of children between 5 and 14 years of age were bilingual, and 73% of the elementary school population attending schools used Basque as a language of instruction, up from 25% in 1982. See Jasone Cenoz, "Multilingual Education in the Basque Country," in Jasone Cenoz and Fred Genesee, eds., *Beyond Bilingualism: Multilingualism and Multilingual Education* (Clevedon: Multilingual Matters Ltd., 1998), pp. 175–192.

CHAPTER 12

1. "Illegal Immigrants Killed in Accident in Spain," *Typically Spanish*, January 5, 2001, <http://www.typicallyspanish.com/news.htm>.

2. "Temas: Inmigración," *El País*, December 19, 2001, <http://www.elpais.es/temas/inmigracion/menua/menua4.html>.

3. Be careful to distinguish "emigrate," to leave or move *out* of one's own country, and "immigrate," to move *in* to the receiving country. The corresponding terms in Spanish are *emigrar* and *inmigrar*. The noun forms are *emigrante* and *inmigrante* in Spanish, "emigré" and "immigrant" in English.

4. Use search features on the pages of online editions of national newspapers such as *El País* and *El Mundo* to look for current information.

5. Figures from the U.S. Census and Immigration and Naturalization Service (INS). Approximately 1.54 million persons were apprehended by the INS in 1999.

6. Ecuador's per capita income for 2000 was estimated at $1,087 (Eurostat).

7. Eurostat, reported in "Temas: Inmigración."

8. See Edwin Harwood, "Can We Solve the Illegal Immigration Problem?" *Business Forum* (Fall 1985): 20–21.

9. Julian L. Simon, "Errors about Immigrants: The Government Spends Much More on the Native Born," Cato Institute, June 25, 1997, accessed December 21, 2001, <http://www.cato.org/dailys/6–25–97.html>. A study by the National Research Council reported that impact of immigration is mixed: positive at the federal level and negative at the local and state level. See also James P. Smith and Barry Edmonston, eds., *The New Americans: Economic, Demographic and Fiscal Effects* (Washington, DC: National

Academy Press, 1997). See a summary of the report online, <http://bob.
nap.edu/html/newamer/index.html#sum>.

10. "Legal Immigration Family Equity (LIFE) Act," news release, Immigration and Naturalization Service (INS), January 15, 2001, <http://www.ins.usdoj.gov/graphics/publicaffairs/newsrels/life245irel.htm>. Spanish and English versions.

11. "Temas: Inmigración." Common abuses included extremely low pay, dangerous and unsanitary working and living conditions.

12. Centro de Investigaciónes Sociológicas, *Boletín* #7, June 1996, accessed December 13, 2001, <http://www.cis.es/boletin/7/est3.html>; *Boletín* #27, January–December 2001, <http://www.cis.es/boletin/27/inmigra.htm>.

13. Hector Becerra and Fred Alvarez, "Census Reflects Large Gains for Latinos," *Los Angeles Times*, May 10, 2001, Section 2, p. 1. Five U.S. urban areas (larger than 100,000 total population) have 80% or more Latino residents: East Los Angeles, 97%; Laredo Texas, 94%; Brownsville, Texas, 91%; Hialeah, Florida, 90%; McAllen, Texas, 80%.

14. U.S. Census Bureau, *Census 2000 Summary*, File 1, 2000, <http://factfinder.census.gov/servlet/BasicFactsServlet>.

15. Kitty Calavitta, "Immigration, Law, and Marginalization in a Global Economy: Notes from Spain," *Law & Society Review* 32(3) (1998): 529–566.

16. "Temas: Inmigración."

17. Mexico was the source of 20% of all immigrants between 1968 and 1993, according to U.S. immigration records, quoted in CQ (Congressional Quarterly) Researcher, <http://library.cqpress.com/cqres/lpext.dll/cqres/bydate/2000/cover20000714/overview>.

18. "Temas: Inmigración."

19. Centro de Investigaciónes Sociológicas, *Boletín* #7, <http://www.cis.es/boletin/7/est3.html>; *Boletín* #27, <http://www.cis.es/boletin/27/inmigra.htm>; and *Boletín* #19, <http://www.cis.es/boletin/19/inmigrantes.html>; Francisco Goldman, "Moro Like Me," in C. Chiawei O'Hearn, ed., *Half and Half: Writers Growing up Biracial and Bicultural* (New York: Pantheon, 1998), pp. 49–70.

CHAPTER 13

1. The *Etymologiae* also enjoyed a readership well into early Modern Period. John B. O'Connor, *The Catholic Encyclopedia*, Online Edition, March 24, 2002, <http://www.newadvent.org/cathen/08186a.htm>. St. Isidore, patron saint of school children and students, was recently designated the patron saint of computer users and computer programmers.

2. Although most famous for its persecution of converted Jews and, later, Protestants, the Inquisition's censorship powers caused long-lasting

damage to the spirit of inquiry inside Spain and its colonies and the introduction of new ideas from outside Spain.

3. Francisco Goya's satirical engravings, *Los Caprichos*, are indicative of the attitudes of many *ilustrados* toward the Church. One of the earliest of Spain's eighteenth-century rationalists was, however, a Galician Benedictine monk: Fray Benito Feijóo.

4. Both sides were guilty of serious atrocities during the civil war. Some 7,000 priests, friars and nuns perished at the hands of republican supporters during the war. A good brief history of the Spanish Civil War is Gabriele Ranzato, *The Spanish Civil War* (New York: Interlink Books, 1999).

5. The affiliation of members with Opus Dei is often not made public. Critics have often complained of its tendency toward secrecy, especially of its internal workings. See James Martin, S.J., "Opus Dei in the United States," *America*, February 25, 1995, pp. 8–17.

6. The Opus Dei provokes strong reactions in its opponents. "The Opus . . . is an instrument of 'recristianization' strongly backed by John Paul II and the Catholic Right. It is a powerful religious, economic and political militia that tries to infiltrate the powers of the state. . . . Opus Dei is transforming the Church into a modern capitalist enterprise. It puts emphasis on 'the santification of work,' favoring the cult of materialism and the reign of capitalism." "Escrivá de Balaguer fundador del Opus Dei: Hitler contra los judíos, es Hitler contra el comunismo," *Chile Hoy*, February 2, 2002, <http://www.chile-hoy.de/internacional/180202_opus_dei.htm>.

7. Edward A. Lynch, "Catholic Social Thought in Latin America," *Orbis* (Winter 1998): 105–120.

8. José Manuel Vidal, "Santificarás las fiestas," *Epoca*, October 29, 2000, p. 46.

9. Ibid.

10. Luis Gómez, "Los musulmanes radicales desplazan a los moderados en la comunidad islámica de España," *El País*, September 19, 2000, February 2, 2002, <http://www.elpais.es>.

11. The more conservative figure comes from Clinton Holland, statistics revised February 22, 1997, quoted on Latin American Mission, <http://www.gospelcom.net/lam/news/population.html>, the higher figure from "Pope Urges New Effort against 'Sects'," *Christianity Today*, May 21, 2001, p. 29.

12. "Protestants on the Rise in Catholic Bolivia," *Christian Century*, October 18, 1995, p. 955.

13. Phillip Berryman, "Church and Revolution," *NACLA Report on the Americas* (March–April 1997): 10–15.

14. "Protestantism Explodes" [interview with Samuel Escobar], *Christian History* 2(3) (1992): 42–45.

15. The area of greatest influence of African religions is Brazil, which falls outside the scope of this book.

16. Nevertheless, critics in the Spanish media say that much of this attention is due to curiosity rather than attachment to the pope or religious fervor.

17. Gerald Renner, "Tactics Aside, the Legion Is Growing,"*National Catholic Reporter Online*, November 3, 2000, accessed May 15, 2002, <http://www.natcath.com/NCR_Online/archives/110300/110300d.htm>.

18. "Legion of Christ on the Advance in Catholic Church," Deutsche Presse-Agentur, December 1, 2001, online, LexisNexis™ Academic, accessed May 30, 2002.

19. Scott Appleby, "Pope John Paul II," *Foreign Policy* (Summer 2000): 12–25.

20. Charo Nogeira, "Over 150 Catholic Groups Give Seal of Approval to Girona's Dissident Clergy." *El País/Herald*, March 9, 2002, <http://www.elpais.es>, pdf file; and Juan Bedoya, "Spain Mulls Ethics of Right to Die," *El País/Herald*, March 23, 2002, p. 3, <http://www.elpais.es>.

21. Charo Nogeira, "Mercedes Carrizosa: Teóloga que desea ser Sacerdote," *El País*, March 28, 2002, <http://www.elpais.es/>.

22. "El obispo de Huelva retira la licencia sacerdotal al cura que proclamó ser gay," *El País*, February 7, 2002, accessed March 9, 2002, <http://www.elpais.es/>.

23. Penny Lernoux, "The Journey from Medellín to Puebla," in Edward L. Cleary, ed., *Born of the Poor: The Latin American Church since Medellín* (Notre Dame, IN: University of Notre Dame Press, 1990). The tone of the documents from the next conference, held in Santo Domingo in 1992, was even more discouraging to liberationists as it indicated a return to traditional church structures.

24. John M. Kirk, "(Still) Waiting for John Paul II: The Church in Cuba," in Edward L. Cleary and Hanna Stewart-Gambino, eds., *Conflict and Competition: The Latin American Church in a Changing Environment* (Boulder, CO: Lynne Rienner, 1992), pp. 147–165.

25. "Human Rights in Cuba 1999," International Society for Human Rights, February 22, 2000, accessed March 26, 2002, <http://www.ishr.org>.

26. John Hooper, *The New Spaniards* (New York: Penguin, 1995), p. 138.

27. Juan G. Bedoya, "La izquierda reclama que la escuela pública enseñe el hecho religioso 'sin confesionalismos,' " *El País* (Educational supplement), March 25, 2002, <http://www.elpais.es>.

28. Paul Rigg, "Re Teacher Sacked for Marrying Divorcee," *The Times Educational Supplement*, June 1, 2001, p. 14; and Paul Rigg, "Religious

Deal Revives Old Tensions," *The Times Educational Supplement*, September 3, 1999, p. 17.

29. Guillermo Garcia-Montufar and Elvira Martinez Coco, "Antecedents, Perspectives, and Projections of a Legal Project about Religious Liberty in Peru," *Brigham Young University Law Review*, no. 2 (1999): 503–536.

30. Porfirio Miranda, "Laicismo es ateísmo," *Proceso*, April 9, 2000, p. 44.

31. Government funds also subsidize schools run by religious organizations in numerous European countries, including England and Germany as well as in Canada.

32. Kevin Sullivan and Mary Jordan, "Reluctant Mexican Church Begins to Question Its Own," *Washington Post*, April 17, 2002, p. A12.

CHAPTER 14

1. Among the victims of the Francoists was the poet Federico García Lorca.

2. ETA is the acronym of Euskadi Ta Askasuna (Basque Land and Liberty), a separatist organization.

3. Oscar Arias, "Confronting Debt, Poverty, and Militarism: A Humane Program of Support for the Developing World," *Journal of Third World Studies* 17(2) (2000): 14.

4. Ibid.

5. Tim L. Merrill and Ramón Miró, eds., *Mexico: A Country Study* (Washington, DC: Federal Research Division, Library of Congress, 1996).

6. The terms "free market" and "neoliberal" reforms refer to economic policies that advocate a virtually unfettered brand of capitalism. Import taxes are cut and nationally owned companies (for example, airlines, telephone and electric companies) are sold to bring in money for the government while other costs of government are kept low and eliminated when possible.

7. See Human Rights Watch, "Reluctant Partner: The Argentine Government's Failure to Back Trials of Human Rights Violators," June 3, 2002, <http://www.hrw.org/reports/2001/argentina/argen1201-01.htm #P53_4982>.

8. Amnesty International Report: Spain, January–December 2001, accessed May 28, 2002, <http://web.amnesty.org/web/ar2002.nsf/eur/spain !Open>.

9. John Hooper, *The New Spaniards* (New York: Penguin Books, 1995), p. 37.

10. Ibid., p. 78.

11. See Margaret Popkin, *Peace without Justice: Obstacles to Building*

the Rule of Law (University Park: Pennsylvania State University Press, 2000).

12. José Pilar Alvarez, quoted in Jeffrey Paul, "Five Years Later, No Peace in Guatemala," *Christian Century*, April 24, 2002, p. 14.

13. See "Cramming Them in," *The Economist*, May 11, 2002, pp. 34–35 and *The Path Out of Poverty: The Inter-American Development Bank's Approach to Reducing Poverty* (Washington, DC: Inter-American Development Bank, April 1998).

14. "Grinding the Poor," *The Economist*, September 27, 2001, p. 13.

15. "Rigged Rules and Double Standards: Trade, Globalization and the Fight Against Poverty," Oxfam, June 2, 2002, <http://www.maketrade fair.com/stylesheet.asp?file=03042002121618>; and Vandana Shiva, "Export at Any Cost: Oxfam's Free Trade: Recipe for the Third World," Oxfam, June 2, 2002, <http://www.maketradefair.com/stylesheet.asp?file=31052002130237>.

16. Claudio Katz, "Free Trade Area of the Americas: NAFTA Marches South," *NACLA Report on the Americas* (January 2002): 27–31.

17. See Marcus J. Kurtz, "Markets and Democratic Consolidation in Chile: The National Politics of Rural Transformation," *Politics & Society* (June 1999): 275–301. The largest drop in both the percent of Chileans living in poverty and the poverty gap came between 1990 and 1992. See also Inter-American Development Bank, *Facing Up to Inequality in Latin America: Economic and Social Progress in Latin America, 1998–1999 Report* (Washington, DC: Inter-American Development Bank [Johns Hopkins University Press]), 1998.

18. See Carlos Salas, "Mexico's Haves and Have-Nots: NAFTA Sharpens the Divide,"' *NACLA Report on the Americas* (January 2002): 32–35.

19. Jubilee Movement International, Data Bank: Ecuador, June 2, 2002, <http://www.jubilee2000uk.org/databank/profiles/ecuador.htm>.

20. Arias, "Confronting Debt, Poverty, and Militarism," p. 18.

21. Budget figures (1998 and 2000) are from Central Intelligence Agency, *CIA World Factbook*, June 6, 2002, <http://www.cia.gov/cia/publications/factbook/index.html>; arms agreement from "Rio Group Backs Social Twist to Political Agenda," Inter Press Service, August 18, 2001, online, LexisNexis™ Academic, accessed June 6, 2002.

Index